# Encountering
# the Living God
# in Scripture

# Encountering the Living God in Scripture

## Theological and Philosophical Principles for Interpretation

# William M. Wright IV and Francis Martin

**Baker Academic**
*a division of Baker Publishing Group*
Grand Rapids, Michigan

© 2019 by William M. Wright IV

Published by Baker Academic
a division of Baker Publishing Group
PO Box 6287, Grand Rapids, MI 49516-6287
www.bakeracademic.com

Printed in the United States of America

Library of Congress Cataloging-in-Publication Data
Names: Wright, William M., IV, author. | Martin, Francis, 1930–2017, author.
Title: Encountering the living God in Scripture : theological and philosophical principles for interpretation / William M. Wright IV and Francis Martin.
Description: Grand Rapids, MI : Baker Academic, [2019] | Includes bibliographical references and index.
Identifiers: LCCN 2018023228 | ISBN 9780801030956 (pbk. : alk. paper)
Subjects: LCSH: Bible—Theology. | Bible—Criticism, interpretation, etc.
Classification: LCC BS543 .W75 2019 | DDC 220.601—dc23
LC record available at https://lccn.loc.gov/2018023228

ISBN 978-1-5409-6154-9 (casebound)

Scripture quotations are from the New Revised Standard Version of the Bible, copyright © 1989, by the Division of Christian Education of the National Council of the Churches of Christ in the United States of America. Used by permission. All rights reserved.

19  20  21  22  23  24  25       7  6  5  4  3  2  1

*In Memoriam*

Fr. Francis Martin
(1930–2017)


Those who are wise shall shine like the brightness of the sky,
and those who lead many to righteousness, like the stars forever and ever.
—Daniel 12:3

Those who love me will keep my word, and my Father will love them,
and we will come to them and make our home with them.
—John 14:23

# Contents

# Foreword

## *Reading and Responding to the Word of God*

### ROBERT SOKOLOWSKI

This book is written to show how we can read the Scriptures as being addressed to us, not only by their particular authors, such as the psalmist or Saint Paul, but also by their primary author, God himself, whose words the Scriptures ultimately are. The book also shows how we can read the Scriptures as our response to the God who speaks to us through them; we may not respond to the particular authors, to the evangelists or to Saint James, but we can and should use the words that have been authored by God when we pray to him, whether in the community of the church or by ourselves. The way God uses the words of Scripture is different from the way its human writers use them, and the best and only correct way for us to read them is in the light of that difference. If we did not read the Scriptures as God's Word to us, we would not be reading them as the Scriptures themselves say that we should. This is the point made by William M. Wright and Fr. Francis Martin in their book, and in their work as authors they help us fulfill the obligation that they describe.

Toward the end of the book the authors give us four examples of people who read the Scriptures in this way: Saint Antony of Egypt, Saint Augustine of Hippo, Saint Francis of Assisi, and Saint Thérèse of Lisieux. These readers lived at different times in the history of the church—the patristic, the medieval, the modern—and each of them is identified not only by their proper name but also by the place they are from, which locates them in a particular human and Christian community that provided them with the Scriptures and with a context for hearing and reading them. In each case, this personal encounter with the words and their author led to achievements that influenced the lives of countless others. The four instances are presented not just as anecdotes but as rhetorical paradigms. As examples of what has been done, they show what we might do on a smaller but still appropriate scale in our time and place. They are tangible instances of what this book is about, and they show us that such things, such readings, do happen; and they imply that we should go and do likewise.

The rest of the book is more theoretical. It is divided, elegantly, into two parts: *Fides*, which is based more immediately on passages from Scripture, and *Quaerens Intellectum*, which involves philosophical and theological reflections.

Part 1, *Fides*, is subdivided into four chapters. First, God's own words are shown to be creative and effective. God achieves the existence of things effortlessly by simply speaking them; he speaks and it is done; what is said comes to be. There is no need for struggle or conquest. Also, God guides people and events through history and brings about coherence in unexpected ways, despite human folly, malice, and disobedience. Second, we are shown that God's Word can be spoken, not just by God, but also by inspired human speakers, the prophets (and lawgivers, narrators, and psalmists) of the Old Testament. They do not speak only in their own voice; when the psalmist, for example, repents for what he has done or praises God's benevolence, he speaks not just as a human poet whose skill we might admire but as someone who speaks the way God wants him to. We can therefore use what he says when we strive to place ourselves in the presence of God. Third, this coordination between God's Word and human words is recapitulated in the New Testament, where the apostles take the place of the prophets, in an adjustment that is appropriate for what occurred when the eternal Word of God became incarnate and brought about a new creation in his redemptive death and resurrection. John the Baptist was a prophet but the apostles were not, because the presence and action of God in the world had changed. The apostles were more than the prophets and were only analogous to them. It was their remembrances, not their anticipations, that were to be the *euangelion*, and their inspiration was different as well. The Holy Spirit, having been promised by Christ, has come and now works in a new, sacramental way. Finally, chapter 4 deals with the transformation of the remembrances of the apostles into a written form, along with the old covenant's prior commitment to writing. This shift from speaking to writing was also carried out under the guidance of the Holy

Spirit. God is not only the author but also the primary editor and publisher of the sacred Scriptures, as well as the one who guides those who read and hear the Scriptures as they were meant to be received. The Word of God has gone through the spoken stages of prophecy and apostolic proclamation and has settled into writing, which is the way it will remain, as read and spoken in the church, for the duration. The development of writing was part of the *praeparatio evangelica.*

Part 2, *Quaerens Intellectum*, uses resources from philosophy and theology to clarify how the Scriptures can truly be what we believe them to be. The authors make use of two forms of philosophy, phenomenology and metaphysics, and in both cases the philosophical style is adjusted to deal with biblical things. It morphs into theology. Thus, we deal not just with the phenomenology of things in the world, but with the understanding of God as radically distinguished from the world as a whole; God is understood as capable of being, in undiminished goodness and greatness, even if there had been no world, and he is disclosed to us as being in this way. This is the background against which the Scriptures must be understood; it is the background described in the Scriptures, and we have inklings of it even apart from them. Ontologically, this understanding of things can be expressed by speaking of God as sheer unqualified existence, with all other things understood to participate in God's activity of being. The core perfection in all entities is their existence, which actualizes each of them in their limited and modified way. What entities are and what they can do depends on and reveals their natures, which in turn reveal the perfection of their being, and this perfection in turn is now seen to have been chosen and granted by the one who is existence itself, *ipsum esse.* Human reason can reach such an understanding of things; it is, therefore, not extinguished when it reaches this kind of transcendence. Rather, it is enlarged and strengthened as it glimpses that which is most worth knowing and most to be loved.

The philosophical and theological material in this book helps us deal with two approaches that raise serious obstacles to a Christian reading of the Scriptures. The first would secularize such reading; it would interpret Scripture simply in the way that we would interpret any human historical or poetic writing; it would take Scripture as a human composition and judge it simply according to standard historical and hermeneutic principles. As the authors show, this way of reading the Bible was initiated in the modern world by Spinoza. The second approach that would derail our reading of Scripture is Kantian; it considers the objects of human knowledge to be human constructs, meanings that we project onto our experience rather than entities that truly show up to us. Kant would claim that we construct the appearance of things according to the a priori forms of human understanding, while a neo-Kantian approach would say that the constructs are historically developed patterns that we inherit from the communities in which we live. In either case, the things themselves are not truly presented to us. Such projections also occur in the case of scriptural belief. The authors deal with such epistemological challenges by showing that we are in fact capable of identifying things of different kinds, and that each kind of thing has its own way of being given to us precisely as an identity in a manifold of appearances. The philosophical and theological task is to clarify what sort of manifold is proper to the kind of thing in question. Such a clarification helps validate the substance or the entity of the thing itself, even in the case of religious belief. Indeed, this entire book could be seen as an effort to spell out various ways in which Christian realities can be intended, experienced, identified, and spoken about.

The authors claim that a proper reading of the Scriptures can occur only if the reader has a personal encounter with Jesus himself as the risen Lord. They present a memorable interpretation of chapter 20 of the Gospel of John to show what this means. So long as Mary Magdalene only sees the stone removed and the tomb as empty, and so long as Peter and John see only the empty tomb and the cloths placed aside, and so long as Thomas the apostle has just heard from others but has not yet heard Jesus speak to him, none of them have reached a full faith in Christ. As the authors say, even the apostle John did not yet have complete faith at this point; the word used to describe his reaction should be translated not as "he believed" but as "he started to believe"; *episteusen* ought to be read as an "ingressive aorist." But once Jesus says "Mary" to Mary Magdalene, and once he addresses the disciples (except Thomas) and says, "Peace be with you," and once he speaks to Thomas directly, they do believe, in the new way that is expressed by Thomas when he says, "My Lord and my God." The Lord whom they now recognize is the one they knew before; he is the one who was able to command the wind and the sea (Mark 4:41); but he is now seen more truly than he was before, from a new perspective, as the Lord God himself, in the person of the Son. And, as the authors observe, just a few lines later the evangelist addresses his readers and speaks about the written word: "But these are written so that you may come to believe that Jesus is the Messiah, the Son of God, and that through believing you may have life in his name." The words of Scripture can mediate the truthful presence of the risen Lord in the way his immediate presence did for the first witnesses of his resurrection. But, the authors say, this mediation cannot occur unless the reader is willing to recognize the Lord and accepts the grace to do so. We might add that this encounter need not require an apparition, and the felt experience and emotion can depend on many contingent factors. However, it does essentially require that the reader believe that he or she can address the Son of God and be addressed by him, whether in the Scriptures, in the sacraments, or even in things that happen in life.

One of the most vivid examples of the encounter with the risen Lord is found in the conversion of Saint Paul. Paul was not a replacement for a fallen apostle, as Matthias was, nor did he know or accompany Jesus in his ministry from the beginning, as Matthias did (Acts 1:21–26). Paul was added to the apostles. Also, he did not originally receive the gospel from them, even though he experienced the witness of Stephen and others whom he persecuted. Like Mary Magdalene and Thomas the apostle, Paul was called by name by Christ himself, which enabled him to read the Scriptures in the light and the authority of the risen Lord (Acts 9:1–9; 26:12–18; Gal. 1:11–17; Phil. 3:4–11). Perhaps the very fact that he persecuted the followers of Jesus gave him a distinct perspective on the law and on how it found its fulfillment in Christ.

In the preface, William Wright speaks about his coauthor, Fr. Francis Martin, and about the origins of this book. They had worked together on projects in the Catholic Biblical Association and on a commentary on the Gospel of John, and Fr. Francis proposed that they jointly write a book on the more general biblical questions that they had discussed during their collaboration. As the years went on, Fr. Francis's health deteriorated, and he passed away on August 11, 2017. He was not able to see the final text of the book he had inspired. Fr. Francis was an extremely learned and insightful biblical scholar. He taught at many institutions, wrote and lectured extensively, and made use of the internet to help people understand the Scriptures and to assist priests in preaching their Sunday homilies. He served for decades as chaplain at the Mother of God Community in Gaithersburg, Maryland, and was a friend, counselor, and source of strength for numerous priests, religious, and laity. He dealt with severe illness and adversity with courage and peace, and helped others to do so. At the core of his relationships with other people was the Word of God as expressed in the Scriptures. His humor, as well as his charismatic spirit, was epitomized in a remark he would make on occasion during his teaching, when he would announce that in this course "we are going to heal your epistemology." May this book, written by him and his devoted friend and colleague William Wright, bear joyful witness to our faith in the risen Lord.

# Preface

Throughout this book, we speak of Scripture as putting people "in living and life-giving contact with the divine realities mediated by the sacred text." This expression comes from the introduction to Francis Martin's edited commentary on Acts of the Apostles in the Ancient Christian Commentary on Scripture. He used these words to describe the powerful encounter with the Word of God, given in Scripture, which the fathers of the church enjoyed in experiential faith. Through their close, spiritual connection to the Word of God, they were able to transmit the life-giving power of the Word. They are "fathers" because through them, life comes into the church.

Fr. Francis Martin, a man of great learning and profound holiness, enjoyed this same kind of faith experience of the Word of God. He knew its reality and sought to share it with others through his preaching, teaching, ministry, and writing. Shortly before beginning my own graduate studies in Scripture, I met Fr. Francis in the summer of 1999 at the Annual Meeting of the Catholic Biblical Association of America. By that time, I was acquainted with his writings, and I also shared many of his interests in modern biblical criticism, the theological tradition expressed in the doctrine of the fourfold sense of Scripture, and the theoretical underpinnings of biblical exegesis. During my graduate studies in Scripture and beyond, I participated in the task force that he started in the Catholic Biblical Association on the integration of historical criticism and the spiritual sense. I continued to work with Fr. Francis for several more years on our commentary *The Gospel of John* in the Catholic Commentary on Sacred Scripture.

As work on that volume was winding down, Fr. Francis proposed that we write a book on what we had been discussing for many years and he had been reflecting on (and living) for much longer: how Scripture enables people to encounter and experience the life-giving reality of God's Word and how we might give a theological and philosophical account of this capacity of Scripture. Shortly after work began, Fr. Francis's health worsened, and though we continued to have many conversations about the project, he was unable to contribute to the composition work on this text. When the draft of the whole manuscript was completed, I planned to deliver the text to Fr. Francis in person. A few days before the very weekend that I had planned to visit, Fr. Francis went to meet the Lord face-to-face.

On behalf of Fr. Francis, I would like to thank the many people who helped in various ways in the composition of this book. In particular, I thank Duquesne University for granting me a sabbatical leave at the outset of this project and the McNaulty College and Graduate School of Liberal Arts for the award of an internal grant from the National Endowment for the Humanities in support of this project. For their input and assistance, I thank Bogdan Bucur, Michael Deem, Edward Feser, Andrea Grillini, Ann Hartle, Carl Holladay, Michael Krom, and Fr. Jared Wicks, SJ. I also thank Bob and Nancy McCambridge and their family as well as the Mother of God Community. I am very grateful to Matthew Levering for reading the entire manuscript and offering helpful feedback. I thank Fr. Guy Mansini, OSB, for sharing a copy of an unpublished paper. Dr. Jim Swindal, dean of the McAnulty College and Graduate School of Liberal Arts at Duquesne University, has been an excellent dean and Catholic intellectual colleague. I thank him for our readings in Aquinas and W. Norris Clarke's interpretation of Thomistic metaphysics. I offer special thanks to Robert Sokolowski. Not only did Fr. Sokolowski graciously contribute the foreword to this book, but he also shared the text of an unpublished paper and offered some helpful suggestions on the manuscript. I am grateful for the help of these and many others, and any mistakes in this text remain my own.

Jim Kinney and his staff at Baker Academic provided excellent editorial and production work, and James Ernest helped get this project started. Many thanks are due to my wife, Michelle, and my son, William, for their constant love, support, and encouragement.

This book is dedicated to Fr. Francis Martin. Those of us who were blessed to have known him can attest that he was a good friend and colleague, a spiritual father, a brilliant scholar, and a holy priest. May the Lord Jesus Christ in his great love and mercy receive Fr. Francis into the house of our heavenly Father.

William M. Wright IV
Feast of St. Athanasius, 2018

# Abbreviations

## Old Testament

| | |
|---|---|
| Gen. | Genesis |
| Exod. | Exodus |
| Lev. | Leviticus |
| Num. | Numbers |
| Deut. | Deuteronomy |
| Josh. | Joshua |
| Judg. | Judges |
| Ruth | Ruth |
| 1–2 Sam. | 1–2 Samuel |
| 1–2 Kings | 1–2 Kings |
| 1–2 Chron. | 1–2 Chronicles |
| Ezra | Ezra |
| Neh. | Nehemiah |
| Esther | Esther |
| Job | Job |
| Ps. (Pss.) | Psalm (Psalms) |
| Prov. | Proverbs |
| Eccles. | Ecclesiastes |
| Song of Sol. | Song of Solomon |
| Isa. | Isaiah |
| Jer. | Jeremiah |
| Lam. | Lamentations |
| Ezek. | Ezekiel |
| Dan. | Daniel |
| Hosea | Hosea |
| Joel | Joel |
| Amos | Amos |
| Obad. | Obadiah |
| Jon. | Jonah |
| Mic. | Micah |
| Nah. | Nahum |
| Hab. | Habakkuk |
| Zeph. | Zephaniah |
| Hag. | Haggai |
| Zech. | Zechariah |
| Mal. | Malachi |

## New Testament

| | |
|---|---|
| Matt. | Matthew |
| Mark | Mark |
| Luke | Luke |
| John | John |
| Acts | Acts |
| Rom. | Romans |
| 1–2 Cor. | 1–2 Corinthians |
| Gal. | Galatians |
| Eph. | Ephesians |
| Phil. | Philippians |
| Col. | Colossians |
| 1–2 Thess. | 1–2 Thessalonians |
| 1–2 Tim. | 1–2 Timothy |
| Titus | Titus |
| Philem. | Philemon |
| Heb. | Hebrews |
| James | James |
| 1–2 Pet. | 1–2 Peter |
| 1–3 John | 1–3 John |
| Jude | Jude |
| Rev. | Revelation |

xviii

**Apocrypha**

Bar.    Baruch
Sir.    Sirach
Wis.    Wisdom of Solomon

**Other Abbreviations**

BZNW    Beihefte zur Zeitschrift für die
        neutestamentliche Wissenschaft
*DV*      *Dei Verbum*

EV      English version(s)
LXX     Septuagint
PG      Patrologia graeca. Edited by J.-P.
        Migne. 162 vols. Paris, 1857–86.
PL      Patrologia latina. Edited by J.-P.
        Migne. 217 vols. Paris, 1844–64.
STGM    Studien und Texte zur
        Geistesgeschichte des
        Mittelalters

# Introduction

T his book is a study of the Christian belief that Scripture can put its readers "in living and life-giving contact with the divine realities mediated by the sacred text."[1] This belief entails that God makes himself known and present to people through sacred Scripture such that properly disposed readers can genuinely encounter his reality and experience his transforming power. This faith-filled understanding of Scripture is grounded in the biblical witness and has been developed in subsequent Christian tradition. As an introduction to our topic, let us consider a few examples from both Scripture and the Christian tradition that display aspects of this belief.

## A First Look at Biblical and Traditional Witnesses

### "Is Not My Word like Fire?"

Throughout Scripture, the image of fire often indicates the presence and power of God. The association of the divine presence and fire is especially prominent in the narrative of the exodus from Egypt and the Sinai covenant. When the Lord first appears to Moses on the mountain and calls him to be his instrument to bring the Israelites out of slavery in Egypt, the Lord reveals himself "in a flame of fire out of a bush" (Exod. 3:2). After the Israelites leave Egypt, the Lord guides them through the wilderness in a column of cloud by day and of fire by night (Exod. 13:21–22). Once the Israelites arrive at Mount

---

1. Francis Martin, introduction to *Acts*, ed. Francis Martin, Ancient Christian Commentary on Scripture: New Testament 5 (Downers Grove, IL: InterVarsity, 2006), xxiii.

Sinai, the Lord offers a covenant relationship to the whole people and declares that he will manifest himself to the whole nation in three days' time. When Exodus describes this theophany at Sinai, it states, "Mount Sinai was wrapped in smoke, because the LORD had descended upon it in fire" (19:18). Deuteronomy speaks in similar terms of the Lord delivering the Torah to Israel: "The LORD spoke to you out of the fire" (Deut. 4:12). Exodus also speaks of "the glory of the LORD"—a sensible display of God's awesome presence—as "a devouring fire" (24:17; cf. Deut. 4:24), which manifested on Mount Sinai and in the wilderness tabernacle (Exod. 40:38).

Deuteronomy continues this figuring of God's presence at Sinai as fire and makes explicit an association of the fires of God's presence with God's speaking. Recounting the awesome gift that God should reveal himself to Israel in this way, Moses asks rhetorically, "Has any people ever heard the voice of a god speaking out of a fire, as you have heard, and lived?" (Deut. 4:33; cf. 5:26). Moses later adds, "On earth he showed you his great fire, while you heard his words coming out of the fire" (4:36). The prophet Jeremiah, in terms redolent of Deuteronomy, describes the Word of God as "something like a burning fire shut up in my bones" (Jer. 20:9). The same image appears in an oracle subsequently spoken by Jeremiah: "Is not my word like fire, says the LORD?" (23:29).

These associations between God's presence, his Word, and the imagery of fire inform another story more familiar to Christian readers of the Bible. On Easter Sunday afternoon, two of Jesus's disciples had left Jerusalem for Emmaus, discussing the report of Mary Magdalene and others that Jesus's tomb was in fact empty. The risen Jesus, withholding recognition of his identity, starts to walk with the two disciples. While they are on the way, Luke writes, "beginning with Moses and all the prophets, [Jesus] interpreted to them the things about himself in all the scriptures" (Luke 24:27). That evening, after the two disciples were given to recognize the risen Jesus, they reflect, "Were not our hearts *burning* within us while he was talking to us on the road, while he was opening the *scriptures* to us" (24:32, emphasis added).

Later, on Easter Sunday evening, the risen Jesus appeared to the apostles and some other disciples in Jerusalem. As he did with the two disciples on the road to Emmaus, the risen Jesus here reveals himself and interprets the Scripture (Luke 24:46–47). He tells them, "Everything written about me in the law of Moses, the prophets, and psalms must be fulfilled" (24:44). Just as rabbis used the exegetical practice of "stringing pearls," the risen Jesus takes the disciples through the three sections of the Bible—"the law of Moses" (the Torah), "the prophets," and "psalms" (the Writings)—and interprets them as speaking of himself: "He opened their minds to understand the scriptures" (24:45).[2]

In these resurrection narratives, the risen Jesus becomes *present* to his disciples and interprets the Scripture—*God's Word*—in light of himself. As Jesus does so, the disciples have within themselves the experience of the *burning fires* of revelation. This manner of interpreting Scripture is not simply an intellectual exercise but rather a transforming encounter with the Lord. The disciples encounter the risen Jesus in connection with the Scriptures, and he sets their hearts on fire with his presence and power. These episodes from Luke's resurrection narrative give particular expression to the belief that Scripture mediates divine reality to people who can experience the power of that reality.

### *Tasting the Word:* Lectio Divina

This biblically founded understanding of Scripture as mediating divine reality and power receives further expression in subsequent Christian tradition. A hallmark example is the Christian practice of *lectio divina*, a mode of praying with Scripture that has flourished (and continues to flourish) within the setting of monasticism and monastically informed spirituality.[3] Although this way of reading Scripture has an ancient Christian pedigree, its four stages were famously articulated by twelfth-century Carthusian monk Guigo II of Chartreuse in his "The Ladder of Monks" (*Scala Claustralium*).[4]

The first stage, "reading" (*lectio*), is, as Guigo puts it, "the careful study of the Scriptures, concentrating all one's powers on it."[5] It is the slow, careful, and attentive reading of the biblical text as it plainly reads. In this stage, the reader ponders the words carefully and prepares to hear the Lord speaking to him or her. Throughout his work (and in keeping with the known monastic metaphor), Guigo compares the slow, prayerful reading of Scripture to the

---

2. The Jewish exegetical tradition of "stringing pearls" (i.e., interpreting Scripture by connecting texts between the Torah, Prophets, and Writings) could likewise be mentioned in this regard. This tradition, along with its subtle resemblances to the Emmaus narrative in Luke 24, is discussed in Francis Martin, "Spiritual Understanding of Scripture," in *Verbum Domini and the Complementarity of Exegesis and Theology*, ed. Fr. Scott Carl (Grand Rapids: Eerdmans, 2015), 12–14.

3. An excellent introduction to the practice and theology of *lectio divina* is Mariano Magrassi, *Praying the Bible: An Introduction to Lectio Divina*, trans. Edward Hagman (Collegeville, MN: Liturgical Press, 1998).

4. Guigo II, *Ladder of Monks and Twelve Meditations*, trans. Edmund Colledge, OSA, and James Walsh, SJ, Cistercian Studies Series 48 (Kalamazoo, MI: Cistercian Publications, 1979). Latin texts from Guigo II, *Scala Paradisi* (PL 40:997–1004).

5. Guigo II, *Ladder* 2 (Colledge and Walsh, 68; Latin from PL 40:998).

eating and enjoying of food.[6] Accordingly, Guigo likens this first stage to putting food in one's mouth.

The second stage, "meditation" (*meditatio*), is "the busy application of the mind to seek with the help of one's own reason for knowledge of hidden truth."[7] Here, the prayerful reader uses his or her intellectual abilities to ponder the meaning of the words and what they are disclosing to the reader. In this stage, the Holy Spirit is at work in the properly disposed reader to open up for him or her the inner depths of the biblical contents.[8] In keeping with the imagery of eating food, Guigo likens this stage to chewing slowly.

The third stage (*oratio*) is "the heart's devoted turning to God to drive away evil and obtain what is good."[9] The reader chews on the words and contents of Scripture, and this stage, Guigo remarks, is like tasting its flavor. The faithful reader here converses with the Lord, asking him for greater understanding both of God's own self (mediated through the biblical text) and of the reader's own self. The reader prays that his or her knowledge and love of God will increase, but such an increase also entails a greater awareness of the reader's own sinfulness and that of which the reader must repent. The Lord enflames our desire for him, and having been so enticed to know him more, we realize that we must give up our sins in order to draw closer to him. Through this praying, the Lord also reveals that of which we must repent, and as we give up our sins, we get to know him better.

The fourth stage (*contemplatio*) is "when the mind is in some sort lifted up to God and held above itself, so that it tastes the joys of everlasting sweetness."[10] This is where the reader rests in the Lord's presence and peace, having been affected and changed through the prayerful reading experience. Contemplation, Guigo writes, "inebriates the thirsting soul with the dew of heavenly sweetness."[11] It is the swallowing of the food and savoring of its goodness. It is, in a sense, being given a small taste of heavenly blessedness.

As he reflects on the movements and experiences of the soul during this practice, Guigo connects this prayerful reading of Scripture to Luke 24 and the familiar imagery of fire: "When you break for me the bread of sacred

6. See Jean Leclercq, OSB, *The Love for Learning and the Desire for God*, trans. Catharine Misrahi (New York: Fordham University Press, 1982), 73.
7. Guigo, *Ladder* 2 (Colledge and Walsh, 68; Latin from PL 40:998).
8. Guigo, *Ladder* 5 (Colledge and Walsh, 71–72), states that such fruits of meditation are a divine gift to the reader: "A man will not experience this sweetness while reading or meditating 'unless it happened to be given him from above.'"
9. Guigo, *Ladder* 2 (Colledge and Walsh, 68; Latin from PL 40:998). Cf. Guigo, *Ladder* 6 (Colledge and Walsh, 72–73).
10. Guigo, *Ladder* 2 (Colledge and Walsh, 68; Latin from PL 40:998).
11. Guigo, *Ladder* 12 (Colledge and Walsh, 79).

Scripture, you have shown yourself to me in that breaking of bread, and the more I see you, the more I long to see you, no more from without, in the rind of the letter, but within, in the letter's hidden meaning. . . . So give me, Lord, some pledge of what I hope to inherit, at least one drop of heavenly rain with which to refresh my thirst, for I am on fire with love."[12] Guigo thus identifies the faith experience of the monk who practices *lectio divina* with the experience of those disciples on the road to Emmaus, who were instructed by the Lord through Scripture and whose hearts were consequently set on fire. It is this capacity of Scripture to mediate an encounter with God and his life-giving power that we explore in this book.

## Charting a Course

With respect to this belief that Scripture can put people in living and life-giving contact with divine reality, we look to do two things. First, we will set forth the biblical substance and warrant for this belief by examining various biblical witnesses pertaining to the Word of God. Second, we will seek a deeper understanding of this biblical teaching through a series of philosophical, theological, and spiritual reflections. That is, we will explicate some basic principles that are appropriate to this understanding of Scripture and help us grasp its intelligibility.

We have structured this book in two parts according to Anselm's famous definition of theology as "faith seeking understanding" (*fides quaerens intellectum*).[13] Part 1, *Fides*, takes up the biblical witnesses that mediate to us the revelation of God in the divine economy. In these chapters, we provide a representative (though not comprehensive) survey of witnesses from both Testaments that pertain to our study of the Word of God.

Chapter 1 focuses on the Word of God as spoken directly by God in the Old Testament and by Jesus in the New Testament. We highlight two related aspects of the Word of God that appear in these texts and that will in turn shape our study. First, the biblical witnesses present the Word of God as having divine causal power. By speaking, God produces a divinely caused effect, such as in creation, in his providential governance of the world, and in the events of salvation history. Second, the Word of God has associations with notions of presence. Admittedly, this second aspect is a bit more nebulous. Under this second aspect, we group together a variety of texts that variously associate the Word of God and modes of presence: for instance, God becomes present

---

12. Guigo, *Ladder* 6 (Colledge and Walsh, 73).
13. Anselm, *Proslogion*, proem (PL 158:225).

to people as he reveals himself and his will through his Word; God causes something to become present by his speaking; the Word of God is a personal reality in its own right (e.g., the personified Word of God as an agent figure).

Chapters 2 and 3 continue this examination of the Word of God but as mediated through inspired human speech. The preeminent cases for study here are the inspired speech of Israel's prophets and the preaching of the apostles, as discussed in Acts and select New Testament epistles. The witnesses examined in these chapters give evidence that the Word of God and its aspects of power and presence can be mediated through the inspired speech of human beings. Chapter 4 extends this line of inquiry one step further. Here, we consider in detail evidence from two texts—the Letter to the Hebrews and the Gospel according to John—that present the Word of God as being mediated through the inspired written discourse of the Scripture to people in their present moment. Taken together, these biblical witnesses provide substance and warrant for the belief that Scripture can mediate divine reality and power to people in their present moment.

Part 2, *Quaerens Intellectum* ("seeking understanding"), reflects theologically and philosophically on these biblically warranted teachings about Scripture. These chapters explore some basic theological and philosophical principles that illumine this biblical teaching and help us grasp its intelligibility. Although the discussion in these chapters delves into some fundamental and technical matters, we look to make our exposition accessible to nonspecialists.

We firmly believe that it is very important for interpreters of Scripture to be familiar with philosophical and theological thinking. All understandings of the Bible and its interpretation depend on various philosophical and theological principles of one sort or another. All biblical interpreters, whether or not they know it (or admit it), are influenced by some forms of philosophical thinking. Moreover, not all philosophical claims are equally truthful and thus equally valuable. Some ideas are better (i.e., more truthful) than others, and faulty premises lead to faulty conclusions. Theologically speaking, not all ideas and related understandings of Scripture are conducive to understanding Scripture as mediating divine reality. Accordingly, if we are going to appreciate and understand more deeply this capacity of sacred Scripture, we must attend to the philosophical and theological principles that show forth its intelligibility and mystery. As we give a positive account of these principles, we will identify and critique certain ideas in modern thought that hinder or obscure reception of this teaching.

It may be helpful to conceive of the exposition in part 2 as a ladder or staircase, with each chapter as a rung or step. We begin at the bottom, with the most basic and fundamental topics, and then ascend each step of the exposition, with new elements building on the previous ones and the application to Scripture becoming more and more focused.

We begin our ascent in chapter 5 (the first step) with the most basic setting for all theological thinking: the doctrine of creation. Drawing largely on the theological writings of Robert Sokolowski, we will focus on the particular understanding of the relationship between God and the world that the biblical doctrine of a free creation entails. This understanding, which we, following Sokolowski, will refer to as "the Distinction," provides the setting for thinking about all theological topics, including Scripture and how it puts people in living contact with divine reality. The Distinction calibrates our thinking so that we do not misconstrue God as a kind of "thing" that exercises causal power in the world in the way that created things do. The Distinction is thus essential for preserving and respecting the mystery of the sacred text, as well as for providing a larger horizon for our reflections on other related topics.

Chapter 6 (the second step) heightens these theological reflections on the world-as-created by reflecting philosophically on some basic structures and dimensions of created reality as such (i.e., metaphysics or ontology). Drawing largely on Thomas Aquinas and some of his interpreters, we will set forth some basic metaphysical principles of the world-as-created, including notions of participation and relationality. Having set forth an account of the Creator-creation relationship, entailed by the Distinction and the conceptually congruent Thomistic metaphysics, we then offer some initial reflections in chapter 7 on what these metaphysical reflections have to do with how we understand the Bible, and we do so with special attention to the notion of transcendence.

These ontological insights about participation and relationality, which are essential to created reality as such, also provide direction for thinking about how human beings can both encounter external reality through words (i.e., cognition) and, specifically, encounter the mystery-bearing realities of salvation history that the biblical text mediates. Accordingly, we ascend to the next step in chapter 8 and bring our reflections on the world-as-created to bear on the relationship between human knowing, words, and the world. Here, we give an account for how human beings can come into cognitive contact with external realities by integrating elements from W. Norris Clarke's analysis of Aquinas on the self-communication of being through action and Robert Sokolowski's phenomenological analyses of intentionality, words, and things. This integration, we suggest, also provides the conceptual means for preserving the connection between human knowing, words, and the world, which much modern philosophy severs.

From here, we move up another step and bring these philosophical and theological reflections to bear on Scripture proper. Given our concern with Scripture as putting people in contact with God and his transforming power, chapter 9 focuses on Scripture in terms of mediation. Scripture mediates God to its audience, but it does so by bearing witness to the mystery-bearing realities of the divine economy. Thus, by putting its audience in cognitive contact with the various realities of the economy, Scripture puts its audience in genuine contact with the mystery of God, which those realities bear.

Although the biblical realities are temporally past, the mystery that they bear is divine: it is eternal and thus ever present. These divine mysteries are available to people in their present moment through Scripture, but a living encounter with these divine mysteries requires both the action of the Holy Spirit and readers properly disposed to the Spirit's action in them. Accordingly, we reach the top of the expository ladder in chapter 10, which treats the personal assimilation of the divine realities mediated by Scripture. Drawing on biblical texts, such as the parable of the sower, as well as other theological resources in the tradition, such as the lives of the saints, we take up how, through the power of the Holy Spirit, the audience of Scripture can experience the divine realities and their life-transforming power that the biblical text mediates. Proper to this faith experience of the Word of God are certain moral and spiritual dispositions by which people are disposed to the action of the Holy Spirit, who impresses the Word of God onto their spirits.

## Further Clarifications

In closing, we clarify a few things about what this project does (and does not) seek to accomplish. First, this book is not so much about method or "how to read the Bible" as it is about "how the Bible works"—or, at least, the way in which the Bible facilitates an encounter with the living God. We address many aspects of this complex topic, but we also acknowledge that much more can be said about it. Other, related areas do not receive substantive consideration in this book (e.g., biblical inspiration, the relationship of the Bible and the liturgy, how to deal responsibly with difficult or problematic passages in Scripture). Therefore, we do not regard this book as a comprehensive statement on the matter. Furthermore, we do not claim that our account is the only viable way for exploring and explicating these teachings about Scripture. Nevertheless, we do offer our account as being congruent with the biblical testimony, philosophically cogent, theologically illuminating, and spiritually resourceful.

By reflecting on this understanding of Scripture and exploring its intelligibility, we look to contribute to biblical and theological studies. This understanding of Scripture as putting people in living and life-giving contact with divine reality is very much ingredient to the classic Christian understanding of the Bible and can be regarded, we think, as an important component of Christian heritage.[14] While we are making a case for this classic understanding of Scripture, we are not rejecting modern biblical criticism—even if we do argue that some of its elements need a better conceptual footing. Historical-biblical criticism is an important component of Christian biblical interpretation today, but it is not the sum total of Christian biblical interpretation.[15] This work on Scripture seeks to open the conceptual space to recognize the legitimacy of other modes of reading Scripture and encountering God through it. At the same time, we do not advocate a wholesale or uncritical retrieval of premodern exegesis either. For a variety of reasons, such an attempt would be both impossible and undesirable.[16] We do, however, believe that much of value remains in the classic understanding of the Bible and in the theology and spirituality that attend it. In the words of Henri de Lubac, "Without either a return to archaic forms or servile mimicry, often by totally different methods, it is a spiritual movement [in traditional Christian exegesis] that we must reproduce."[17] The contemporary church only stands to benefit from a philosophically and doctrinally sound integration of the wisdom of the Christian past with the genuine insights of the present.

Finally, we hope that this book will serve a practical and pastoral purpose. A key component of our exposition is that through Scripture, people can genuinely encounter the living God and his life-giving and life-changing power as people consent to God's work in them. By introducing and explicating the understanding of Scripture as mediating divine reality and God's transforming power, we hope that our readers will come to experience the life-giving power of God's Word in their own lives and transmit it among their families, relationships, communities, and the world.

14. So too Henri de Lubac, *History and Spirit: The Understanding of Scripture according to Origen*, trans. Anne Englund Nash and Juvenal Merriell (San Francisco: Ignatius, 2007), 431.

15. See Lewis Ayres and Stephen E. Fowl, "(Mis)Reading the Face of God: The Interpretation of the Bible in the Church," *Theological Studies* 60 (1999): 527–28.

16. We might cite in this regard the impossibility of contemporary Christian biblical interpretation ignoring the advances and challenges offered by modern biblical criticism as well as the limits and defects in much premodern exegesis (e.g., textually loose interpretations, anti-Jewish polemics); cf. Martin, introduction to *Acts*, xxii–xxiii.

17. De Lubac, *History and Spirit*, 450.

# PART 1

*Fides*

# 1

# The Word of God

*Power and Presence*

We begin with the biblical witness concerning the Word of God. This chapter focuses specifically on the Word spoken directly by God as distinguished from God's Word given through human intermediaries (e.g., prophets and apostles). Two overarching motifs come to light in these texts. First, the Word of God has causal power. Through his Word, God produces a divinely caused effect in the world, such as in creating, his providential governance of the world, and his immediate acts of divine power in the world. Second, the Word of God has associations with forms of presence. For instance, the Word of God can cause something to be or to occur (e.g., God creates by his Word). The Word of God also puts people in cognitive contact with divine reality or truth by imparting knowledge of God (e.g., God reveals himself and his designs by his Word). Moreover, some texts present the Word of God as an agent figure, a form of presence. Given the volume of material pertinent to this topic, the survey in this chapter (as well as the others) is representative, including texts from different historical periods and literary genres to show that these teachings about the Word of God span the entire canon.

## Old Testament Witnesses

### God's Word and Creation

An appropriate place to begin this study of Old Testament teaching about the Word of God is with creation. The seven-day account of creation in

Genesis 1:1–2:4a depicts God creating and ordering the world (i.e., "every-thing that is not divine") by spoken commands.[1] Although this account is not the oldest biblical evidence (historically speaking) for the power and presence of God's Word, it certainly is quite prominent in terms of both its dramatic depiction and its placement at the opening of the canon.

Four aspects of the creation narrative's depiction of God's Word stand out for present purposes. First, God brings everything into an ordered exis-tence by his speaking. The phrase "God said" opens each of the six days of creation, and thus it introduces the creation of each thing that God makes part of the cosmos (Gen. 1:3, 6, 9, 11, 14, 20, 24, 26). Moreover, all the other Hebrew verbs employed in this account for God's creative action—"make" (*'āśâ*), "create" (*bārā'*), "separate" (*bādal*)—never appear without reference to God's speaking. So prominently does God's Word figure into this narrative that God's creating cannot be conceived of apart from it.

Second, the Genesis narrative presents God's Word as an exercise of his almighty power. The narrative depicts God's creating as being veritably ef-fortless and as happening in perfect accord with his Word. Scholars have pointed out that the creation account in Genesis 1:1–2:4a reflects (and, in some cases, subverts) certain stock images and motifs common to other ancient Near Eastern accounts of creation.[2] The significance of God's creating by his Word in Genesis 1 can be appreciated when compared with the ancient combat myth of creation such as that given in the Babylonian account of origins, Enuma Elish.[3] This famed Babylonian account depicts creation as stemming from battle between gods: the Babylonian hero god Marduk and the sea monster Tiamat and her cohort.[4] In contrast with the violence in the Babylonian myth of origins, Genesis 1 narrates creation as resulting from the simple, placid fiat of the one almighty God, not a violent contest between rival deities.[5] Not only does the Genesis narrative lack any hint of contest or

1. Robert Sokolowski, "Creation and Christian Understanding," in *Christian Faith & Human Understanding: Studies on the Eucharist, Trinity, and the Human Person* (Washington, DC: Catholic University of America Press, 2006), 38.
2. See Claus Westermann, *Genesis 1–11: A Commentary*, trans. John J. Scullion, SJ (Minne-apolis: Augsburg, 1984), 80–81; Gordon J. Wenham, *Genesis 1–15*, Word Biblical Commentary 1 (Dallas: Word, 1987), 8–10, 37.
3. Westermann (*Genesis 1–11*, 111–12) points out that the idea of creation by divine com-mand is also present in Egyptian Memphite creation theology.
4. Cf. the version of Enuma Elish as "The Epic of Creation" in *Myths from Mesopotamia: Creation, the Flood, Gilgamesh, and Others*, trans. Stephanie Dalley (New York: Oxford Uni-versity Press, 1989), tablet 4 (252–55), tablet 6 (261).
5. Westermann, *Genesis 1–11*, 80. While the Genesis account and other ancient Near Eastern creation stories do contain real differences in content and emphasis, they should not be taken as hermetically sealed off from one another. Thus, other biblical texts (e.g., Pss. 74:12–17; 89:5–18;

struggle; it also subtly rebuts the combat myth by counting "the sea monsters" among God's creatures (1:21).

The Genesis narrative also underscores that creation happens in perfect accord with God's Word. This point comes to light in two ways through the language of the narrative. First, the text frequently follows God's creative speech with the simple phrase "And it was so" (1:7, 9, 11, 15, 24, 30). The terseness of this expression reinforces the uncontested nature of God's creative activity and the perfection with which the divine fiat is executed. Second, the narrative frequently repeats the language used in the divine creative command in the description of a thing's coming-to-be. For instance, on the first day (1:3), God issues the creative pronouncement "Let there be light" (yəhî 'ôr), and the description of the resulting, created state of affairs both follows immediately and is given in the exact same language as God's speech: "and there was light" (wayəhî-'ôr). The repetition of language between God's spoken pronouncement and the creation of a particular thing indicates that there is no disconnect between what God says and what results. God creates effortlessly by a spoken command, and what results happens in perfect accord with God's Word. These two features—the effortlessness of God's creating by his Word and the perfectly corresponding result—point to the almighty sovereignty of God. God's Word is an exercise of the divine will and power, and as Gordon Wenham writes, the Word of God "brings into existence what it expresses."[6]

Not only is God's creating by his Word an exercise of the divine will, but it is also revealing of God's wisdom and intention—a third aspect of God's Word in Genesis 1. As the passage describes God's creating by his Word, it not only declares *that* God speaks ("Then God said . . .") but also gives the content of *what* God says ("Let there be light"; 1:3). The text spells out the divine intention to create by articulating it in the direct, declarative speech of God himself. By providing the reader with the content of God's pronouncement, the narrative presents God's Word as revealing his intention to create and his intentions for various creatures: the heavenly lights are "to separate the day from the night . . . and . . . be for signs and for seasons and for days and years" (1:14); human beings are to "have dominion" over the birds, the fish, and the creeping things on the land (1:28); the green plants and fruit are to serve as food for both human beings and other creatures (1:29–30). God's

---

114; Isa. 51:9–11) employ the imagery of the combat myth when talking about God. The biblical authors thought and wrote in an ancient Near Eastern context and idiom, and therefore it should not be altogether surprising that they should appropriate conventional religious imagery and motifs in their compositions.

6. Wenham, *Genesis 1–15*, 18.

speech reveals him as one who provides for the well-being and sustenance of his creatures. Not only is God's Word an exercise of the divine will, but it is also revealing of God's wisdom and his intentions for creation.[7]

Fourth, God imparts blessing by his Word. On two occasions in Genesis 1, God "blesses" his creatures, and the declaration of blessing is connected with God's speech (1:22, 28). God blesses his creatures as he instructs them to "be fruitful and multiply," a command given to the birds, the fish, and the human beings. God blesses these creatures by endowing them with the capacity for reproduction. In doing so, God allows creatures to participate in God's own creative activity.

The creation account of Genesis 1:1–2:4a, with its distinctive emphasis on God's creating by his Word, is verbally and thematically echoed in Psalm 33. The psalm, a hymn of praise, celebrates God's providence and sovereignty over all things.[8] The hymn contains a subsection (33:6–9) that speaks of God's action as the Creator. Mention of God's creating by his Word both opens and closes this subsection, forming an *inclusio*. This movement of the psalm opens with the statement "By the word of the LORD the heavens were made, and all their host by the breath of his mouth" (33:6). The psalmist then exhorts the world's population to stand in awe before the Lord and cites as the warrant for such reverence the Lord's creating the world by his powerful Word: "For he spoke, and it came to be; he commanded, and it stood firm" (33:9).[9] References to the Lord's creating by his Word—either as a noun (*dābār*) or as a verb (*'āmar*)—frame this section. Like the creation account in Genesis 1, Psalm 33 depicts God effortlessly creating the world by his Word, a simple and powerful fiat that instantiates his will. This connection between God's Word and his activity is anticipated in verse 4, which reads, "For the word of the LORD is upright, and all his work is done in faithfulness." The parallel construction of the two lines aligns the Lord's Word and his working. As Terence Fretheim puts it, "The word of God is the vehicle for the will of God;

---

7. Cf. Wenham, *Genesis 1–15*, 38. This implication of the Genesis text is what Thomas Aquinas later articulated in a different register as regarding divine simplicity: "The will of God is not distinct from the divine intellect and God's essence." Thomas Aquinas, *Aquinas's Shorter Summa: Saint Thomas Aquinas's Own Concise Version of His "Summa Theologica,"* trans. Cyril Vollert, SJ (Manchester, NH: Sophia Institute Press, 2002), 1.33 (p. 32).

8. J. Clinton McCann Jr., "The Book of Psalms," in *The New Interpreter's Bible*, ed. Leander E. Keck, 12 vols. (Nashville: Abingdon, 1994–2004), 4:809–11.

9. The phrasing of Ps. 33:9 ("he spoke, and it came to be ['*āmar wayyehî*]") recalls the pairing of *'āmar* and *hāyâ* in Gen. 1—e.g., Gen. 1:3 ("Then God said, 'Let there be light'; and there was light [*wayyōmer 'ĕlōhîm yəhî 'ôr wayəhî-'ôr*]"). The language of Ps. 33 also appears in Ps. 148, which likewise summons people to praise the Creator: "for he commanded and they were created [*hû' ṣiwwâ wənibrā'û*]" (Ps. 148:5); "he commanded, and it stood firm [*hû'-ṣiwwâ wayyaʿămōd*]" (Ps. 33:9).

the word expresses what God intends."[10] Just as in Genesis 1, God's creative Word was revealing of his wisdom and intentions for created things, so here too, his Word reveals him as being "upright" and "faithful."

### God's Word and His Providential Governance

The hymn in Sirach 42:15–43:33 associates God's Word with his creating and his providential governance of the world. The hymn opens, "I will now call to mind the works of the Lord, and will declare what I have seen. By the word of the Lord his works are made; and all his creatures do his will" (42:15). Reminiscent of Genesis 1 and Psalm 33:6, Sirach 42:15c mentions God creating by his Word and seemingly envisions God speaking things into being. The chiastic structuring of 42:15c–d also associates God's Word and his will:

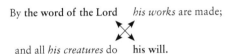

This literary-rhetorical structure implies that God both creates the world and providentially governs the world by his Word. The "creatures" that "do his will" are the various created things that follow God's wise, providential arrangement. This point receives further support from this hymn's other references to created things that follow God's Word. Ben Sira speaks of the sun as following God's Word: "At his orders [*logois*] it hurries on its course" (Sir. 43:5); and similarly the stars: "On the orders [*logois*] of the Holy One they stand in their appointed places" (43:10). After his review of various created things that are governed by providence, Ben Sira concludes, "By his word [*logō*] all things hold together" (43:26). It is because God creates, orders, and governs all things by his providential Word that creation can be said to be suffused with and reflective of God's glory (42:16–17, 25; 43:1, 9, 12) and beauty (43:9, 18). Both Psalm 33 and Sirach 42:15–43:33 thus speak of created things obeying God's Word by living out their essential natures and activities (e.g., the motions of heavenly bodies), which the Creator's wise providence ordains.

Other texts likewise display the connection between God's Word and his providential governance of creation. There are affirmations of God's Word as holding sway over the angels in the concluding movement of Psalm 103, a hymn of praise to God the benevolent and merciful Savior. After setting the heavenly scene with an introductory remark, "The LORD has established

10. Terence E. Fretheim, "Word of God," in *The Anchor Bible Dictionary*, ed. David Noel Freedman, 6 vols. (New York: Doubleday, 1992), 6:963.

his throne in the heavens" (103:19), the psalmist exhorts the angels to bless God the heavenly King. He addresses the angels as "you mighty ones who do his bidding, obedient to his spoken word [dābār; LXX: logos]" (103:20; LXX 102:20). This identification of the angels as those who carry out the commands of the heavenly King is reaffirmed in the next verse: "Bless the LORD, all his hosts, his ministers that do his will" (103:21). The parallelism between these two verses points to the familiar association with God's "spoken word" and "his will." Psalm 119:89 likewise declares the heavenly permanence of God's Word: "The LORD exists forever; your word is firmly fixed in heaven." The psalmist associates the permanent rule of God's Word with God's very life, as well as his governance of the world and his faithfulness (119:90). Precisely because God's Word is so permanent and reliable, the psalmist can speak of it as his "delight" (v. 92), source of life (v. 93), and hope (v. 95).

Another kind of association between God's Word and his providential governance appears in texts that present God causing things to happen in the world by his Word. Especially significant in this regard are three aspects of Psalm 147. First, the psalmist speaks of God's Word in terms of his providential governance of nature. Psalm 147:15 introduces a unit of the psalm (vv. 15–18) that discusses God's providence in terms of the example of cold-weather phenomena.[11] The movement begins, "He sends out his command to the earth; his word runs swiftly" (v. 15). The psalmist then lists the effects of this command with three meteorological examples: God "gives snow," "scatters frost," and "hurls down hail" (vv. 16–17). After a rhetorical declaration of the power of God manifested in the cold weather, "who can stand before his cold?" (v. 17b), the psalmist follows up with the meteorological reversal of these frozen states, which is likewise brought about by God's Word, "sent out" by him: "He sends out his word, and melts them; he makes his wind blow, and the waters flow" (v. 18; cf. v. 15).

Second, Psalm 147 speaks of God's Word in connection with his providential activity in the history of Israel. Immediately after speaking of God reversing the cold-weather conditions by his Word, the psalmist shifts to God's Word in the history of Israel: "He declares his word to Jacob, his statues and ordinances to Israel" (v. 19). By repeating the term for "word" (dābār) in verses 15, 18, 19, the psalmist identifies the Word by which God providentially governs nature as the same Word given to Israel in the Torah.[12] As in Genesis 1,

---

11. McCann writes, "The mention of God's 'word' in verse 18a makes it clear that these phenomena cannot be subsumed simply under the category of meteorology. For the Psalmist, because God rules the world, even the weather is a theological matter!" "Psalms," 1268.

12. God's Wisdom is also identified with the Torah in Bar. 3:36–4:2; Sir. 24:22.

God's Word not only enacts God's providential power but also is revealing of who God is. As J. Clinton McCann writes of Psalm 147:19–20, "God's word—formerly addressed to snow and hail and wind—is now addressed to Israel. To know God's word is to know God's will and, indeed, God's very self."[13] By associating God's providence with his being both Creator and Savior, the psalmist creates an *inclusio* with the opening of the psalm, where this same association also appears (cf. vv. 2–4).[14]

Third, the poetic discourse of the psalm speaks of God's Word as an agent or a subject who acts. The parallelism in Psalm 147:15 associates God's "word" (*dābār*) with his "command" (*'imrâ*).[15]

He sends out   his command to the earth;

his word   runs swiftly.

Just as God "sends out" (*šālaḥ*) "his command" (v. 15) to bring about the cold-weather phenomena, so too God "sends out" (*šālaḥ*) "his word" to undo those conditions (v. 18).

Having been dispatched, the Word of God "runs swiftly" (Ps. 147:15) on a mission in the world, and the Word carries out God's providential will. Through this poetic discourse, Psalm 147 coheres with the more substantive personification of God's Word as an agent in other biblical texts.

The Wisdom of Solomon speaks of God's creating by his Word, but here, God's Word is spoken of in more substantive terms. Wisdom 9:1–18 is a prayer that amplifies Solomon's petition for God to send him wisdom to assist in his service as king (cf. 1 Kings 3:6–9). The prayer opens with an address: "O God of my ancestors and Lord of mercy, who have made all things by your word [*logos*], and by your wisdom have formed humankind" (Wis. 9:1–2). The chiastic construction clearly associates God's Word (*logos*) with his Wisdom (*sophia*), which are said to be, respectively, that by which God made "all things" and that by which he made "humankind."

who have made all things   by your word [logos],

and by your wisdom [sophia]   have formed humankind

---

13. McCann, "Psalms," 1268–69.

14. Psalm 147:2, 4 reads, "The Lord builds up Jerusalem; he gathers the outcasts of Israel. . . . He determines the number of the stars; he gives to all of them their names."

15. The Hebrew noun *'imrâ* can be a synonym for God's Word (e.g., Deut. 33:9).

While the prayer does not again speak of God's Word specifically, it goes on to explicate the various roles and functions of God's personified Wisdom. Wisdom "was present when [God] made the world" (Wis. 9:9) and "sits by [God's] throne" (v. 4), from which God sends her (vv. 6, 10). Solomon prays for Wisdom, "who knows [God's] works, . . . understands what is pleasing in [his] sight and what is right according to [his] commandments" (v. 9). He prays that God will send Wisdom to teach, direct, and protect him (vv. 10–11), just as Wisdom did for Israel's great ancestors from Adam to Moses (10:1–11:4).

The identification of God's Word with his wisdom, which is personified at length here and elsewhere in the Wisdom literature, imparts a kind of substantiveness (or hypostatization) to God's Word. Whereas Genesis 1, Psalm 33, and Sirach 42:15–43:33 focus on God's *act* of speaking creation into being, Wisdom 9:1, by identifying his Word with personified Wisdom, presents God's creative Word as an instrumental agent, a "who" by whom God creates and acts. In this way, Wisdom 9:1 coheres with other texts that speak of God's Word as an agent and thus a kind of presence.

The author of Wisdom depicts God's Word as an agent even more dramatically in 18:15–16. We have already seen how the author identified God's Word with God's Wisdom personified (9:1–2) and spoke of God's Wisdom (or Word) as coming from heaven and at work in the history of Israel's ancestors (10:1–11:4). Continuing this theme, 18:15–16 presents the Word of God as an acting subject, who descends to earth to carry out God's judgment on the Egyptians in the exodus. The author thus describes the climactic tenth plague, the death of the firstborn: "Your all-powerful word leaped from heaven, from the royal throne, into the midst of the land that was doomed" (18:15; cf. Exod. 12:29). The text continues by calling God's Word "a stern warrior carrying the sharp sword" of God's "authentic command"; this Word "stood and filled all things with death" (Wis. 18:15–16). By serving as the heavenly agent of God's will on earth, the Word has a kind of intermediary role: the Word "touched heaven while standing on the earth" (v. 16). This presentation of the divine Word as an intermediary figure has much in common with other Jewish speculation about the personified Word of God, such as in the Logos figure in Philo of Alexandria as well as the *memra* in the Aramaic Targumim.[16]

16. See Richard Bauckham, *Jesus and the God of Israel: God Crucified and Other Studies on the New Testament's Christology of Divine Identity* (Grand Rapids: Eerdmans, 2008), 7–17; Daniel Boyarin, *Border Lines: The Partition of Judaeo-Christianity* (Philadelphia: University of Pennsylvania Press, 2004), 89–147; Thomas H. Tobin, "Logos," in *Anchor Bible Dictionary*, 4:348–56; William M. Wright IV, "Logos," in *The Routledge Encyclopedia of Ancient Mediterranean Religions*, ed. Eric Orlin (New York: Routledge, 2016), 546.

### God's Word and His Action in History

As some texts identify God's Word and the Torah (e.g., Ps. 147) and others present God's Word as a substantial agent in the exodus (e.g., Wis. 18:15–16), other texts associate the Word of God with his action in the history of salvation—past, present, or future.

A variety of biblical texts speak of God's Word in connection with the (*past*) events of the exodus. Psalm 105 recounts God's covenant faithfulness to Israel in building up the descendants of Abraham and rescuing them from slavery in Egypt. When discussing the plagues—the "signs" (v. 27) that God worked through Moses and Aaron—the psalmist twice speaks of plagues being accomplished by God's speaking. Psalm 105:31 reads, "He spoke ['*āmar*], and there came swarms of flies, and gnats throughout their country" (cf. Exod. 8:16–24). A similar description is given with regard to the plague of locusts: "He spoke ['*āmar*], and the locusts came, and young locusts without number" (Ps. 105:34; cf. Exod. 10:3–6). As with creation, God's speaking enacts God's will by virtue of his almighty sovereignty.

Sirach 39:16–21 also speaks of the events of the exodus as being accomplished by God's spoken Word. This text appears within a hymn (vv. 12–35) that praises God for his providential arrangement of the world as a whole and for the individual things within it by which God accomplishes his purposes. The hymn predominantly focuses on created things, but verse 17 suggests a subtle allusion to the exodus. The text reads, "At his word the waters stood in a heap, and the reservoirs of water at the word of his mouth" (v. 17). The expression "the waters stood in a heap" echoes the description of the parting of the sea in Exodus 15:8: "The floods stood up in a heap."[17] Subsequent biblical texts employ the same language with respect to the exodus sea crossing either in recounting it (e.g., Ps. 78:13: "He divided the sea and let them pass through it, and made the waters stand like a heap") or through a deliberate typological allusion (e.g., the parting of the Jordan in Josh. 3:13, 16). Significant for our purposes is Ben Sira's explicit claim that the exodus sea parting came about by God's Word (*en logō autou*) (Sir. 39:17).

The Wisdom of Solomon also reflects on the power of God's Word that was made manifest during Israel's time in the wilderness. In Wisdom 11–19, the author deploys a series of contrasts between what God did to the Egyptians in the exodus and what he did for the Israelites.[18] For instance, God

---

17. The Hebrew expression in Exod. 15:8 speaks of "waters" (*mayim*) as standing or being dammed up in a single place (*kəmô-nēd*).

18. David Winston, *The Wisdom of Solomon: A New Translation with Introduction and Commentary*, Anchor Bible 43 (Garden City, NY: Doubleday, 1979), 6–9.

struck the Egyptians through "the bites of locusts and flies" (Wis. 16:9; cf. Exod. 8:24; 10:14–15), and he afflicted the Israelites with snakebites in the wilderness (cf. Num. 21:6–9). But whereas "no healing was found for [the Egyptians]" (Wis. 16:9), God did heal the repentant Israelites of their bites. The author explicitly speaks of God healing the Israelites through his Word: "Neither herb nor poultice cured them, but it was your word, O Lord, that heals all people" (16:12).

The author also recalls the fire that fell on the Egyptians in the hailstorms of the exodus and destroyed their crops (i.e., their food) (Wis. 16:16–19; cf. Exod. 9:22–26). In contrast, the author cites God's gift of manna to Israel and its relation to God's Word. Developing the description of the manna being "as fine as frost on the ground" (Exod. 16:14), the author of Wisdom evidences a Jewish interpretation of the manna as being like snow.[19] Despite being snow-like, the manna was not destroyed by fire (Wis. 16:22), although it would melt in the sun (vv. 27–28). The behavior of the manna vis-à-vis natural forces attests to creation's being subject to God's will. Thus, in addition to being a food source to sustain the Israelites in the wilderness, the manna taught them. "It served your all-nourishing bounty," the author writes, "so that your children, whom you loved, O Lord, might learn that it is not the production of crops that feeds humankind but that your word sustains those who trust in you" (vv. 25–26). This statement recalls Deuteronomy 8:3, which likewise discerns a pedagogical purpose in the manna: "He humbled you by letting you hunger, then by feeding you with manna . . . in order to make you understand that one does not live by bread alone, but by every word that comes from the mouth of the LORD."

The Old Testament books provide a variety of other examples that speak of God helping people in *present* times of need by his Word. Psalm 107 describes a series of perilous situations from which God delivers the afflicted. In one such situation are those who are mortally ill, and their illness is attributed to their own sinfulness (vv. 17–22). The psalmist states that these sick people cry out to God for help, and God responds by healing them through his Word: "He sent out his word and healed them, and delivered them from destruction" (v. 20). The book of Proverbs praises God's Word for its reliability and security: "Every word of God proves true; he is a shield to those who take refuge in him" (30:5). Moreover, one can also point to Psalm 119, the longest of the

---

19. Winston, *Wisdom of Solomon*, 299. Among other Jewish instances of this exegetical tradition, Winston cites Josephus, *Antiquities of the Jews* 3.1.6, and the fragments of Artapanus (the latter can be found in *Fragment* 3.37 in Carl R. Holladay, *Fragments from Hellenistic Jewish Authors*, vol. 1, *Historians*, Texts and Translations 10 [Chico, CA: Scholars Press, 1983], 224–25).

psalms, which praises God for the gift of the Torah, his Word. Within this psalm, God's Word and its role in daily life are praised many times: among other things, God's Word is cause for "delight" (vv. 14, 16, 24, 35, 47, 70, 77, 92, 143, 174); it contains "wondrous things" (v. 18) and is a "word of truth" (v. 43; cf. v. 160); it is the source of strength and life (vv. 25, 28, 107); it is full of God's faithfulness (vv. 89–90). God's Word is to be loved (vv. 47–48, 97, 113, 119, 127, 159, 163, 167), contemplated (vv. 15, 23, 48, 97), and observed (vv. 4–5, 8, 32–35, 57, 166). God's Word is a sure source of guidance and direction for life: "Your word is a lamp to my feet and a light to my path" (v. 105).

Previously, we noted the identification of God's Word with the Torah given to Israel at Mount Sinai (Ps. 147). This identification informs the place of God's Word in the eschatological *future* as set forth in the new-covenant oracle of Jeremiah 31:31–34 (cf. 32:37–41). The new-covenant oracle appears within a larger section of Jeremiah (30:1–31:40) that speaks of the eschatological act of salvation that the Lord will work for Israel, who had been sent into exile and scattered among the nations as punishment for their sins. Among the things God promises to do for his people in this eschatological action are the following: to regather all Israel from their state of exile (30:3, 10; 31:8–11) and return them to the promised land (30:3); to restore the Davidic monarchy to rule over restored Israel (v. 9); and to provide a time of great joy and abundant prosperity (31:12–14). God's promise to make a new covenant with restored Israel is another component in this vision of eschatological salvation.

The element in this oracle that is most pertinent for our purposes is God's promise to put his Torah (i.e., his Word) inside his redeemed people: "I will put my law [*tôrâ*] within them, and I will write it on their hearts" (Jer. 31:33). This statement encapsulates the continuity and discontinuity between the Sinai covenant and the eschatological new covenant. On the one hand, God's gift of the Torah is at the heart of both the Sinai covenant and the new covenant.[20] However, the Lord contrasts the eschatological new covenant with the Sinai covenant: "[The new covenant] will not be like the covenant that I made with their ancestors when I took them by the hand to bring them out of the land of Egypt" (v. 32). As Jack Lundbom notes, in the Sinai covenant, the Torah was written on stone tablets, and Deuteronomy teaches that it "was supposed to find its way into the human heart."[21] These aspects imply a kind of exteriority of the Torah to the people Israel. But in the new covenant, God will act on people's interiority by writing his Torah "on their hearts" (v. 33).

---

20. So Gerhard von Rad, *Old Testament Theology*, vol. 2, *The Theology of Israel's Prophetic Traditions*, trans. D. M. G. Stalker (Edinburgh: Oliver & Boyd, 1965), 213.
21. Jack R. Lundbom, *Jeremiah 21–36: A New Translation with Introduction and Commentary*, Anchor Yale Bible 21B (New Haven: Yale University Press, 2004), 468.

But since, as Jeremiah puts it, "sin . . . [was] engraved on the tablet of their hearts" (17:1), hearts in restored Israel would need to be changed in order to receive the Torah, which God would write on them.[22] Thus, the Lord says through Jeremiah, "I will give them a heart to know that I am the LORD; and they shall be my people and I will be their God" (24:7). God promises to change the hearts of his redeemed people, making them able to receive this interiorized Torah.[23]

God promises to so internalize his Torah within people, enabling it to sink in and permeate his people's lives. Resulting from this action of God on his people's interiority is a profound, intimate knowledge of God and newly enabled covenantal obedience: "No longer shall they teach one another, or say to each other, 'Know the LORD,' for they shall all know me, from the least of them to the greatest" (Jer. 31:34). By putting his Torah, his Word, within his people, God will create with his people a new relationship of intimacy and close, personal knowing. The indwelling Word of God will be a kind of presence within the new-covenant community.

## New Testament Witnesses

The same overarching motifs of the Word spoken by God—its associations with power and presence—continue into the New Testament writings. The associations of the Word of God and presence are even more profound in the New Testament, with its identification of the Word of God not only as intrinsic to the "identity of God" but also as a person who becomes incarnate in Jesus of Nazareth.[24] The divine Word speaks directly and humanly in Jesus. Accordingly, since his are the words of the divine Word, the words of Jesus possess divine causal power—the other focal aspect of the Word of God.

### The Personal Reality of the Word: Jesus Christ

Christian theological reflection on the Word of God must be centered on the New Testament's identification of the Word of God as the person of Jesus Christ. With the incarnation, the reality of the Word of God is expressed most robustly. While only two New Testament texts explicitly designate Jesus as

22. So Lundbom, *Jeremiah 21–26*, 468–69.

23. As von Rad puts it, "God would himself change the human heart and so bring about perfect obedience." *Old Testament Theology*, 2:217.

24. Our use of "identity" here and elsewhere is indebted to Bauckham, *Jesus and the God of Israel*.

God's "Word" (John 1:1–18; Rev. 19:13), many New Testament writings affirm the preexistence of the Son or Word of God, who became incarnate in Jesus.[25] Very often this teaching appears in texts that speak of Jesus as the agent by whom God created the world. To articulate this identification of Jesus as the preexistent agent of creation, New Testament writers appropriate the biblical language and imagery of God's personified Word or Wisdom, who was present when God created the world.

The most prominent identification of Jesus as the preexistent Word (or Son) of God is the prologue of the Gospel according to John (1:1–18).[26] The prologue begins with a deliberate allusion to the creation narrative in Genesis 1, with its phrase "In the beginning" (John 1:1). The Gospel begins by rereading, in light of the revelation in Jesus, Genesis 1 and its presentation of God creating all things by speaking. In this way, John signals that he is looking anew at all (creation, history, God's activity in them, and even God himself) in light of Christ. Through the revelation in Christ, John teaches that the Word by which God creates is a divine person. The Word is both one with God the Father ("the Word was God") and yet distinct from God the Father ("the Word was with God") (v. 1). Moreover, God (the Father) and the Word (the Son) exist in a dynamic relationship with each other. While the Greek phrasing in 1:1b is accurately translated as "the Word was *with* God," the Greek preposition used here, *pros*, also connotes dynamic movement toward something.[27] The subtle hint at dynamism here coheres with the Fourth Gospel's larger presentation of the life of God as the eternal exchange of life and love between the Father and Son—that is, the divine communion.[28]

The Word (or Son; cf. John 1:14, 18) is the agent by whom God the Father created the world: "All things came into being through him, and without him not one thing came into being" (v. 3). All that exists, therefore, exists in relation to (and by virtue of) God and his Word. Moreover, as the psalmist praises God's Word as "a light to [his] path" and as a source of "life" (Ps. 119:105, 107), so, similarly, does John speak of the divine Word as the source of "life" and spiritual "light of all people" (John 1:4).

---

25. Bauckham, *Jesus and the God of Israel*, 18–59.

26. See Raymond E. Brown, SS, *The Gospel according to John: Introduction, Translation, and Notes*, 2 vols., Anchor Bible 29, 29A (New York: Doubleday, 1966, 1970), 1:23–36; Daniel Boyarin, "The Gospel of the *Memra*: Jewish Binitarianism and the Prologue to John," *Harvard Theological Review* 94 (2001): 243–84; Francis Martin and William M. Wright IV, *The Gospel of John*, Catholic Commentary on Sacred Scripture (Grand Rapids: Baker Academic, 2015), 31–41.

27. So too Francis J. Moloney, SDB, *The Gospel of John*, Sacra Pagina 4 (Collegeville, MN: Liturgical Press, 1998), 35.

28. Martin and Wright, *Gospel of John*, 23–25, 33.

Daniel Boyarin has offered a thought-provoking and illuminating analysis of John's prologue along similar lines.[29] Boyarin argues that John's prologue reflects the interpretive dynamics of Jewish homiletic midrash, in which a text from the Torah is interpreted in light of another, related text from another part of the canon. In the case of John's prologue, Boyarin argues, the evangelist is reading Genesis 1 (where God creates by speaking) in tandem with Proverbs 8:22–31 (a poetic account of God's Wisdom being present at creation). Emerging from these intertextual dynamics is the hypostatization of the divine Word (Gen. 1) along the lines of personified Wisdom (via Prov. 8).[30] The prologue also incorporates the conventional motif of Wisdom seeking a home in the world (cf. Sir. 24:1–12) as it narrates the activity of the preincarnate divine Word in the world (John 1:9–13). According to Boyarin, the prologue makes the decidedly Christian turn when it speaks of God's Word/Wisdom becoming incarnate in Jesus (v. 14). Among the merits of Boyarin's case is his demonstration of how John's prologue is deeply embedded within Jewish thinking about God's Word and Wisdom, while at the same time taking a new turn in light of the Christian belief in the incarnation.

Paul also identifies Jesus's person as a preexistent, divine figure through whom God the Father created all things.[31] In 1 Corinthians 8, Paul begins his discussion over whether it is permitted for Corinthian Christians to eat meat that came from animal sacrifices to pagan gods with a strong affirmation of biblical monotheism. In a Christian rereading of the famous "Shema, Israel" (Deut. 6:4–9), Paul writes, "There is one God, the Father, from whom are all things and for whom we exist, and one Lord, Jesus Christ, through whom are all things and through whom we exist" (1 Cor. 8:6). Here, the "identity" of the Lord God is articulated as consisting of the Father, the source of all things, and Jesus, the agent of creation.[32] Similarly, the hymn in Colossians 1:15–20 contains a series of profound affirmations about Jesus, beginning with his being "the image of the invisible God" (v. 15). To underscore the sovereignty and ultimacy of Christ, who "is before all things" (v. 17), Paul writes, "In him [or 'by him'] all things in heaven and on earth were created, things visible and invisible. . . . All things have been created through him and for him" (v. 16). The Colossians hymn also speaks of Christ as an agent or instrument of God's activity to reconcile a sinful world to himself. In both 1 Corinthians 8:6 and Colossians 1:16, therefore, Christ is spoken of as the

29. Boyarin, "Gospel of the *Memra*"; Boyarin, *Border Lines*, 93–111.
30. Boyarin, "Gospel of the *Memra*," 268–71.
31. See James D. G. Dunn, *The Theology of Paul the Apostle* (Grand Rapids: Eerdmans, 1998), 267–93.
32. See Bauckham, *Jesus and the God of Israel*, 26–30.

one "through" whom all things have been created, but not without some reference to God the Father.

The Letter to the Hebrews begins with a similar set of claims. The text begins by recounting the history of God's revelation: "Long ago God spoke to our ancestors in many and various ways by the prophets" (Heb. 1:1). This history of divine communication culminates in the eschatological revelation through God's "Son," whom the author identifies as "the reflection of God's glory and the exact imprint of God's very being" (vv. 2–3). The Son also has a role in God's creation and preservation of the world. The author identifies the Son as the one "through whom [God] created the worlds" (v. 2), and the one who "sustains all things by his powerful word" (v. 3).

Such appropriation by New Testament writers of biblical imagery for God's Wisdom or Word also appears in the Gospel presentations of Jesus's earthly life. For purposes of illustration, we will comment briefly on two Gospel texts that identify Jesus as the Word or Wisdom of God made flesh.

First, the bread of life discourse (John 6:35–59) uses biblical traditions pertaining to God's Word and Wisdom to present Jesus as the bread of life, the revelation of God in the flesh, which he in turn gives to people in the Eucharist.[33] In verse 27, Jesus sets up the discourse by speaking of "the food that endures for eternal life, which the Son of Man will give."[34] These words about food enduring for eternal life run throughout the discourse and reflect biblical traditions in which God's Wisdom and Word—that is, the Torah—were likened to food and drink. The psalmist prays, "How sweet to my palate are your words, sweeter than honey to my mouth" (Ps. 119:103, translation ours). Proverbs depicts God's Wisdom inviting people to understand her as a woman making a dinner invitation: "Come, eat of my bread and drink of the wine I have mixed!" (Prov. 9:5). Sirach likewise uses the imagery of food and eating to describe learning from God's Wisdom and law: "Whoever fears the Lord [and] . . . holds to the law will obtain wisdom. . . . She will feed him with the bread of learning, and give him the water of wisdom to drink" (Sir. 15:1, 3).[35]

In Sirach 24, God's Wisdom likewise invites people to come and learn from her, and she does so with the imagery of food: "Come to me, you who desire me, and eat your fill of my fruits" (v. 19). Here, the imagery of eating food points to learning from God's wisdom teaching, taking it in, making it a part of one's life. Wisdom says that those who partake of her will want

---

33. See Martin and Wright, *Gospel of John*, 123–31.

34. The remainder of this paragraph appears in Martin and Wright, *Gospel of John*, 120–21, with the biblical translations adapted to reflect the NRSV.

35. God's Word is also likened to the manna in Philo, *Allegorical Interpretation* 3.162. Cf. Genesis Rabbah 70:5.

more: "Those who eat of me will hunger for more, and those who drink of me will thirst for more" (v. 21). In the bread of life discourse, Jesus issues similar declarations, inviting people to partake of him—that is, receive in faith his revelation of God as Father and himself as Son (John 6:35, 47–51). But unlike personified Wisdom in Sirach 24, Jesus promises eternal satisfaction for those who eat and drink of him: "I am the bread of life. Whoever comes to me will never be hungry, and whoever believes in me will never be thirsty" (John 6:35).

Along similar lines, Jesus identifies himself in terms of the manna in the wilderness to show that he is both like and unlike the manna.[36] Like the manna, Jesus speaks of himself as "bread that came down from heaven" (John 6:51). But unlike the manna, Jesus promises eternal life to those who eat of him: "Unlike your ancestors who ate and died, the one who eats this bread will live forever" (v. 58, translation ours; cf. v. 49). As Jesus is both like and unlike the manna, so too is Jesus the divine Wisdom but something more. Jesus not only imparts divine wisdom and teaching (as does personified Wisdom) but also gives his crucified and glorified flesh and blood in the Eucharist. By partaking in Jesus's resurrected flesh and blood in the Eucharist, Jesus's disciples will share his life ("Those who eat my flesh and drink my blood abide in me, and I in them"; v. 56) and partake also in the reality of his resurrection on the last day ("Those who eat my flesh and drink my blood have eternal life, and I will raise them up on the last day"; v. 54).

Another Gospel passage that presents Jesus as the divine Word or Wisdom made flesh is the "Father and Son" saying in Matthew 11:25–27 (cf. Luke 10:21–22). The larger narrative context of this saying (we focus on Matthew's here) is important for discerning the associations with God's Wisdom. Having instructed the twelve apostles for their missionary endeavors (Matt. 10:1–42), Jesus continues his preaching and teaching in Galilean towns (11:1). The narrative material that follows deals in large part with the messianic authority of Jesus and the various responses of people to him. The opening sequence of scenes in Matthew 11 concerns the identity of Jesus as the promised Messiah, who performs the messianic tasks set forth in Isaiah (cf. Isa. 35:5–6; 61:1), and the identification of John the Baptist as the eschatological return of Elijah (Matt. 11:7–14; cf. Mal. 4:5–6). Jesus then speaks of the rejection and slander that both he and John the Baptist have received: "John came neither eating nor drinking, and they say, 'He has a demon'; the Son of Man came eating

---

36. See Brant Pitre, *Jesus and the Last Supper* (Grand Rapids: Eerdmans, 2015), 193–244; William M. Wright IV, "Jesus' Identity and the Use of Scripture in John 6:1–21," *Josephinum Journal of Theology* 17 (2010): 24–40, 39.

and drinking, and they say, 'Look, a glutton and a drunkard, a friend of tax collectors and sinners!'" (Matt. 11:18–19).

Jesus then follows up by saying, "Yet wisdom is vindicated by her deeds" (Matt. 11:19). With these words, Jesus seemingly identifies himself with divine Wisdom.[37] He appeals to the good deeds performed by divine Wisdom as vindicating him against the slander leveled at him. He similarly identifies himself as the Messiah to the disciples of John the Baptist indirectly by citing his miracles: "The blind receive their sight, the lame walk, the lepers are cleansed, the deaf hear, the dead are raised, and the poor have the good news brought to them" (11:4–5). These miracles are among those Jesus has already performed in the Gospel narrative.[38] W. D. Davies and Dale Allison thus articulate the import of this, saying: "Despite the poor response of people, the works of God in Jesus have made plain to all Jesus' identity (cf. 11.2–6) and the need to respond to him favourably."[39]

After pronouncing woes of condemnation on those cities that did not repent and receive him in faith, despite having seen his miraculous works (Matt. 11:20–24), Jesus offers a prayer of praise to the Father for those disciples who have in fact received him in faith (vv. 25–26). The Father has "revealed [apokalyptein]" sacred things to "infants" (v. 25), and this revelation comes by way of the Son: "No one knows the Son except the Father, and no one knows the Father except the Son and anyone to whom the Son chooses to reveal [apokalyptein] him" (v. 27). Jesus's identification of himself as the Son, the only one who knows and reveals the Father, echoes certain things said of divine Wisdom.[40] For instance, Wisdom 9 (a text discussed above) speaks of Wisdom as knowing God: "With you is wisdom, she who knows your works" (9:9). Solomon then asks God to dispatch Wisdom from heaven so that Solomon himself might learn from her: "Send her forth from the holy heavens . . . that I may learn what is pleasing to you. For she knows and understands all things" (9:10–11).

Jesus then invites weary people: "Take my yoke upon you, and learn from me" (Matt. 11:29). The image of the yoke is common in Jewish tradition as

37. So too W. D. Davies and Dale C. Allison Jr., *A Critical and Exegetical Commentary on the Gospel according to Saint Matthew*, 3 vols., International Critical Commentary (Edinburgh: T&T Clark, 1988, 1991, 1997), 2:264.

38. Already in Matthew's Gospel, Jesus has healed the blind (9:27–31), cured the paralyzed (9:2–8), made lepers clean (8:1–4), raised the dead (9:18–26), and proclaimed the gospel (4:23–7:29). The only task Jesus has not performed thus far in Matthew is making the deaf hear (cf. Mark 7:31–37).

39. Davies and Allison, *Matthew*, 2:265.

40. References here are taken from those provided in Davies and Allison, *Matthew*, 2:272. See also André Feuillet, "Jésus et la Sagesee Divine d'après les Évangiles Synoptiques: Le 'logion johannique' et l'Ancien Testament," *Revue biblique* 62 (1955): 161–96.

a symbol of the Torah (God's Word), and those who study Torah take this yoke upon themselves.[41] The prophet Jeremiah castigates those who know God's ways and still reject them: "Then I said, '. . . surely they know the way of the LORD, the law of their God.' But they all alike had broken the yoke" (Jer. 5:4–5). The Mishnah also records a saying of Rabbi Nehunya ben Ha-Kanah that encourages the man "that takes upon himself the yoke of the Law."[42] Since God's Word and Wisdom are effectively synonymous, yoke imagery can also be applied to God's Wisdom. As has been pointed out, Jesus's words in Matthew 11:29 echo the invitation issued in Sirach 51 to learn from divine Wisdom, whose teaching is likened to a "yoke."[43] Ben Sira invites his audience, "Put your neck under her yoke, and let your souls receive instruction" (Sir. 51:26). Moreover, as Jesus says, "My yoke is easy, and my burden is light" (Matt. 11:28), so does Ben Sira speak of the ease of taking upon himself the yoke of Wisdom: "I have labored but little and found for myself much serenity" (Sir. 51:27).

Taken together, Jesus's words about Wisdom in Matthew 11:19, his self-identification as the Son who alone knows and reveals the Father, and his invitation to take on his "yoke" and "learn" from him all point to Jesus as the incarnation of God's Word (Torah) or Wisdom. Davies and Allison summarize it well: "The identification of Jesus with Torah makes Jesus the full revelation of God and of his will for man. . . . [Jesus] is the perfect embodiment of God's purpose and demand and the functional equivalent of Torah. Law-giver and law are one."[44]

### The Power of Jesus's Word: A Case Study from Luke

Throughout his Gospel narrative, Luke uses "the word of God" (and some related expressions) to designate *that which Jesus speaks*. When Jesus first begins his public ministry, he tells his disciples, "I must proclaim the good news of the kingdom of God [*euangelisasthai . . . tēn basileian tou theou*] to the other cities also; for I was sent for this purpose" (4:43). To proclaim the gospel of the kingdom is central to what Jesus says and does. Immediately after this saying, Luke describes Jesus's proclamation of the gospel of the kingdom in two similar phrases. First, Luke adds that Jesus "continued

41. For references, see Davies and Allison, *Matthew*, 289n241.
42. Mishnah Aboth 3:5, in Herbert Danby, trans., *The Mishnah* (Oxford: Oxford University Press, 1933), 450.
43. See Daniel J. Harrington, SJ, *The Gospel of Matthew*, Sacra Pagina 1 (Collegeville, MN: Liturgical Press, 1991), 168–70.
44. Davies and Allison, *Matthew*, 2:290.

proclaiming the message [*kēryssōn*] in the synagogues of Judea" (4:44). For Luke, the Greek verb *kēryssein*, referring to Jesus's preaching in general, is a veritable synonym for *euangelizein*, "proclaim the good news." For Luke uses the verb *kēryssein* to present Jesus as (1) doing what he had just identified as his mission (to "proclaim the good news") and (2) indicating what he planned to do next (to do so in "other cities").

A second phrase related to proclaiming the gospel appears in the very next narrative scene. After an unspecified passage of narrative time, Luke reports that Jesus was teaching beside the Sea of Galilee and that "the crowd was pressing in on him to hear the word of God" (5:1), and this crowd leads Jesus to begin teaching them from Simon Peter's boat. Luke explicitly identifies that which Jesus teaches as "the word of God" (v. 1), and presumably Jesus continues to teach from the boat (cf. v. 3). This identification of Jesus's teaching as the Word of God is further corroborated by Luke's language in the episode of Jesus with Martha and Mary (10:38–42). Luke introduces Mary as the one who "sat at the Lord's feet and listened to his word" (10:39, translation ours), and this posture identifies Mary as a student of Jesus the Teacher. Given that "Lord" (*kyrios*) is a title articulating Jesus's divine identity in Luke, the designation of Jesus's teaching as "the word" of the "Lord" further supports the identification of Jesus's teaching as "the word of God."[45]

By aligning these three articulations—"proclaiming the good news" (*euangelizein*), "proclaiming the message" or preaching (*kēryssein*), and "the word of God"—in such close sequence, Luke invites us to take them as equivalents. That is, "the word of God" is synonymous with the gospel of the kingdom of God; it is that which Jesus teaches and preaches.

Luke presents Jesus's teaching the Word of God as an essential component to his messianic ministry and identity. As such, Jesus's teaching the Word is related to his being anointed with the Holy Spirit and power. From the beginning of the Gospel, Luke presents Jesus as being in intimate and constant contact with the Holy Spirit. The Holy Spirit brings about Jesus's virginal conception in the womb of the Virgin Mary upon her acceptance of God's invitation, spoken by the angel Gabriel (1:35, 38). John the Baptist says of the Messiah, the one to come after him, "He will baptize you with the Holy Spirit and fire" (3:16). That is, he will be the one in whom God will make good on his promise to pour out his Spirit in the end time.[46] At the baptism of Jesus, Luke reports, "The Holy Spirit descended upon him in bodily form

---

45. On the title "Lord" in Luke as expressing Jesus's divine identity, see C. Kavin Rowe, *Early Narrative Christology: The Lord in the Gospel of Luke* (Grand Rapids: Baker Academic, 2009).

46. See John P. Meier, *A Marginal Jew: Rethinking the Historical Jesus*, 5 vols., Anchor Yale Bible Reference Library (New Haven: Yale University Press, 1991–2016), 2:54–55.

like a dove" (3:22). The Father's voice from heaven is a revelation of Jesus's identity as the Messiah, God's beloved Son (in the multiple dimensions of that term), and the Suffering Servant: "You are my Son, the Beloved; with you I am well pleased" (3:22).[47] After the baptism, Luke states that "Jesus, full of the Holy Spirit . . . was led by the Spirit in the wilderness" (4:1) to confront Satan. Having overcome Satan's temptations in the wilderness, Jesus goes back to Galilee, "filled with the power of the Spirit" (4:14).

The first major event of Jesus's public ministry in Luke is the so-called Nazareth inaugural (Luke 4:16–30).[48] The Nazareth inaugural is a telescoping of Jesus's public ministry into a single episode, for much of what Jesus says in this scene, he does elsewhere in Luke's narrative—and does so in the power of the Spirit. In this scene, Jesus reads from the Scripture (a combination of Isa. 61:1–2; 42:7; 58:6) and pronounces this prophetic text to be fulfilled in his audience's present. Jesus uses the Isaiah text to identify himself as the Messiah, the promised bringer of salvation, who is anointed by the Holy Spirit. By declaring to his audience, "Today this scripture has been fulfilled in your hearing" (Luke 4:21), Jesus indirectly identifies himself as the one spoken of in the Isaiah text. By using the words of Isaiah, Jesus thus says of himself, "The Spirit of the Lord is upon me, because he has anointed me" (Luke 4:18, quoting Isa. 61:1). As the Messiah, Jesus has been anointed with the Holy "Spirit of the Lord."

Continuing to so employ the Isaiah text, Jesus implicitly identifies many of the activities that he will perform in his ministry as the Spirit-anointed Messiah. What the Isaiah text lists as activities performed by the anointed one, Luke presents Jesus performing in his public ministry.[49] For instance, Isaiah 61:1 lists as the first task of the Messiah "to bring good news [*euangelisast-hai*] to the oppressed" (cf. Luke 4:18, with "to the poor"). Shortly after the Nazareth inaugural, Jesus says that his "purpose" is to "proclaim the good news [*euangelisasthai*] of the kingdom of God" (4:43). Isaiah 42:7 says that the Servant of the Lord will "open the eyes that are blind" (cf. Luke 4:18: "proclaim . . . recovery of sight to the blind"), and in a summary statement, Luke mentions that Jesus "gave sight to many who were blind" (7:21). Isaiah

47. The expression "You are my Son" recalls multiple texts that speak of the Davidic king (e.g., Ps. 2:7) and the people Israel (e.g., Exod. 4:23; Hosea 11:1) as God's son. The use of the modifier "beloved" with "Son" links Jesus to Isaac, who is Abraham's beloved son (Gen. 22:2). The phrase "with you I am well pleased" recalls Isa. 42:1, where similar language is predicated of the Servant of the Lord.

48. We adopt the title "the Nazareth inaugural" for Luke 4:16–30 from Carl R. Holladay, *A Critical Introduction to the New Testament*, 2 vols. (Nashville: Abingdon, 2005), 1:257.

49. Luke Timothy Johnson, *The Gospel of Luke*, Sacra Pagina 3 (Collegeville, MN: Liturgical Press, 1991), 81.

58:6 speaks of the anointed one's commission "to let the oppressed go free" (Luke 4:18). Arguably, in Luke's narrative, this phrase refers to Jesus's ministry of exorcism (cf. 4:31–37, 41; 6:18; 7:21; 8:2, 29; 9:42; etc.), for later, in Acts 10:38, Peter speaks of Jesus as "healing all who were oppressed by the devil."[50]

When Luke presents Jesus performing the messianic works of healing the sick and driving out demons, he speaks of Jesus's "power" (Greek: *dynamis*). Luke has already established that Jesus's "power" is the power of the Holy Spirit, which he possesses as Messiah and Lord (cf. Luke 2:11; 4:14). The power of the Spirit animates and infuses all aspects of Jesus's messianic ministry. Luke introduces the episode of Jesus healing the paralytic (5:17–26) by stating that "the power of the Lord was with him to heal" (v. 17). Likewise, Luke speaks of a crowd of the infirm and afflicted seeking to touch Jesus, "for power came out from him and healed all of them" (6:19; cf. 8:46). Similar expressions appear in Luke's accounts of Jesus's exorcism ministry. In the scene that immediately follows the Nazareth inaugural, Jesus goes to teach in the synagogue at Capernaum (4:31–37). Provoked by the "authority" of his teaching (v. 32), a demon that has taken possession of a congregant manifests itself and tries to assert power over Jesus by using his name (v. 34). Jesus immediately silences and exorcizes the demon by simple command. Upon witnessing what Jesus has done, the synagogue congregation marvels at the power of Jesus's word: "What is this word? For with authority and power he commands the unclean spirits, and out they come" (v. 36, translation ours). When he commissions the Twelve, Jesus gives them a delegated share in his ministry and power: he "gave them power and authority over all demons and to cure diseases, and he sent them out to proclaim the kingdom of God and to heal" (9:1–2).

This pairing of "Spirit" and "power" and their association with Jesus's messianic ministry likewise appear in Peter's speech to Cornelius's household in Acts 10. In recounting Jesus's life, death, and resurrection, Peter begins with John the Baptist and states, "God anointed Jesus of Nazareth with the Holy Spirit and with power" (10:38). Then immediately Peter summarizes Jesus's healing miracles and exorcisms: "He went about doing good and healing all who were oppressed by the devil, for God was with him" (10:38).

Since Luke uses the language of "power" with reference to Jesus's messianic tasks of healing and exorcism (both of which he performs by his speaking), it seems warranted to view his messianic task "to bring good news" (Luke 4:18) as likewise infused with the power of the Holy Spirit. When Jesus proclaims

---

50. Note, however, that different Greek verbs are used for "oppressed" in Luke 4:18 (*thrauein*) and Acts 10:38 (*katadynasteuein*), respectively.

the good news (or teaches the Word of God), he does so in the power of the Holy Spirit. Jesus's word has causal power because it is his word as the Lord and Messiah, and as such, it is infused with the power of the Holy Spirit.

A further point is that the Word of God proclaimed by Jesus makes present the reality that it articulates. To clarify, we turn again to the Nazareth inaugural. When Jesus interprets the Isaiah texts as speaking of him and his ministry, he declares that that which the Isaiah texts are talking about—the messianic age—is now, in a very real respect, a present reality: "Today this scripture has been fulfilled in your hearing" (Luke 4:21). Moreover, the fact that Jesus performs in his ministry those tasks that the Isaiah text prophesies of the messianic age further corroborates the presence of that age in Jesus. Luke thus invites his audience to recognize the kingdom of God—God's eschatological coming in power to rule as King and exercise that power in healing, forgiving, and delivering his people—as present in the world in Jesus and his ministry.[51] In his words, deeds, and very self, Jesus makes the kingdom of God a present reality in the world.

Particularly illustrative of the presence and power of the kingdom of God in Jesus's ministry are his exorcisms.[52] Like Matthew and Mark, Luke records a controversy over the source of power whereby Jesus exorcized demons, with some accusing Jesus of manipulating occult powers (Luke 11:14–28; cf. Matt. 12:22–30; Mark 3:22–27). Within his account of this controversy, Luke—like Matthew—features a Q saying [Q is a hypothetical source used by Matthew and Luke] in which Jesus specifies the source of his exorcistic power: "If it is by the finger of God that I cast out the demons, then the kingdom of God has come to you" (Luke 11:20). The Matthean version of the saying reads "the Spirit of God," whereas Luke's version has "finger of God" (Matt. 12:28; Luke 11:20). But even without recourse to the Matthean version, Luke's insistence that the Spirit's power infuses Jesus's words and deeds strongly suggests that we are to take "the finger of God" as referring to the Holy Spirit. The import of the saying, therefore, is that the kingdom's presence and power are instantiated in Jesus's exorcizing demons by the power of the Holy Spirit. Put differently, in Jesus, God is now coming in power as King to deliver his people, heal them, and defeat their demonic enemies—"to let the oppressed go free" (Luke 4:18).

As Luke invites his audience to see Jesus's exorcisms and healings as instances of the presence and power of the kingdom, so too does he invite his audience to understand Jesus's teaching the Word of God in the same terms.

51. On Jesus's kingdom of God ministry as situated within the horizon of Second Temple Judaism, see Meier, *Marginal Jew*, 2:238–506.
52. See Graham H. Twelftree, *In the Name of Jesus: Exorcism among Early Christians* (Grand Rapids: Baker Academic, 2007); Meier, *Marginal Jew*, 2:404–22.

To "bring good news" is a task for the Spirit-anointed Messiah as much as to give "recovery of sight to the blind, [and] to let the oppressed go free" (Luke 4:18). They are all instances of the presence of the messianic age, which has arrived in Jesus. Taken in this light, the kingdom of God becomes present in the act of Jesus's preaching and teaching. That is, Jesus's Spirit-infused preaching of "the good news of the kingdom of God" (v. 43) makes God's ruling in power as King a manifest and powerful reality in the world.

We might, therefore, conceive of the Word of God spoken by Jesus in the power of the Spirit as making present the divine reality of the kingdom that his words articulate. Jesus's word is a linguistic means, a vehicle, by which the kingdom comes into the world and its power becomes operative. In a sense, "the good news of the kingdom of God" is the reality of the kingdom in verbal form. The Word makes present the divine reality of which it speaks.

## Looking Back and Looking Forward

This survey of texts from both Testaments of the Christian Bible gives evidence for conceiving of the Word spoken by God as having associations with power and forms of presence. The review of Old Testament texts points to a number of associations between God's Word and his being the Creator and providential governor of all things. By depicting God as creating by a simple word of command, these selected texts underscore the almighty sovereignty of the Creator over his creation. God's creative Word not only brings things to be, but also reveals God's intentions for creation. By the same Word, God providentially governs the created world and the events within it. Biblical witnesses present God acting by his Word in the course of events, such as the past events of the exodus, the present life of his covenant people Israel, or the eschatological future of the new covenant. Through the works and words, God reveals some of his attributes—his fidelity and righteousness (Ps. 33:4), his glory and beauty (Sir. 43)—as well as his being Israel's savior and provider. Through his Word, God reveals something of himself and his designs for the world, and in doing so, he becomes present to people in the modality of being known. Some texts also present the Word of God in personified terms as an agent figure. The Word can be sent by God on a mission, instruct people in God's ways, and carry out his will.

The survey of New Testament witnesses provides further teaching about God's Word and its associations with power and presence. Multiple New Testament writings teach that Jesus is the preexistent One through whom God the Father created all things. Jesus is the Son, the Word/Wisdom/Torah of God, made flesh—the Word of God present in the world as a human being. To articulate this teaching, New Testament writers employ the resources provided by the biblical wisdom tradition. Focusing on the presentation of Jesus in the Gospel of Luke, we see that the Word of God, that which Jesus teaches as part of his ministry as Messiah and Lord, has causal power. The power of the Word of God, proclaimed by Jesus, is closely connected with the Holy Spirit. In Luke's Gospel, the Holy Spirit rests upon Jesus as the Messiah and infuses his messianic ministry with power. The Spirit-anointed Word, proclaimed by Jesus, also mediates the reality of which it speaks. Jesus's proclamation of the kingdom of God makes the kingdom of God present and operative in the world.

This chapter has focused on the Word of God, spoken directly by God. In the next two chapters, we expand the focus to consider the Word of God as spoken by human intermediaries: the biblical prophets and apostles. As we will see, the Word of God, proclaimed in the inspired (or Spirit-touched) speech of prophets and apostles, continues to have these same associations with causal power and presence.

# 2

# The Word of God in the Inspired Speech of the Prophets

The preceding survey focused on the Word spoken directly by God and highlighted two aspects of the Word. First, the Word of God has causal power by which God produces a divinely caused effect in the world. Second, the Word of God has associations with various modes of presence. Through his Word, God reveals himself and his designs and thus makes something of himself present to people through knowing. The Word of God can cause something to be or to occur, and in the cases of God's personified Word and especially in the incarnation, the Word of God is a reality in itself.

Both biblical Testaments also affirm that the Word of God can be communicated through human speech that has been empowered and touched by God (i.e., inspired). In this chapter, we will consider the Word of God as given in the inspired discourse of the biblical prophets of Israel. As we will see, the same two aspects of the Word of God that we have highlighted carry into the Word spoken by the prophets. The Word of God, given through inspired, human speech, can produce a divinely caused effect in the world. Moreover, the Word of God has associations with forms of presence—for instance, by imparting knowledge of God, by bringing about a particular state of affairs in the world, or by the Word being an agent figure in its own right.

## God's Word Received by the Prophets

As studies of biblical prophecy have shown, the prophets prophesied in diverse ways, their roles and the historical settings in which they ministered varied,

37

their messages were received and redacted in many ways, and the personality and temperament of each left a stamp on his work.[1] Yet all true prophets receive their message from one source: God. The prophet is called and empowered by God to deliver a word from God to an audience.[2]

The prophetic writings relate the divine call and commissioning of prophets in different ways. In some cases, the divine call of a prophet comes in the form of a theophany or vision. The prophets Isaiah and Ezekiel, for instance, receive a vision of God wherein they are summoned to prophesy, and they receive the Word that they are to communicate to God's people (e.g., Isa. 6:1–13; Ezek. 1:28–2:8; 3:4–27). The call narratives of Isaiah and Ezekiel also accent the speaking role of the prophet through gestures that involve the prophets' mouths. In Isaiah, a seraph touches the prophet's mouth with a hot coal from God's temple to purge him of his sins and make his mouth apt for speaking the Word of God (Isa. 6:6–7). In Ezekiel's call vision, the prophet eats a scroll to denote his receiving and taking in the Word that he has been called to speak (Ezek. 2:8–3:3; cf. Rev. 10:8–10).

Other prophetic books speak of the "word" received by the prophet as something "seen" (i.e., the prophets receive God's Word in a vision).[3] The book of Isaiah introduces the famous oracle of the eschatological Zion as the pilgrimage destination for gentiles with the phrase "The word [*haddābār*] that Isaiah son of Amoz saw [*ḥāzâ*] concerning Judah and Jerusalem" (2:1). Similarly, the book of Micah begins, "The word of the Lord [*dəbar-YHWH*] that came to Micah . . . , which he saw [*ḥāzâ*] concerning Samaria and Jerusalem" (Mic. 1:1). In other cases, the prophet's reception of a word from God is related in a simple statement that opens a prophetic book. This is often the case in the Minor Prophets (the Book of the Twelve), which begin with phrasing such as "the word of the Lord that came to Hosea" (Hos. 1:1) or "The word of the Lord came to the prophet Zechariah" (Zech. 1:1).[4]

1. Helpful discussions from historical, literary, and theological perspectives include Joseph Blenkinsopp, *A History of Prophecy in Israel: Revised and Enlarged* (Louisville: Westminster John Knox, 1996); David L. Petersen, *The Prophetic Literature: An Introduction* (Louisville: Westminster John Knox, 2002); Luis Alonso Schökel, SJ, *The Inspired Word: Scripture in Light of Language and Literature*, trans. Francis Martin, OCSO (Montreal: Palm, 1965).

2. On prophetic speech, considered from different perspectives, see Gene M. Tucker, "Prophetic Speech," in *Interpreting the Prophets*, ed. James Luther Mays and Paul J. Achtemeier (Philadelphia: Fortress, 1987), 27–40; Gerhard von Rad, *Old Testament Theology*, vol. 2, *The Theology of Israel's Prophetic Traditions*, trans. D. M. G. Stalker (London: Oliver & Boyd, 1965), 80–98; Schökel, *Inspired Word*.

3. Other examples include Nah. 1:1; Hab. 1:1; Obad. 1. The same pattern carries into the LXX, which renders the Hebrew *dābār* as *logos*—i.e., as that which the prophet saw (Greek: *eiden*) (Mic. 1:1). Cf. the appearance of "the word of the Lord [*dəbar-YHWH*]" to Abram "in a vision [*bammaḥāzeh*]" (Gen. 15:1).

4. Cf. Joel 1:1; Jon. 1:1; 3:1; Mic. 1:1; Zeph. 1:1; Hag. 1:1; Mal. 1:1.

That a true prophet receives a word from God, which he (or she) then delivers to people, has a prominent place in the promise of the prophet-like-Moses (Deut. 18:15–22). A hallmark descriptor of this prophet is that he will faithfully speak all that the Lord gives him to say: "I will put my words in the mouth of the prophet, who shall speak to them everything that I command" (18:18).[5] Since this prophet faithfully speaks only that which the Lord gives him to speak, the Lord "will hold accountable" those who do not receive the word spoken by this prophet (18:19). The faithful speaking of God's Word distinguishes a true prophet from a false prophet: the false prophet delivers a message from gods other than the Lord or purports to speak a word from the Lord that the Lord has not in fact given him (18:20). Deuteronomy then prescribes a negative test as to whether a supposed message is from the Lord: "If a prophet speaks in the name of the LORD but the thing does not take place or prove true, it is a word that the LORD has not spoken" (18:22). However, even the fulfillment of a prophet's word does not of itself suffice to prove that a prophet is true. As Deuteronomy 13 specifies, even if a prophet's word comes to pass, if the prophet speaks a message encouraging Israel to follow other gods, he is a false prophet (13:1–3). For by this false prophet, the Lord may be testing the love and fidelity of his people.

The prophets receive a message from God, which God empowers and commissions them to deliver. As the word that a prophet speaks is ultimately God's Word, the same associations of the Word of God with power and forms of presence extend into the prophet's discourse. Through the inspired discourse of a prophet, God causes certain things to happen in the world. In other cases, God reveals his wisdom and providential designs to people by announcing things to come or interpreting the theological significance of various realities. Some prophetic texts likewise conceive of the Word of God as a reality or agent figure in its own right.

In what follows, we shall look at select examples from prophetic narrative texts and from the writings associated with the prophets themselves.

## God's Word Spoken by the Prophets: Narrative Examples

### The Deuteronomic History

Among the various associations of the Word of God with modes of presence is God's revealing his own reality or wisdom to people through his Word.

---

5. As will be later discussed, the Hebrew phrasing of this claim—"I will put my words in the mouth of the prophet, who shall speak to them everything that I command"—is significant, for it likewise appears in the descriptions of the prophetic work of Elijah and Jeremiah.

That is to say, God makes himself or some reality or truth cognitively present to people through his Word. This basic teaching finds different expressions in the so-called Deuteronomic history.[6]

One example is the divine revelation of things to come through the prophets' word. Such revelation through the prophetic word figures prominently into the Deuteronomic history's prophecy-fulfillment dynamic. Across this history, there are cases where a prophet delivers a word from the Lord at one point in the narrative, and what the prophet says comes to pass later on in the narrative.

For instance, the early chapters of 1 Samuel narrate the downfall of the priestly family of Eli. According to 1 Samuel 2 (and in contrast to the piety of young Samuel), Eli's two sons, Hophni and Phinehas, were corrupt priests: they "were scoundrels; they had no regard for the LORD or for the duties of the priests to the people" (vv. 12–13). The narrative details their sinful conduct, which includes the dereliction of priestly duties, habitual violation of the protocols for sacrificial offerings for personal gain (vv. 12–17), and engaging in sexual relations with women at the sanctuary (v. 22). On account of their sins and their refusal to repent at their father's pleading, "it was the will of the LORD to kill them" (v. 25).

The Lord sent a prophet to deliver an oracle to Eli that foretold the downfall of his priestly family (1 Sam. 2:27–36). The oracle, "a classic example of a prophetic judgment speech," brings an indictment against the house of Eli (vv. 27–29) and pronounces the judgment to fall on them for their sins (vv. 30–36).[7] Through the prophet, the Lord declares, "No one in your family will live to old age," and (with one exception), "All the members of your household shall die by the sword" (vv. 31, 33).[8] The oracle singles out the specific fate of Hophni and Phineas as a "sign" to Eli, for "both of them shall die on the same day" (v. 34).

The very thing spoken by this prophet to Eli in 1 Samuel 2 comes to pass in 1 Samuel 4. The narrative recounts a Philistine attack on the Israelites wherein the Israelites suffer a significant defeat (4:1–2). The defeated Israelites then

6. "Deuteronomic history" is a scholarly designation for the sustained narrative of Israel's history from the entrance into Canaan until the Babylonian conquest of Jerusalem, and it is given in the books of Deuteronomy, Joshua, Judges, 1–2 Samuel, and 1–2 Kings. For secondary discussion, see Peter R. Ackroyd, *Exile and Restoration: A Study of Hebrew Thought of the Sixth Century BC* (Philadelphia: Westminster, 1968), 62–83; Gerhard von Rad, *Old Testament Theology*, vol. 1, *The Theology of Israel's Historical Traditions*, trans. D. M. G. Stalker (New York: Harper & Row, 1962), 334–47; Blenkinsopp, *History of Prophecy*, 161–65.

7. Bruce C. Birch, "The First and Second Books of Samuel," in *The New Interpreter's Bible*, ed. Leander E. Keck, 12 vols. (Nashville: Abingdon, 1994–2004), 2:988.

8. The one exception is Eli's descendant Abiathar (see Birch, "Books of Samuel," 988).

send for the ark of the covenant to be brought to their camp, thinking that the Lord will necessarily join them in battle against the Philistines. Eli's sons, Hophni and Phinehas, bring the ark to the camp (4:4), and despite the presence of the ark, the Israelites suffer far greater losses than before (4:10). In the second battle, the narrator tersely reports, "The ark of God was captured; and the two sons of Eli, Hophni and Phinehas, died" (4:11). When news of the Israelites' defeat and the Philistines' capture of the ark reaches Eli, the old priest falls backward off his chair, breaks his neck, and dies (4:18). The judgment that the Lord decreed and revealed through his prophet (2:34) has come to pass in the course of events (4:11).

A second kind of example wherein the prophetic word reveals God's wisdom and designs appears in places where the narrator offers a "prophetic interpretation of reality" (to use the apt phrase of Walter Kasper).[9] On several occasions in the Deuteronomic history, the narrator interrupts his account to offer commentary on the deeper (often hidden) meaning of the events that he is recounting. This narratorial commentary can be called a "prophetic interpretation of reality" because the authors are prophetically laying bare for their audience the inner, theological significance of certain historical events.

An example of this prophetic interpretation of reality appears in 2 Kings 17, where the Deuteronomist recounts the Assyrian conquest of the northern kingdom of Israel. The account begins with the narrator recounting certain actions of King Hoshea of Israel, which prompted the Assyrian conquest (17:1–4). During Hoshea's reign, the Assyrian army (led by Sargon II) invaded and destroyed Israel, taking much of the surviving population into exile (17:5–6) and resettling other conquered peoples in that territory (17:24–28). After recounting these historical events, the narrator proceeds to interpret their inner, theological meaning (17:7–18). The narrator is very explicit: "This occurred because the people of Israel had sinned against the LORD their God" (17:7). This theological interpretation emphasizes repeatedly that the conquest and exile of the northern kingdom resulted from a long history of unrepented sins, despite the Lord's repeated calls to repent given through the prophets (17:13–14). Thus, the narrator concludes: "Therefore the LORD was very angry with Israel and removed them out of his sight; none was left but the tribe of Judah alone" (17:18).

The Deuteronomist teaches that the Assyrian conquest of the northern kingdom in 722/721 BC was not just the end result of political and military maneuvers in the eighth-century ancient Near East. Rather, within these

---

9. Walter Kasper, *The God of Jesus Christ*, trans. Matthew J. O'Connell (New York: Crossroad, 1984), 66–67.

movements and actions of these kingdoms, the Deuteronomist discerns the hand of God punishing his people for their sins. Such a prophetic interpretation of reality is ingredient to the theological interests of the Deuteronomic historians. Gerhard von Rad thus writes of the Deuteronomist, "He was not interested in drawing up a secular history, or a history of the faith and worship of Israel. His concern was rather with the problem of how the word of Jahweh functioned in history."[10] By so narrating the history of Israel and interpreting the events in it, the Deuteronomic narrator aligns himself somewhat with the prophets whom he presents in the narrative proper: both reveal God's action in the world and his designs, and in doing so, they make something of God cognitively present to people.

Through both means—the prophecy-fulfillment dynamic and the prophetic interpretation of reality—the Deuteronomist presents the Word of God, delivered by the prophets, as revelatory. By so narrating Israel's history, the Deuteronomists underscore God's providential governance of history and his action in the course of human events to bring about his will. These judgments of God, whether the fall of the house of Eli or the conquest of the northern kingdom, are revealed to God's people through a word given by a prophet.

### Elijah and Elisha

The preeminent narrative examples of the power of God's Word, spoken by the prophets, are the ministries of Elijah and Elisha. Like other biblical prophets, Elijah and Elisha are gifted with the Spirit and speak the Lord's Word (cf. 2 Kings. 2:9, 15; Sir. 48:12). Like the ministry of Moses, a prophet through whom God performed "signs and wonders" (Deut. 34:10–12), the ministries of Elijah and Elisha feature the actions of divine power (i.e., miracles). These miracle stories are cases where the power of God's Word, spoken by the prophets, comes most prominently to light.

Elijah first appears (and does so quite abruptly) in 1 Kings 17. From the first mention of this prophet, the narrator calls attention to the power of the Word spoken by Elijah. Elijah goes to King Ahab of Israel, who, on account of his marriage to the Sidonian princess Jezebel, introduced the worship of Canaanite gods and goddesses into Israel (16:29–34), and Elijah declares, "As the LORD the God of Israel lives, before whom I stand, there shall be neither dew nor rain these years, except by my word" (17:1). The Word of the Lord, spoken by Elijah, exercises power over nature, and in this case, the rainfall. The religious backdrop for this stage of Elijah's ministry is the apostasy in Israel

---

10. Von Rad, *Old Testament Theology*, 1:343.

from the Lord for the worship of Baal, the Canaanite god of the storm.[11] By commanding the rain to stop, Elijah demonstrates that the Lord, not Baal, is the living God, who truly provides life, survival, and sustenance for his people.[12]

An even more dramatic demonstration of the Lord's reality and the power of his Word is the showdown at Mount Carmel between Elijah and the 450 prophets of Baal (1 Kings 18:1–46). To demonstrate that the Lord, not Baal, is the true God of Israel, Elijah publicly challenges the prophets of Baal to call upon their god to send fire to consume sacrificial offerings, and Elijah will pray to the Lord to do the same (18:24). After very lengthy, vocal, and self-mutilating prayers, the prophets of Baal are unable to make fire come and burn up the sacrifices. Elijah then orders that the sacrifice to the Lord be drenched three times with water. In a public prayer spoken to the Lord, Elijah asks that the Lord reveal to Israel his true deity and Elijah's faithful following of his commands, so that Israel might repent and return to the Lord (18:36–37). In response to Elijah's words, "the fire of the LORD fell and consumed the burnt offering, the wood, the stones, and the dust, and even licked up the water that was in the trench" (18:38). Upon seeing this display of divine power, "all the people . . . fell on their faces and said, 'The LORD indeed is God'" (18:39). And as Israel returned to the Lord, the rain returned to the land (18:45).

The Lord performs other acts of power through the Word spoken by Elijah. When the drought and famine have settled in the land, Elijah is sent to non-Israelite territory to meet a widow and her son in Zarephath. Upon receiving her hospitality, Elijah speaks an oracle that the widow's supply of flour and oil will not run out, thus sustaining them during the famine: "Thus says the LORD the God of Israel: The jar of meal will not be emptied and the jug of oil will not fail until the day that the LORD sends rain on the earth" (1 Kings 17:14). The narrator later points out that this very thing happened on account of the power of God's Word that Elijah spoke (v. 16). At a later time, the same widow's son dies from an illness, and Elijah prays

---

11. C. L. Seow thus explains the significance of the drought in light of Canaanite polytheism and the Baal mythology: "In Canaanite religion, Baal the storm god is the one who brings rain, and thus, the possibility of life on earth. When there is drought, it is presumed that death (which is deified in Canaanite mythology) has been victorious and that Baal is dead. Conversely, when there is rain, it is presumed that Baal is alive and that death has been defeated." Seow, "The First and Second Books of Kings," in *The New Interpreter's Bible*, ed. Leander E. Keck, 12 vols. (Nashville: Abingdon, 1999), 3:126. For historical discussion, see John Bright, *A History of Israel*, 3rd ed. (Philadelphia: Westminster, 1981), 243–47; J. Maxwell Miller and John H. Hayes, *A History of Ancient Israel and Judah*, 2nd ed. (Louisville: Westminster John Knox, 2006), 313–15.

12. Seow, "Books of Kings," 126.

that the Lord would restore the boy's life (v. 21). The Lord brings the boy back to life, and the widow declares to Elijah, "Now I know that you are a man of God, and that the word of the LORD in your mouth is truth" (v. 24). In 2 Kings 1, Elijah delivers an oracle to King Ahaziah of Israel, pronouncing his coming death as God's punishment for the king's seeking answers from the Canaanite god Baal-zebub (v. 16). The narrator then says, "So [Ahaziah] died according to the word of the LORD that Elijah had spoken" (v. 17). Earlier in the same account, Elijah calls down fire from heaven twice more to destroy the two detachments of soldiers that King Ahaziah dispatched to bring Elijah to him (vv. 9–12).

One further example of the power of the God's Word spoken by Elijah is the judgment oracle that he pronounces on Ahab and Jezebel for the murder of Naboth and seizure of his ancestral land (1 Kings 21:20–24). This is a further example of the Deuteronomic history's prophecy-fulfillment dynamic wherein the prophet delivers a Word from the Lord at one point in the narrative, and what the prophet says comes to pass later in the narrative. Thus, in 1 Kings 21, Elijah announces that the royal house of Ahab will fall in the next generation (vv. 21–22) and that Jezebel, the main villain in the Naboth incident, will die a particularly violent death: "The dogs shall eat Jezebel within the bounds of Jezreel" (v. 23).[13] Later, in 2 Kings 9–10, these two things come to pass, and the narrator explicitly points out that they happened in accordance with the Word of the Lord, spoken by Elijah (cf. 2 Kings 9:36; 10:10, 17)

Very appropriately, therefore, does Ben Sira praise Elijah by saying that he "arose, a prophet like fire, and his word burned like a torch" (Sir. 48:1). He identifies the Word of God, spoken by Elijah, as that by which these acts of divine power were wrought: "By the word of the Lord he shut up the heavens, and also three times brought down fire" (v. 3), and "raised a corpse from death ... by the word of the Most High" (v. 5).

Much of the same applies to miracles performed in the ministry of Elijah's prophetic successor, Elisha. When God appears to Elijah at Mount Horeb in the quiet, whispering sound, he gives Elijah three prophetic tasks, one of which is to anoint Elisha as his prophetic successor (1 Kings 19:16).[14] In the very next narrative episode, Elijah does so, and Elisha leaves his family to become Elijah's follower (vv. 19–21).

13. Jezreel was the location of Naboth's vineyard (1 Kings 21:1), and the specification of this location as the place where Jezebel would die underscores the connection between her sins and the punishment.
14. The other two tasks are to anoint Hazael as king of Aram and to anoint Jehu as king of Israel (to replace the house of Ahab over Israel) (1 Kings 19:15–16). Elisha, not Elijah, completed these two tasks (see 2 Kings 8:15; 9:1–6).

Before Elijah is taken away to heaven, Elisha requests (and Elijah accordingly prays) that "a double share of [Elijah's prophetic] spirit" be given him (2 Kings 2:9). The Lord grants this request, and as a result, the ministry of Elisha features even more miracles, many of which resemble those performed through Elijah. For instance, like Elijah, Elisha assists a widow, who is in danger of losing her children to debt slavery, by commanding that from her limited supply enough oil be produced to pay off her family's debt (4:1–7). Also like Elijah, Elisha raises from the dead the deceased son of the Shunammite woman, who was one of his benefactors (vv. 32–37). Elisha heals the Syrian general Naaman of his leprosy at a distance by commanding him to wash seven times in the Jordan River (5:10, 14).[15] Also by Elisha's spoken prayer, an Aramaean army, which is attacking Israel, is struck with blindness and later has that blindness taken away (6:18, 20).

A bit more germane to our study of God's Word, spoken by the prophet, are those miracle stories that explicitly contain an oracle from God. Upon coming to a city with an undrinkable water supply, Elisha throws salt into the spring and says, "Thus says the LORD, I have made this water wholesome; from now on neither death nor miscarriage shall come from it" (2 Kings 2:21). The narrator then comments on the efficacy of Elisha's word: "So the water has been wholesome to this day, according to the word that Elisha spoke" (v. 22). In an episode that anticipates the feeding miracles of Jesus, Elisha also feeds a multitude of people with only twenty loaves of bread. Elisha's command to the man with the loaves to feed the crowd features an oracle: "Give it to the people and let them eat, for thus says the LORD, 'They shall eat and have some left'" (4:43). Once again, the narrator calls attention to the power of God's Word, spoken by Elisha: "He set [the bread] before them, they ate, and had some left, according to the word of the LORD" (v. 44). Another prophetic oracle spoken by Elisha grants water and victory to a coalition of armies from Israel, Judah, and Edom in their campaign against Moab (3:16–19). These miracles, which contain an oracle, make clear that God is the one performing the miracles through the Word spoken by the prophet.

Thus, Elisha, much like his prophetic master and predecessor, performed mighty deeds of power by virtue of God's Word that he spoke. And Ben Sira, just as he praised the power of the Word spoken by Elijah, praises Elisha: "He performed twice as many signs, and marvels with every utterance of his mouth" (Sir. 48:12).

---

15. Elisha also commands Naaman's leprosy to come to afflict Elisha's duplicitous servant Gehazi, who connived to take payment for this miracle (2 Kings 5:27).

## God's Word Spoken by the Prophets: Examples from the Prophets' Writings

### *Jeremiah*

In addition to these narrative accounts of the power and presence of God's Word spoken by the prophets, there are also relevant descriptions in the writings associated with prophets as such. A constellation of related passages from the book of Jeremiah is especially helpful.

The call narrative in Jeremiah relates the revelation in which God calls and empowers Jeremiah for his task (1:4–19).[16] The call narrative introduces several details and phrases that are relevant for the book's teaching about the Word of God. First, the call narrative underscores the presence of God's Word in Jeremiah, who will in turn speak that Word. After God makes the introductory revelation wherein he tells Jeremiah, "I appointed you a prophet to the nations" (v. 5), Jeremiah, as is customary, voices his own reluctance to undertake this role: "Truly I do not know how to speak, for I am only a boy" (v. 6).[17] God's reassuring response to Jeremiah underscores the prophet's role of speaking God's Word: "You shall speak whatever I command you" (v. 7). The prophet then relates, "The LORD put out his hand and touched my mouth . . . and said to me, 'Now I have put my words in your mouth'" (v. 9). The phrases "speak whatever I command you" and "I have put my words in your mouth" allude to the description of the prophet-like-Moses, about whom the Lord says, "I will put my words in the mouth of the prophet, who shall speak to them everything that I command" (Deut. 18:18). The same language will reappear later in the book when Jeremiah will comment on the power of God's Word within him.

Second, the call narrative introduces the theme that Jeremiah's message will feature oracles of both destruction and restoration. The Lord announces, "See, today I appoint you over nations and over kingdoms, to pluck up and to pull down, to destroy and to overthrow, to build and to plant" (1:10). Moreover, the Lord tells Jeremiah that he will encounter much opposition from his contemporaries, who will reject his message (vv. 8, 14–18). These motifs of Jeremiah's message of impending destruction as well as opposition from his contemporaries anticipate the conflict between Jeremiah and the false prophets.

16. Jeremiah's statement "The LORD put out his hand and touched my mouth" (1:9) suggests that this revelation involved a vision that Jeremiah saw. So Jack R. Lundbom, *Jeremiah 1–20: A New Translation with Introduction and Commentary*, Anchor Bible 21 (New York: Doubleday, 1999), 234.

17. For helpful discussion of Jeremiah's call, see Patrick D. Miller, "The Book of Jeremiah," in *The New Interpreter's Bible*, ed. Leander E. Keck, 12 vols. (Nashville: Abingdon, 2001), 6:579–86.

Third, the call narrative also hints that although Jeremiah was summoned to be a prophet while "only a boy" (1:7), he did not undertake his active ministry until he was a bit older.[18] When the Lord asks Jeremiah about what his eyes are beholding at his call, the prophet reports seeing an almond tree (v. 11). The Lord replies, "You have seen well, for I am watching over my word to perform it" (v. 12). This seemingly odd exchange involves a play on words in Hebrew that does not come across in translation. The Hebrew verb for God's "watching" in verse 12 ($š\bar{o}q\bar{e}d$) picks up the Hebrew noun for "almond tree" in verse 11 ($š\bar{a}q\bar{e}d$). God will preserve the Word that he has given to Jeremiah so that God may later bring about that which his Word, spoken by Jeremiah, will articulate.[19]

Later in the book, Jeremiah develops many elements from the call narrative as he voices his experience of having the Word of God within him. In one of his laments (15:10–21), Jeremiah speaks of the time, later in life, when his prophetic ministry was "activated." Seemingly, the occasion for the activation of Jeremiah's prophetic ministry was the discovery of the "book of the law" by the high priest Hilkiah during King Josiah's renovation of Solomon's temple in 622/621 BC (2 Kings 22:8).[20] The discovery of this book—a version of the book of Deuteronomy—prompted King Josiah to renew the covenant with the Lord and launch a wide-ranging series of reforms (cf. 2 Kings 23). Of this time, Jeremiah states, "Your words were found, and I ate them" (15:16). He likens his faith experience of "receiving" or "taking in" God's Word to eating food. In doing so, Jeremiah anticipates the faith experiences of later prophets, such as Ezekiel and John the visionary (in the book of Revelation), who in a symbolic vision receive the Word by eating a scroll (cf. Ezek. 3:1–3; Rev. 10:8–11). Having so devoured the Word of God, Jeremiah describes the experience of having God's Word within him: "Your words became to me a joy and the delight of my heart" (Jer. 15:16). Moreover, through this taking in of the Word of God, Jeremiah came to understand himself in a unique relationship with God. According to Patrick Miller, the phrase in 15:16, "for I am called by your name, O Lord," expresses legal ownership. Miller continues, "Just as God claims ownership of the Temple, for which this same formulation is used (7:10), so also, Jeremiah says, God has claimed him as a special possession."[21]

As introduced in the call narrative, the Word spoken by Jeremiah will contain a message of impending doom for Judah and will provoke much

18. Lundbom, *Jeremiah 1–20*, 233–35, 743.
19. Lundbom, *Jeremiah 1–20*, 236.
20. Lundbom, *Jeremiah 1–20*, 743.
21. Miller, "Jeremiah," 698.

opposition. Thus, in a later lament, Jeremiah says, "The word of the LORD has become for me a reproach and derision all day long" (20:8). The prophet entertains the possibility of quitting his prophetic vocation, of not speaking God's Word anymore on account of all the hostilities that this Word has aroused (v. 9). But Jeremiah finds that he cannot but speak the Word of God. He writes, "Then within me there is something like a burning fire shut up in my bones; I am weary with holding it in, and I cannot" (v. 9).

Jeremiah thus speaks of the Word of God as a present reality within him, and this reality has power. For instance, Jeremiah likens the Word of God in him to "burning fire" (similar to the descriptions of the Sinai revelation that we discussed in the introduction). Moreover, Jeremiah's description of God's fiery Word—"I am weary with holding it in, and I cannot"—recalls an earlier description of God's wrath which is about to fall upon Jerusalem.[22] In this earlier statement, Jeremiah remarks, "I am full of the wrath of the LORD; I am weary of holding it in" (6:11). This impending doom is due in part to the fact that the "word of the LORD is to [Jeremiah's contemporaries] an object of scorn; they take no pleasure in it" (v. 10). Thus, according to Jeremiah, the Word of God is a reality within him that has a power of its own: it burns like fire and pressures to burst forth from within the prophet.

Jeremiah's description of the Word of God as being like fire coheres with two other passages in the book. First, Jeremiah 5:10–17 frames a contrast between Jeremiah and the "false prophets of peace" by recalling certain details from the call narrative.[23] Whereas Jeremiah says that the Lord is going to bring judgment on his people for their unrepented sins, other prophets claim that the Lord will do no such thing: the false prophets declare, "He will do nothing. No evil will come upon us" (v. 12). These prophets, Jeremiah writes, "are nothing but wind, for the word is not in them" (v. 13). The Lord tells Jeremiah that, unlike these false prophets, Jeremiah will be effective: "I am now making my words in your mouth a fire" (v. 14)—much as he did at Jeremiah's call (cf. 1:9). This Word, which Jeremiah "ate" (15:16; Hebrew: *'ākal*) and which became "like a burning fire" in him (20:9), is going to "eat up" the people of Judah: "The fire shall devour [*'ākal*] them" (5:14). Moreover, the fiery Word will "devour" the people of Judah by bringing about the reality that it articulates: God's judgment on Judah, carried out through the Babylonian conquest. The prophet underscores this connection by repeatedly using the same verb for "eating," which he applied to the Word in 5:14, to denote the destruction to come at the hands of Babylon. In verse 17, the

22. Lundbom, *Jeremiah 1–20*, 856–57.
23. See Lundbom, *Jeremiah 1–20*, 395; Miller, "Jeremiah," 620.

prophet says four times that the "ancient nation" (i.e., Babylon; v. 15) will "eat up" (Hebrew: *'ākal*) various parts of Judah's life. The Word of God, spoken by Jeremiah, will cause the reality that it signifies: the Babylonian conquest.

A second text that speaks of the power of God's Word by likening it to fire is Jeremiah 23:28–29. As in 5:10–17, Jeremiah here voices a polemic against the prophets who proclaim a false peace and no judgment on sin to come from the Lord. The text contrasts the prophets of false peace, who claim revelation through dreams, with Jeremiah, who actually has the Word of the Lord: "Let the prophet who has a dream tell the dream, but let the one who has my word speak my word faithfully" (23:28). Jeremiah then speaks of the Lord's Word as a powerful reality: "Is not my word like fire, says the LORD, and like a hammer than breaks a rock in pieces?" (v. 29). The likening of God's Word to fire and a rock-shattering hammer is in keeping with the word of impending judgment that Jeremiah speaks. But at his calling, God's message to Jeremiah also involved a word of hope and consolation: "to build and to plant" (1:10). As the fiery Word will "devour" the people of Judah for their sins, so too can we anticipate the same Word as going to fulfill the promises of eschatological restoration and salvation that the prophet also speaks (cf. 30:1–31:40).

### Second Isaiah

This basic message of future restoration, consolation, and forgiveness constitutes the heart of Isaiah 40–55, so-called Second Isaiah. This material is normally attributed to an unspecified prophet, living in Babylon, near the end of the Babylonian exile, who writes in the spirit and tradition of Isaiah of Jerusalem (d. 704 BC). For our purposes, we note that Second Isaiah begins and ends with mention of the power and reality of God's Word, spoken by the prophet.[24]

We start with a part of the oracle that closes Second Isaiah (chap. 55). Here, the prophet compares God's Word with the rain and snow. He begins by stating that both rain and snow "come down from heaven" (i.e., the sky) and produce an effect on earth for people's benefit: "making [the earth] bring forth and sprout, giving seed to the sower and bread to the eater" (v. 10). The rain and snow "do not return" to the heavens (i.e., evaporate) until they bring these things about on the earth (v. 10). The natural rhythm of precipitation descending to earth, producing a benefit, and returning to the heavens

---

24. So Brevard S. Childs, *Isaiah*, Old Testament Library (Louisville: Westminster John Knox, 2001), 437–38; Christopher R. Seitz, "The Book of Isaiah 40–66," in *The New Interpreter's Bible*, ed. Leander E. Keck, 12 vols. (Nashville: Abingdon, 2001), 6:336.

provides a natural analogue to the Word of God.[25] Through the prophet, the Lord says, "So shall my word be that goes out from my mouth" (v. 11). Just as the rain and snow "do not return" (Hebrew: *lō'-yāšûb*) until they produce their effects, so too the Word "shall not return" (Hebrew: *lō'-yāšûb*) to the Lord until it produces its effect in the world (v. 11). The prophet presents the Word of God in quasi-personal terms, which cohere with the more robust hypostatization of the Word in later Jewish and Christian writings. In Isaiah 55, the Word of God is a reality that can be sent on a purposeful mission from God—the Word is an agent that does what God wills.

God adds, "My word . . . shall accomplish that which I purpose, and succeed in the thing for which I sent it" (Isa. 55:11). When verses 10–11 are placed in the larger context of the closing oracle, God's purpose for which the Word is sent is the work of redemption. The oracle begins with an invitation to God's people who are in exile for their sins (vv. 1–2). The Lord exhorts his people, "Listen carefully to me, and eat what is good" (v. 2). These words are reminiscent of divine Wisdom, who hosts a dinner and invites all to come learn from her: "Come, eat of my bread and drink of the wine I have mixed" (Prov. 9:5).[26] So too, the Lord invites people to "listen" and "eat"—that is, to take in his word of salvation that he offers freely to all (Isa. 55:2). God promises to glorify his people and make a new covenant with them (vv. 3–5). He summons his people to repent of their sins and seek his abundant mercy (vv. 6–9). The oracle's closing verses, which immediately follow the passage about the Word of God in verses 10–11, promise the restoration of God's people from the exilic state of punishment for sins and the transformation of creation (vv. 12–13).

These teachings about the Word of God in Isaiah 55:10–11 form a bookend with the earlier mention of the Word of God in 40:6–8, part of the programmatic opening of Second Isaiah in Isaiah 40. Like 55:10–11, 40:6–8 compares the Word of God to natural phenomena. Here, human beings and their ways are likened to grass and flowers (v. 6). Whereas 55:10–11 turns on an analogical likeness between the rain and snow and the Word of God, 40:6–8 accents the difference between human beings and God's Word. The text highlights the passing, transitory nature of human beings and their ways. Like the grass and the flowers, humanity "withers" and "fades" before God (v. 7). But the Word of God is unlike these worldly realities, for it is permanent and unfading: "the word of our God will stand forever" (v. 8). As Joseph Blenkinsopp reads the

---

25. Joseph Blenkinsopp, *Isaiah 40–55: A New Translation with Introduction and Commentary*, Anchor Bible 19A (New York: Doubleday, 2002), 372.
    26. So too Blenkinsopp, *Isaiah 40–55*, 369 (contra Seitz, "Isaiah 40–66," 481).

contrast: "The transforming power of the prophetic word ('the word of our God') [is] contrasted with, or pitted against, the political powers and principalities, which appear to be indestructible but are in reality impermanent."[27]

The permanently abiding Word, which the prophet speaks, announces that God is coming with salvation for people. It is "comfort" for Judah (Isa. 40:1), for "she has served her term, . . . her penalty is paid" (v. 2). God will come to restore his people from exile (i.e., the state of covenantal punishment for sin), and in doing so, he will manifest himself to all peoples: "The glory of the LORD shall be revealed, and all people shall see it together, for the mouth of the LORD has spoken" (v. 5).

Put differently, the Word of God is the "good tidings" (Isa. 40:9) or "good news" (52:7), announced by a herald to Jerusalem. Namely, "the Lord GOD comes with might," and he "will feed his flock like a shepherd; he will gather the lambs in his arms" (40:10–11). This "good news" is a word of "peace" and "salvation" (52:7), for the Lord will return to Zion to reign as King (vv. 7–8). It is the message that the Lord "has comforted his people . . . has redeemed Jerusalem" (v. 7), and "all the ends of the earth shall see the salvation of our God" (v. 10). The Hebrew verb used in the participial phrases rendered as "herald of good tidings" and the one "who brings good news" (40:9; 52:7; Hebrew: *bāśar*) is rendered in the Septuagint with the Greek verb *euangelizein*. This is the verbal form of the term used throughout the New Testament for "the gospel" (cf. Mark 1:14). Taken in this light, the Word of the Lord, which "will stand forever" (Isa. 40:8), is the good news of the eschatological salvation wrought by God, who comes in saving power as King. It is the gospel, "the good news of the kingdom of God" (Luke 4:43).

## Looking Back and Looking Forward

This examination of Old Testament texts has provided evidence that the Word of God, with its associations of power and presence, can be given through inspired human speech. The biblical witnesses affirm this point in the case of the biblical prophets whom God summons and empowers to speak his Word to people. The Deuteronomic history presents the Word of God as mediating divine truths, either about future things or the interior, theological significance of realities in the world. The Word of God can thus make things cognitively present to people by imparting knowledge. The power of God's Word, spoken by the prophets, appears in the narratives of Elijah and Elisha. By virtue of

27. Blenkinsopp, *Isaiah 40–55*, 183.

the Word, which the prophets speak and have in their mouths, God produces divinely caused effects in the world. The prophet Jeremiah speaks of the Word of God as a reality that he has taken in and that has a power of its own. According to Jeremiah, the Word of God has power to bring about that which it signifies, be it God's judgment or promises of salvation. Anticipating the substantive presentations of God's Word as a personal, causal agent in later Jewish writings, Second Isaiah presents God's Word as an agent, sent on a mission by God to accomplish his work of salvation. Unlike the transitoriness of human life, the Word of God is permanent and utterly reliable; it "will stand forever" (Isa. 40:8).

Having examined relevant witnesses from the Old Testament, we now turn to consider examples from the New Testament. As we will see, much of what is the case with the inspired speech of the Old Testament prophets of Israel extends into the New Testament with the case of the apostles.

# 3

## The Word of God in the Inspired Speech of the Apostles

We continue to examine the biblical witness concerning the Word of God given through inspired human discourse by taking up the New Testament's presentation of the apostolic preaching. Our survey of New Testament material focuses on three major witnesses. First, we will examine the narrative presentation of the apostolic preaching in Acts of the Apostles. Second, we will consider several instances of Paul's discussion of his own apostolic preaching in his letters. Third, we will look closely at elements in 1 Peter, and in particular, the remarks in 1:23 about Christians being "born anew . . . through the living and enduring word of God." As we will see, the inspired preaching of God's Word by the apostles bears divine causal power, and it constitutes a means by which the risen Jesus himself becomes present to people.

### The Apostles in Acts

In chapter 1, we looked at aspects of Jesus's teaching the Word of God in the Gospel according to Luke. We saw that Luke presents Jesus's teaching of the Word, "the good news of the kingdom of God" (Luke 4:43), as essential to his ministry as the Spirit-anointed Messiah and Lord. Jesus's words are totally infused with the power of the Holy Spirit, and through them, the kingdom of God becomes present in power in the world. Much of what Luke presents with regard to Jesus's preaching in the Gospel gets extended and transposed into the preaching of the apostles in Acts. We will highlight three specific areas: (1) like Jesus, the apostles teach the "Word of God," (2) there is some manner of connection between the Word proclaimed and the Holy Spirit, and (3) the Word proclaimed in the Holy Spirit has causal power and can make present what it articulates.

### Teaching the Word of God

First, just as Luke in his Gospel identified the Word of God as that which Jesus teaches, so too does he identify the Word of God as that which the apostles and other Christians proclaim in Acts. In Acts 6, the Twelve identify "the ministry of the Word" as their primary task as apostles (v. 4, translation ours). Hence, the seven assistants were appointed to assist in the Jerusalem church's food distribution so that the twelve apostles might not "neglect the word of God in order to wait on tables" (v. 2). Upon hearing about the arrest and subsequent release of Peter and John, the early Christians petition God in communal prayer: "Grant to your servants to speak your word with all boldness" (4:29). God grants their request with a manifestation and outpouring of the Holy Spirit: "They were all filled with the Holy Spirit and spoke the word of God with boldness" (v. 31). When the persecution in Jerusalem begins to drive Christians (and thus the gospel) to territories outside the city, Luke states, "Those who were scattered went from place to place, proclaiming the word" (8:4). The ensuing account of the Christian mission in Samaria reports that "the word of God" was being taught there by Philip (vv. 12, 14) as well as by Peter and John (v. 25). Luke also identifies "the word of God" as that which Peter and Paul proclaim in their evangelization.[1]

Luke's specification that Peter and Paul proclaim the Word of God in their evangelization invites a consideration of the sermons in Acts as providing further insight into the *content* of the proclaimed Word. Throughout Acts, speeches and sermons are an important vehicle for theological teaching, and scholars have endeavored to put the speeches into different categories.[2] For present purposes, we will attend briefly to two of these sermons—Peter's

1. Luke identifies "the Word of God" or "the Word of the Lord" as that which Peter proclaims in Acts 11:1 (cf. 10:44) and as what Paul proclaims in Acts 13:5–7; 14:3; 15:35–36; 16:32; 17:13; 18:11; 19:10; 20:24 (cf. 14:25; 16:6; 18:5).

2. The speeches in Acts have attracted much scholarly attention. For a sense of the critical issues involved in their study, see Joseph A. Fitzmyer, *The Acts of the Apostles: A New Translation with Introduction and Commentary*, Anchor Bible 31 (New York: Doubleday, 1998), 103–8; Carl R. Holladay, *Acts: A Commentary*, New Testament Library (Louisville: Westminster John Knox, 2016), 40–46; Eduard Schweizer, "Concerning the Speeches in Acts," in *Studies in Luke-Acts*, ed. Leander E. Keck and J. Louis Martyn (Mifflintown, PA: Sigler, 1999), 208–16.

sermon to the household of Cornelius (10:34b–43) and Paul's sermon in the synagogue in Antioch in Pisidia (13:16b–41)—for Luke explicitly identifies both of them as conveying "the word" (10:44; 13:44).

Like other sermons in Acts, these two have in common several basic elements of content.[3] First, both sermons center on Jesus Christ and what God has done for the salvation of the world in the life, death, and resurrection of Jesus (10:36–41; 13:27–31). Second, God's action in Jesus stands in continuity with his previous actions in the history of Israel, and thus in Jesus, God has fulfilled his promises of salvation that he had made through the prophets (10:43; 13:17–23, 32–37). Third, the apostles have been divinely chosen to be "witnesses" of the risen Jesus to all peoples (10:41–42; 13:31–32). Fourth, God's gifts of salvation, the forgiveness of sins, and eternal life are available through the risen Jesus (10:43; 13:38–39, 46, 48). Fifth, there is a call to repent and turn to Jesus in faith, and so receive the gifts offered by God in him (10:43; 13:38–41). Given that Luke identifies both speeches as voicing "the word," we can, at the very least, identify these five elements as articulating the basic contents of the Word of God proclaimed by the apostles.

Luke also uses other phrases to designate the contents of the apostles' teaching. For instance, he calls it "the good news of God's grace" (20:24) or "the word of his grace" (14:3). On several occasions, Luke speaks of the apostles and other early Christians as teaching "the word of the Lord."[4] In the Gospel, Luke identifies the teachings of "the Lord" as the teachings of Jesus (Luke 10:39), and Luke does the same in Acts. In Acts 11:16, Peter states, "I remembered the word of the Lord, how he had said, 'John baptized with water, but you will be baptized with the Holy Spirit.'" This statement about John's baptism, which Peter here identifies as "the word of the Lord," is a saying of Jesus reported in Acts 1:5: "For John baptized with water, but you will be baptized with the Holy Spirit not many days from now." The "word of the Lord" is the Word of Jesus. Furthermore, as he does with respect to Jesus in the Gospel, Luke also cites "the kingdom of God" as that which the apostles preach.[5] Acts concludes with a description of Paul's teaching in Rome that draws together elements from both of Luke's volumes: Paul was "proclaiming the kingdom of God and teaching about the Lord Jesus Christ with all boldness" (28:31). By speaking of "the kingdom of God" (characteristic of Jesus's teaching in the Gospel) together with "teaching about the

---

3. The five elements listed below also appear in Peter's sermons at Pentecost (2:14b–39) and in the temple (3:12b–26). See also C. H. Dodd, *The Apostolic Preaching and Its Developments* (New York: Harper & Row, 1964), 7–35.

4. See Acts 4:29; 8:25; 13:44, 48–49; 15:35–36; 16:32; 19:10.

5. See Acts 8:12; 19:8; 28:23, 31.

Lord Jesus Christ" (characteristic of the apostles' teaching in Acts), Luke shows the essential continuity between Jesus's teaching and the apostolic teaching about Jesus.[6]

### Proclaiming the Word in the Power of the Holy Spirit

A second point of continuity between the Word of God proclaimed by Jesus and by the apostles concerns the Holy Spirit. As we have seen, Luke articulates a close relationship between the Holy Spirit and Jesus's Word. Whereas the Holy Spirit totally suffuses Jesus's humanity from the moment of his conception, the apostles must receive a derivative share of the Holy Spirit from Jesus.

Acts presents the apostles as divinely chosen "witnesses" of the risen Jesus, whom the Holy Spirit empowers for this mission (Luke 24:48–49; Acts 1:8). The apostles' role as witnesses is based in their own experiences of being with Jesus before and after the resurrection. When the very first Christians meet to choose a replacement for Judas Iscariot as one of the Twelve, Peter sets forth a criterion for candidacy: a suitable replacement should be "one of the men who have accompanied us during all the time that the Lord Jesus went in and out among us, beginning from the baptism of John until the day when he was taken up from us" (Acts 1:21–22). In his speech to Cornelius's household, Peter reiterates that firsthand experiences with Jesus are the basis for being an apostolic witness. He says of himself and his apostolic confreres, "We are witnesses to all that he did both in Judea and in Jerusalem" (10:39). He later adds that the risen Jesus appeared only to those "who were chosen by God as witnesses, and who ate and drank with him after he rose from the dead" (10:41). Similarly, Paul states in his first sermon, "For many days [Jesus] appeared to those who came up with him from Galilee to Jerusalem, and they are now his witnesses" (13:31). Paul's own personal encounter with the risen Jesus on the road to Damascus enables Paul to "be his witness to all the world of what [Paul has] seen and heard" (22:15; cf. 9:15; 23:11; 26:16).

To assist the apostles in their mission of being his witnesses to the whole world, the risen Jesus promises them heavenly "power." This promise appears in accounts of the postresurrection commissioning of the apostles in both the Gospel and Acts. Just as in the Gospel account of Jesus's ministry, Luke associates "power" with the Holy Spirit, so also does he identify the divine empowerment given to the apostles as the Holy Spirit (Luke 24:49; Acts 1:8).

6. Holladay remarks about this closing to Acts that it is "an emphatic—and triumphant—conclusion to the narrative, an exclamation point, as it were, confirming what Gamaliel has wisely predicted, 'If it is of God, you will not be able to destroy them' (5:39)." *Acts*, 513.

Throughout Acts, the Holy Spirit inspires the apostles and empowers their proclamation of the Word of God. In Acts 2, Peter delivers his first sermon, having been "filled with the Holy Spirit" at Pentecost (v. 4). In the second (large) summary statement of the church's life in Jerusalem, Luke states, "With great power the apostles gave their testimony to the resurrection of the Lord Jesus" (4:33).[7] As Peter proclaims the Word in the household of Cornelius, the Holy Spirit descends upon them (10:44; 11:15)—an episode illustrating what was later known as baptism in the Holy Spirit.[8] Moreover, Luke states the Holy Spirit directs the proclamation of the Word by both Peter (11:12) and Paul (16:6).

A particular way in which Luke expresses the Holy Spirit enabling the apostles and other early Christians to speak the Word of God powerfully is with mention of "bold speech" (*parrhēsia*). After Peter and John have been arrested and brought before the Sanhedrin, Peter gives his third speech in Acts and proclaims the Word of God (4:8–12). Luke introduces this speech by stating Peter was "filled with the Holy Spirit" (v. 8). After this Spirit-infused speech of Peter, the Sanhedrin recognizes "the boldness [*parrhēsia*] of Peter and John" (v. 13). As mentioned previously, after Peter and John return to the Jerusalem church after being released, the church petitions God that they might "speak [God's] word with all boldness [*parrhēsia*]" (v. 29). God answers their prayers with a manifest outpouring of the Spirit: "They were all filled with the Holy Spirit and spoke the word of God with boldness [*parrhēsia*]" (v. 31). After Paul's baptism and consequent reception of the Holy Spirit, he stays in Damascus and later goes to Jerusalem. Luke reports that in both places Paul was "speaking boldly [*parrhēsiazomenos*] in the name of the Lord" (9:28; cf. v. 27). Later, while in Iconium on Paul's first missionary expedition, Paul and Barnabas were "speaking boldly [*parrhēsiazomenoi*] for the Lord, who testified to the word of his grace by granting signs and wonders to be done through them" (14:3). At the conclusion of Acts, Luke likewise speaks of Paul preaching in Rome "with all boldness [*parrhēsias*]" (28:31). While Luke sometimes uses *parrhēsia* in other senses, these examples suffice to illustrate that for Luke, "bold speech"

---

7. Throughout Acts, Luke provides both large and small summary statements. The large summaries appear in 2:42–47; 4:32–35; 5:12–16. The small summaries appear in 2:41, 47; 4:4; 5:14; 6:7; 9:31, 42; 11:21, 24; 12:24; 14:1; 16:5; 19:20; 28:31. For discussion, see Fitzmyer, *Acts*, 97–98; Holladay, *Acts*, 46–48.

8. For more information on "baptism in the Holy Spirit," see Francis Martin, ed., *Baptism in the Holy Spirit: Reflections on a Contemporary Grace in the Light of the Catholic Tradition* (Petersham, MA: Saint Bede's Publications, 1998); Martin, *The Life-Changer: How You Can Experience Freedom, Power and Refreshment in the Holy Spirit* (Ann Arbor, MI: Servant, 1990).

(*parrhēsia*) is often a veritable synonym for the Spirit-filled proclamation of the Word of God.[9]

### The Spirit-Infused Proclamation of the Word Mediates Divine Reality and Power

Having been "promised" by the Father (Luke 24:49) and sent by the risen Jesus, the Holy Spirit clothes the apostles' proclamation of the Word of God with power. Luke provides his audience with examples of the Word's power in action wherein the proclaimed Word makes present the spiritual realities that it articulates. Put differently, when the apostles proclaim "the kingdom of God and . . . the Lord Jesus Christ" in the power of the Holy Spirit, these divine realities become present and active (Acts 28:31). Acts presents two interrelated displays of the power of the Word to make present the reality it articulates, and they are, in a sense, two sides of the same coin. When the Word is proclaimed in the power of the Holy Spirit, (1) it can cause faith in those who receive it and (2) it defeats the spiritual powers of evil.

First, the Spirit-infused proclamation of the Word causes faith in those who receive it. Upon hearing Peter's Spirit-filled proclamation of the Word on Pentecost, his audience was "cut to the heart" (Acts 2:37), and as a result, many "received his word and were baptized" (v. 41, translation ours). Similarly, after Peter proclaimed the Word of God in the Jerusalem temple, "many of those who heard the word believed" (4:4). While on his first missionary expedition and shortly after his sermon in Antioch of Pisidia, Paul announces that he and his team will be "turning to the Gentiles" in the face of Jewish resistance to his Gospel (13:46). The gentiles who learned of this news "praised the word of the Lord; and as many as had been destined for eternal life became believers" (v. 48).

The same causal relationship between the apostolic proclamation of the Word and faith arising in the hearts of those who receive it appears in the account of Paul and Silas in Philippi. Soon after Paul arrives, he meets a woman, Lydia, a textile merchant from Thyatira (16:14). In a statement that reminds us of the audience's reaction to Peter's Pentecost speech (i.e., being "cut to the heart," 2:37), Luke states that "the Lord opened her heart to listen eagerly to what was said by Paul" (16:14). Later, she and her household "were baptized" (v. 15). Similarly, after the Philippian jailer finds Paul and Silas freed from their restraints and the prison doors open, he falls down before them in fear, asking, "What must I do to be saved?" and as part of their response, calling for

---

9. For instance, *parrhēsia* seems to suggest skill in rhetorical argumentation (18:26; 19:8) or direct, frank speech (26:26).

faith, Paul and Silas "spoke the word of the Lord to him and to all who were in his house" (vv. 30, 32). Upon hearing and receiving the proclaimed Word, the jailer and his household are baptized and rejoice "that he had become a believer in God" (v. 34).

A second display of the power of the proclaimed Word is that when the Word of God is proclaimed in the power of the Holy Spirit, the spiritual powers of evil are defeated. As the Word proclaimed in the power of the Spirit leads many to faith in Jesus, it also confronts and conquers the spiritual powers of evil.

On several occasions in Acts, when the gospel begins to be proclaimed in a new geographical region or at the start of a new missionary endeavor, it confronts and conquers the spiritual powers of evil in that region as it brings people to faith in Jesus. For instance, when the gospel begins to move outside Jerusalem as a result of the persecutions there, the narrative follows the work of Philip in Samaria. He "proclaimed the Messiah" to the Samaritans (8:5), and the Samaritans "received the word of God" (v. 14, translation ours). Luke also specifies that Philip's proclamation of the Word of God was accompanied by the performance of exorcisms and healing miracles (v. 7). Philip's proclamation of "the good news about the kingdom of God and the name of Jesus Christ" turned many Samaritan men and women away from their attraction to the magic of Simon Magus and to baptism and faith in Jesus (v. 12).

The same basic elements—the gospel moves into a new area; it confronts and defeats the spiritual powers of evil; it brings many to faith in Jesus— appear near the beginning of each of Paul's three missionary expeditions. The first stop on Paul's first missionary expedition is Cyprus (13:4–12). Upon his arrival there, Paul "proclaimed the word of God in the synagogues" (v. 5). Soon thereafter, Paul was summoned by the proconsul Sergius Paulus, who himself "wanted to hear the word of God" (v. 7). However, Elymas, a magician and Jewish false prophet (presumably the same person called "Bar-Jesus" in v. 6), "opposed [Paul and Barnabas] and tried to turn the proconsul away from the faith" (v. 8). In response to the magician's opposition, Paul, "filled with the Holy Spirit," speaks a word of condemnation against Elymas, whom he calls a "son of the devil" (vv. 9–10). By Paul's powerful word, Elymas is struck temporarily blind (vv. 9–11). So amazed at Paul's proclamation as well as his overpowering of the magician, the Roman proconsul comes to believe in Jesus (v. 12).

One of the locations visited in the early stages of Paul's second missionary expedition is Philippi. Immediately after the conversion of Lydia and her household, Paul is confronted by a slave girl who has a spirit for divination (16:16). After the spirit/girl has harassed Paul's group for several days, the apostle exorcizes the spirit from the girl (v. 18). This incident also leads to the imprisonment of Paul and eventually to the conversion of the Philippian jailer and his household. Thus in Philippi, as in Samaria and Iconium, when the gospel begins to be proclaimed powerfully in a new area, many come to faith in Jesus, and the spiritual powers of evil are defeated.

This same dynamic appears in Paul's visit to Ephesus—the first episode in Paul's third missionary expedition. This scene provides a vivid example of the power of the apostolic proclamation of the Word. Luke begins by presenting Paul as proclaiming the Word of God in the power of the Holy Spirit at Ephesus (19:9–10). As in Philip's ministry in Samaria, God performs "extraordinary acts of power" through Paul, and in particular, Luke singles out healings and exorcisms (v. 11, translation ours).

Luke then provides a counterpoint to these teachings about the power of the Word by narrating the failures of some Jewish exorcists (19:13–16). In Ephesus, a group of traveling Jewish exorcists attempt to exorcise a demon from a possessed man by invoking the name of Jesus (v. 13). The phrasing of the Jewish exorcists' command—"I adjure you by the Jesus whom Paul proclaims" (v. 13)—is significant, for it reveals the personal distance between the exorcists and Jesus. They do not believe in Jesus, but they attempt to manipulate the power of Jesus's name as if it were a kind of magic.[10] The Jewish exorcists fail, in part because they themselves have not received the Word proclaimed by Paul and do not have faith in Jesus. Not only do these exorcists fail to drive out the demon, but also the demon in turn delivers a humiliating defeat to the Jewish exorcists: "The man with the evil spirit leaped on them, mastered them all, and so overpowered [*ischysen*] them that they fled out of the house naked and wounded" (v. 16).

Luke proceeds to report the reaction to the news of this event. The power of the Word proclaimed by Paul, along with the contrasting failure of the Jewish exorcists, prompts many to conversion: a confession of sins and a radical breaking off from sinful practices. Many Ephesians abandon their magical practices and publicly burn their spell books, and in doing so, they incur extraordinary financial loss: the value of the burned magic books was "fifty thousand silver coins" (Acts 19:19).

With so many people turning away from magic and the spiritual powers of evil and then coming to believe in Jesus, Luke concludes with a summary statement: "In this way, the word of the Lord was increasing and conquering

10. In this regard, these Jewish exorcists are somewhat comparable to Simon Magus, who attempted to buy the power of the Holy Spirit from Peter in order to manipulate the Spirit at will (8:18–19).

[*ischyen*] with power" (Acts 19:20, translation ours). The language of this statement brings to light the contrast between the ministry of Paul (and the fruits that it produces) and the failures of those Jewish exorcists. Whereas the demon "overpowered" (*ischysen*) the exorcists who did not have faith in Jesus, the Word of God, proclaimed by Paul in the power of the Holy Spirit, "conquered" (*ischyen*) the spiritual powers of evil in Ephesus and brought many to faith in Jesus. The Word of God, proclaimed by the apostles in the power of the Holy Spirit, increases the number of disciples and conquers the spiritual powers of evil. It makes present in power those spiritual realities that it articulates—"the kingdom of God . . . and the Lord Jesus Christ" (28:31).

## The Letters of Paul

Throughout his letters, Paul identifies the proclamation of the gospel of Jesus Christ as his foremost task as an apostle. Writing to the churches of Galatia, he speaks of the revelation of the divine sonship of Jesus Christ that he received as ordered to this purpose: "God . . . was pleased to reveal his Son to me, so that I might proclaim him among the Gentiles" (Gal. 1:16). Paul also uses the language of "Spirit" and "power" with reference to his evangelization—the familiar pair that we previously saw associated with the proclamation of the Word of God in Luke-Acts.[11]

In the survey that follows, we will focus on three major texts from Paul's letters—1 Corinthians 1:18–2:5; 1 Thessalonians 2:13; Romans 1:16—wherein he speaks of the gospel or the Word that he proclaims in terms of divine causal power and often with a subtle affirmation of the Word as a mode of Jesus's presence. While other relevant Pauline texts could be adduced (e.g., Col. 1:5, 25–29; 3:16; Eph. 6:17; 2 Tim. 3:15–17), these three focal texts suffice to illustrate the major contours of the Pauline witness.

### *"The Message about the Cross . . . Is the Power of God"*
### *(1 Cor. 1:18–2:5)*

Our study of material from 1 Corinthians will focus on the interconnections that Paul articulates between the crucified and risen Jesus, Paul's proclamation of Jesus in his gospel, and the power of God working in both.

---

11. The pairing of "Spirit" and "power" appears in Rom. 1:4; 15:13, 19; 1 Cor. 2:4; Gal. 3:5; Eph. 3:16. Given that Luke was most likely a member of Paul's missionary team (cf. Col. 4:14; 2 Tim. 4:11; Philem. 24), it may very well be the case that Luke derived this pairing of terms from Paul himself.

In 1 Corinthians 2:1–5, Paul reminds the Corinthian Christians of his earlier preaching to them and how they came to believe in Jesus. Paul begins, "I did not come proclaiming the mystery of God to you in lofty words or wisdom" (v. 1). On the contrary, Paul tells the Corinthians, "I decided to [make known] nothing among you except Jesus Christ, and him crucified" (v. 2).[12] The "mystery of God," which Paul proclaims, centers on Jesus, the crucified and risen Messiah. Paul also proclaims this mystery in a form that corresponds to its content. As the cross is "God's weakness" (1:25), so does Paul proclaim the crucified Jesus "in weakness" (2:3).[13] As the Christ is "the power of God and the wisdom of God" (1:24), so Paul proclaims him "in fear and in much trembling" (2:3)—with "fear and trembling" being the human response, compelled by the awesome power and glory of God (cf. Exod. 20:18; Ps. 2:11).

Paul introduces a further contrast with his statement, "My speech and my proclamation were not with plausible words of wisdom, but with a demonstration of the Spirit and of power" (1 Cor. 2:4). Here, Paul juxtaposes his preaching "with a demonstration of the Spirit and of power" with a mode of speaking with "plausible words of wisdom." By the latter, Paul arguably has in mind the kind of verbal eloquence associated with rhetoric, which was a vital part of public life in Greco-Roman antiquity and which Paul by his own admission did not possess in great measure.[14] Paul then specifies the resulting purpose of his mode of preaching: it is "so that [the Corinthians'] faith might rest not on human wisdom but on the power of God" (v. 5). The Corinthians came to believe in Jesus as the crucified and risen Messiah not because Paul was a sophisticated rhetorician who could persuade his audience through verbal eloquence. Rather, Paul preaches Christ crucified in an object-appropriate manner, and his teaching is marked by "Spirit" and "power." The power of God, actively communicated through Paul's apostolic proclamation of Jesus Christ, brings the Corinthians to faith and continues to ground their belief (v. 5).

We can amplify our understanding of Paul's remarks in 1 Corinthians 2:1–5 by taking them together with his words in 1:18–30, for this section features many of the same elements and points of contrast. In 1:17, Paul reports that Christ sent him "to proclaim the gospel" but not to do so "with eloquent wisdom." As he does in 2:4–5, Paul here contrasts preaching "with eloquent wisdom" to the power of God. The reason why Paul was not to preach with

---

12. Bracketed text is a slight amending of the NRSV translation.

13. The coming together of "power" and "weakness" in Christ crucified and risen, as well as in Paul's proclamation, likewise finds expression in the risen Jesus's words to Paul in 2 Cor. 12:9: "My grace is sufficient for you, for power is made perfect in weakness."

14. Joseph A. Fitzmyer, SJ, *First Corinthians: A New Translation with Introduction and Commentary*, Anchor Yale Bible 32 (New Haven: Yale University Press, 2008), 172–73.

rhetorical eloquence was "so that the cross of Christ might not be emptied of its power" (1:17).[15]

This statement segues into Paul's exposition of "the message about the cross" (1:18). His exposition features a contrast between how the crucified Jesus is perceived by unbelieving outsiders and by believing insiders. The knowledge provided by faith enables believers to perceive the cross of Jesus, which Paul proclaims, for what it truly is: "the power of God" (v. 18). The crucified and risen Jesus is "the power of God and the wisdom of God" (v. 24); he is "righteousness and sanctification and redemption" (v. 30). The death of Jesus on the cross is "God's foolishness" and "God's weakness," which is "wiser than human wisdom" and "stronger than human strength" (v. 25). Believers can recognize the cross of Jesus for what it truly is because, in faith, they have been given a share in "God's wisdom" (2:7) and see things in its light: "We have the mind of Christ" (v. 16).

By contrast, those without Christian faith perceive Paul's proclamation of the crucified Christ to be nonsensical or highly problematic. To Jewish outsiders, Paul's proclamation of a crucified Messiah is "a stumbling block" (1 Cor. 1:23), for it runs contrary to Torah (if Torah is taken as the ultimate standard of righteousness).[16] To gentile outsiders, Paul's proclamation of the crucified Jesus is "foolishness" (v. 23). For, in gentile eyes, how could this Jesus, executed as an enemy of Rome by means of crucifixion—the most shameful, torturous, degrading form of death in Greco-Roman antiquity—be "the power of God and the wisdom of God" (v. 24)?[17] And yet, that is precisely what Paul proclaims. The reality of Jesus, as the crucified and risen Messiah, both defies all categories by which people might want to evaluate him and requires that such categories be reconfigured around him.

As Jesus Christ, crucified and risen, is "the power of God and the wisdom of God" (1 Cor. 1:24), so also is Paul's proclamation of him marked by "power" (2:4). The key implication here is that the power of God, at work in Christ's death and resurrection, is also communicated through Paul's proclamation of

15. Although "power" is not explicitly mentioned in the Greek text, which simply reads "might not be emptied"—one might justifiably regard "power" as implied. For argumentation, see Jan Lambrecht, SJ, "The Power of God: A Note on the Connection between 1 Corinthians 1, 17 and 18," in *Collected Studies on Pauline Literature and on the Book of Revelation*, Analecta biblica 147 (Rome: Pontificio Istituto Biblico, 2001), 35–42.

16. Arguably, the primary text of Torah that Paul has in mind here, which leads many Jews to see the cross as a "stumbling block," is Deut. 21:22–23; cf. Gal. 3:10–14. See the discussion in Fitzmyer, *First Corinthians*, 159.

17. For a survey of attitudes in the Greco-Roman world toward crucifixion, see Martin Hengel, *Crucifixion in the Ancient World and the Folly of the Cross*, trans. John Bowden (Philadelphia: Fortress, 1977).

the Word of God, the gospel. Paul proclaims the reality of the crucified and risen Jesus in his preaching, and in so doing he also communicates the power of God at work in that reality. Indeed, Paul reports a sensible manifestation of God's power in his proclamation of Christ. He speaks of "a demonstration of the Spirit and of power" (v. 4). This demonstration features the working of miracles in connection with Paul's preaching, for Paul later uses the same Greek word for "power" (*dynamis*) to designate the charismatic gift of miracle working (cf. 1 Cor. 12:10, 28–29).

Less dazzling but ultimately more important, the very fact of the Corinthians' own conversion to Christ is a manifestation of God's power. Paul has already established that there are certain aspects of his proclamation that, in a sense, could stand in the way of anyone coming to faith. Paul spoke of the crucified Jesus as "foolishness" and a "stumbling block" (1 Cor. 1:23) to unbelieving outsiders. Paul did not proclaim Jesus with rhetorical eloquence, a customary means by which people would be moved to adopt a certain line of thinking or action. And yet these Corinthians, "both Jews and Greeks" (1:24), have come to believe in Jesus through Paul's proclamation of the gospel in "Spirit" and "power" (2:4). They have been brought to faith and "called into the fellowship of . . . Jesus Christ our Lord" (1:9) through God's powerful action in them.

Paul hints that this powerful action of God came to operate in the Corinthians through his proclamation of Jesus Christ in other sections of 1 Corinthians. In 1 Corinthians 4:15, Paul speaks of himself as the spiritual father of the Corinthians: "In Christ Jesus, I became your father through the gospel." Through Paul's preaching, the Corinthians came to believe in Jesus, and through baptism received a new life in him: they have become members of his body through the Holy Spirit (cf. 12:12–13). At the same time, Paul recognizes that he is an instrument of God in the Corinthians' lives. Before speaking of himself as the Corinthians' father, Paul employs agricultural imagery to talk about the instrumental character of himself and his companions. Having identified himself and his coworker Apollos as "servants through whom [the Corinthians] came to believe" (3:5), Paul continues, "I planted, Apollos watered, but God gave the growth" (v. 6). The Corinthians are "God's field," and Paul and his coworkers are "God's servants, working together" (v. 9). God causes the Corinthians' faith and new life in Christ, and his power came to work in them through Paul's preaching of the gospel.

The power of God, communicated through the gospel, continues to work in the Corinthians' lives beyond their initial conversion.[18] In 1 Corinthians 15,

18. As James D. G. Dunn observes, Paul uses the term "power" (*dynamis*) throughout his letters with respect to different aspects and moments of the Christian life. Dunn observes that

Paul opens his extensive treatment of the resurrection of the body by saying, "I would remind you . . . of the gospel that I proclaimed [*to euangelion ho euēngelisamēn*] to you, which you in turn received, in which you have stood, and also through which you are being saved" (vv. 1–2).[19] Paul's use of the present tense and passive voice in the phrase "you are being saved" (*sōzesthe*) suggests the ongoing action and power of God in Christians' lives. The gospel that the Corinthians "received" from Paul in the past continues to indwell them by their faith. As the gospel continues to indwell them by faith, it continues to be a source of God's transforming and saving power.[20] Moreover, the same power of God, at work in the death and resurrection of Jesus as well as in the gospel proclaimed by Paul, will cause the bodily resurrection of the Corinthians themselves on the last day.[21] As Paul writes, "God raised the Lord and will also raise us by his power" (6:14; cf. 15:23). Thus, the power of God is at work throughout the lives of the Corinthians, from their initial conversion to their eschatological glorification. This power of God flows into the Corinthians from the crucified and risen Jesus, whose reality Paul mediates through his Spirit-touched proclamation of the Word of God.

### *"The Word of God at Work in You Believers" (1 Thess. 2:13)*

The exercise of divine power through Paul's proclamation of the Word of God, as well as the Word of God as an abiding form of presence and power, also appears in 1 Thessalonians. In 1 Thessalonians 2:13, Paul writes the following: "We also constantly give thanks to God for this, that when you received the word of God that you heard from us, you accepted it not as a human word but as what it really is, God's word, which is also at work in you believers." This statement appears in a larger context where Paul commends the Thessalonian Christians for their conduct and reminds them of

---

for Paul, God's power is a transformative force "evident particularly in conversion . . . and resurrection . . . and providing a source of energy to sustain that qualitatively different [Christian] life." Dunn, *Romans 1–8*, Word Biblical Commentary 38A (Dallas: Word, 1988), 39.

19. Translation ours: it is deliberately literal to accent the verb tenses.

20. This point is suggested by Paul's qualifying phrase, "if you hold firmly to the message that I proclaimed to you—unless you have come to believe in vain" (15:2).

21. This language about God raising Christians "by his power [*dia tēs dynameōs autou*]" (6:14) obliquely suggests the activity of the Holy Spirit, for Paul elsewhere mentions the Holy Spirit as a causal agent in the resurrection of the dead. As Paul writes in Rom. 8:11, "If the Spirit of him who raised Jesus from the dead dwells in you, he who raised Christ from the dead will give life to your mortal bodies also through his Spirit that dwells in you [*dia tou enoikountos autou pneumatos en hymin*]." When 1 Cor. 6:14 and Rom. 8:11 are taken together, there again appears the close relationship between the Holy Spirit and God's power. Through the power of the Spirit, God the Father causes the resurrection of the dead.

their history with him. Paul's statement in 2:13 has a number of linguistic and thematic connections with its surrounding context, and attending to this statement in its context does much to illumine what Paul teaches here about the Word of God and its power.

In 1 Thessalonians 2:13, Paul identifies that which the Thessalonians heard from him as "the word of God." But much more frequently in 1 Thessalonians, Paul uses the word "gospel" to designate that which he proclaims (cf. 1:5; 2:2, 4, 8, 9). Paul also specifies that God is the source of what he teaches, for he speaks of himself and his companions as having been "entrusted [by God] with the message of the gospel" (2:4). Accordingly, the gospel proclaimed by Paul is not principally a "human word," but rather, his human speech mediates to his audience the Word of God (v. 13).

Like Luke in his account in Acts 17, Paul reports that he and his companions "proclaimed to [the Thessalonians] the gospel of God" and met local opposition there (1 Thess. 2:9; cf. 2:2; Acts 17:5–9). Paul also speaks of his proclamation of the gospel to the Thessalonians with the familiar pair of the Holy Spirit and power: "Our message of the gospel came to you not in word only, but also in power and in the Holy Spirit and with full conviction" (1 Thess. 1:5). Just as Paul's proclamation of the Word of God was not that of a "human word," it was not simply an exercise in human speaking. His proclamation of the Word of God was also clothed by the Holy Spirit, who worked acts of divine power in connection with Paul's proclamation.

Despite the opposition met by Paul and his companions, a group of Thessalonians converted to Christianity from gentile polytheism. As he does in 1 Thessalonians 2:13, so too in chapter 1 Paul praises these Christians for receiving the Word of God that he proclaimed: "For in spite of persecution you received the word with joy inspired by the Holy Spirit" (v. 6).[22] For Paul, the Thessalonians' receiving the Word of God and their coming to faith in Christ are intimately connected. The Word of God, proclaimed in power and the Holy Spirit by Paul, causes the Thessalonians' conversion to Christian faith as they receive that Word.

The Word of God exercises its power in the transformation of the Thessalonians. As Paul writes, they "turned to God from idols, to serve a living and true God" (1 Thess. 1:9). The Thessalonian Christians have come to faith in Jesus and have embraced a new mode of conduct. On account of these changes, the Thessalonian Christians have been harassed and opposed by some of their neighbors (2:14), and they have still remained faithful. In

---

22. There is a slight difference in the verbs translated in the NRSV as "receive": *dexamenoi* (1:6) and *paralabontes* (2:13).

doing so, they have become "imitators" of Jesus and Paul and the Jerusalem church (1:6; 2:14–16), who have likewise persevered in faithfulness and with the Spirit's joy despite suffering at the hands of others. Indeed, Paul praises the young Thessalonian church as an example of faith amid adversity to other Christian churches in that region and goes so far as to say, "The word of the Lord has sounded forth from you" (1:8). The Thessalonian church is a living witness, a practical mode of evangelization by which the Word of God radiates out into the world.

However, the power of God's Word is not limited to what has happened to the Thessalonian Christians in the past but continues to be a reality in their present. The present-tense verbs in Paul's formulation—"God's word, which is also at work [*energeitai*] in you believers [*pisteuousin*]" (1 Thess. 2:13)—underscores that the Word of God remains a present and active reality in the Thessalonians' lives. That is, the same Word of God that Paul proclaimed to them in the past continues to indwell and work in the Thessalonians in their present. By speaking of the Word's ongoing work in the Thessalonians in connection with their being "believers"—and doing so with the present active participle *pisteuousin* (literally, "you who are believing")—Paul suggests that faith is the way in which the Word of God continues to dwell and work within the Thessalonians.[23] Faith, therefore, is not just a subjective disposition of the Thessalonians, but it is also an objective indwelling of the reality of the Word of God in them. The Word of God, which indwells the Thessalonians by faith, can continue to exercise its transformative power in them as they await the parousia (1:9–10). Hence, Paul offers various moral and spiritual exhortations to the Thessalonians (4:1–5:28) with the prayer that "the God of peace himself sanctify you entirely . . . [and keep you] sound and blameless at the coming of our Lord Jesus Christ" (5:23).

### *"The Gospel Is the Power of God" (Rom. 1:16)*

Paul's Letter to the Romans also speaks to the power of the Word in ways redolent of 1 Corinthians and 1 Thessalonians. Of particular importance are certain elements given in Romans 1:16–17. These dense and complex verses provide the thesis statement to Romans as a whole, and as such, they establish many central points to be developed throughout the letter.[24] For present

23. So understood, 1 Thess. 2:13 would also resonate with the claim in Eph. 3:16–17: "I pray that, according to the riches of his glory, he may grant that you may be strengthened in your inner being with power through his Spirit, and that Christ may dwell in your hearts through faith."

24. Scholarship in the last quarter of the twentieth century made the case that Romans reflects an established form of Greco-Roman rhetorical composition known as the scholastic

purposes, we focus on Paul's statement that "the gospel . . . is the power of God for salvation to everyone who has faith" (v. 16).

Throughout Romans, Paul identifies "the gospel" as an essential component of his apostolic ministry. At the very beginning of the letter, Paul introduces himself as one "called to be an apostle, set apart for the gospel of God" (1:1). When these two expressions—"called to be an apostle" and "set apart for the gospel of God"—are taken in light of their biblical background, they come to light as veritable parallels. For the notion of being "called" or chosen by God involves being "set apart" for a role or task, such as in the case of the election of Israel, which was chosen by God to be his "holy nation" (Exod. 19:3–6). Paul's identity and vocation as an apostle *are* his ministry to proclaim the gospel. Similarly, near the end of Romans, Paul speaks of proclaiming the gospel as the hallmark characteristic of what he does throughout his apostolic travels: "From Jerusalem and as far around as Illyricum I have fully proclaimed the good news of Christ" (Rom. 15:19).

Paul also speaks of his apostolic task of evangelization as a priestly act, employing liturgical language to present it. In Romans 1:9, Paul associates his worship of God with the gospel. He speaks of God, "whom I worship [*latreuein*] with my spirit in the gospel of his Son."[25] Paul thus presents his own task of evangelizing as a form in which he gives worship and praise to God.[26] Later in the letter, Paul employs liturgical language to speak of his evangelizing work as a priestly action and of his gentile converts as a liturgical sacrifice offered to God. He speaks of his gift "to be a *minister* of Christ Jesus to the Gentiles in the *priestly service* of the gospel of God" (15:16, emphasis added). As gentiles come to Christian faith through his evangelizing, Paul speaks of them as a liturgical sacrifice that he offers to God as a priest: "so that the offering of the Gentiles may be acceptable, sanctified by the Holy Spirit" (15:16).[27]

Paul's "gospel" is "the proclamation of Jesus Christ" (16:25). He presents what God, fulfilling the promises that he made in Scripture, has done for the

---

diatribe. Along with many characteristic features of style, this rhetorical pattern involves a routine sequence of argumentative components through which the rhetor unfolds his case. According to this convention, Rom. 1:16–17 provides the thesis statement that Paul will develop over the course of Romans (and that he will restate in 3:21–26). See Luke Timothy Johnson, *Reading Romans: A Literary and Theological Commentary*, Reading the New Testament (Macon, GA: Smyth & Helwys, 2001), 1–18, 26–30.

25. Translation ours. Throughout the LXX, the verb *latreuein* designates the liturgical worship given to God (e.g., Exod. 3:12; 4:23; 23:25; Deut. 6:13) or to a false god (Exod. 20:5; Lev. 18:21; Deut. 4:28; Dan. 3:12).

26. As Joseph Fitzmyer tersely puts it, "By preaching the Gospel, [Paul] worships God." Fitzmyer, *Romans: A New Translation with Introduction and Commentary*, Anchor Yale Bible 33 (New Haven: Yale University Press, 2008), 243.

27. So too Fitzmyer, *Romans*, 711.

salvation of fallen humanity in Jesus Christ (3:21–26). The "redemption" (v. 24), accomplished by Christ's sacrificial death on the cross, is communicated freely to all people, who accept this gift by receiving it in obediential faith (vv. 22, 26; cf. 1:5) and baptism (6:3–11). God's saving action in Christ reveals his love, goodness, and righteousness (1:17; 5:8), and by his gracious action, the Father makes the baptized his adopted children by incorporating them into the reality of his Son, the risen Jesus, through the indwelling Holy Spirit (8:15–17). The same risen Jesus will also sit in eschatological judgment on all people (2:16) and "will repay according to each one's deeds" (v. 6).

Paul also speaks of his gospel in relation to God's action to give strength to believers. He writes of "God who is able to strengthen you according to my gospel and the proclamation of Jesus Christ" (16:25). As Joseph Fitzmyer comments on this verse, "The gospel that he has been preaching not only stems from Jesus Christ but also proclaims him as the source of such strength and constancy for all believers."[28] This identification of God as a continual source of strength for believers leads us to consider another major element in Romans 1:16: "the gospel . . . is *the power of God*" (emphasis added).

Shortly before identifying the gospel as "the power [*dynamis*] of God" in 1:16, Paul speaks of divine "power" with respect to the risen Jesus and does so within the setting of his gospel. Paul speaks of "the gospel concerning his Son, who was descended from David according to the flesh and was declared to be Son of God with power [*dynamis*] according to the spirit of holiness by resurrection from the dead" (1:3–4). As with the pattern he followed in Philippians 2, where Jesus is "in the form of God," takes "the form of a slave," and is then "exalted" by the Father (vv. 6–7, 9), Paul contrasts the human birth of the Son of God ("descended from David according to the flesh") with the subsequent glorification of his humanity and revelation of his divinity in the resurrection ("declared to be Son of God with power . . . by resurrection from the dead"). In the resurrection, the Father totally transforms and divinizes Jesus's humanity through the Holy Spirit, making it the source of divine life, power, and grace for humanity. This is the reality that Paul presents in his gospel, as Fitzmyer notes: "The gospel now reveals that Jesus is not merely God's son, born in a human way of Davidic lineage, but God's Son as a source of power."[29] Having first connected the risen Jesus with divine "power" in 1:4, Paul invites his readers to have this association in mind when he later identifies the gospel as "the power of God" in 1:16.

28. Fitzmyer, *Romans*, 754.
29. Fitzmyer, *Romans*, 235.

As he does elsewhere, Paul presents himself as an instrument by which the risen Jesus works in the world. He explicitly mentions his instrumental role vis-à-vis the risen Jesus in 15:18: "I will not venture to speak of anything except *what Christ has accomplished through me* to win obedience from the Gentiles" (emphasis added). The risen Jesus works in and through Paul as "a chosen instrument" to bring gentiles to faith (Acts 9:15, translation ours). Paul then enumerates various means by which the risen Jesus works through him. He mentions Christ working through him "by word and deed" (15:18), "by the power of signs and wonders" (v. 19)—that is, the working of miracles—and "by the power of the Spirit of God" (v. 19). The telos, or goal, of Christ's working powerfully through Paul's evangelization is to bring the gentiles to "the obedience of faith" (1:5; cf. 15:18; 16:26). The risen Jesus exercises his divine power to cause faith in gentiles who receive the Word proclaimed by Paul.

To summarize the identification of "the gospel" as "the power of God" (Rom. 1:16): Paul proclaims the gospel of Jesus Christ—that is, what God has done for the salvation of sinful humanity in Jesus's life, death, and resurrection.[30] Through Paul's apostolic proclamation of the gospel, the realities that Paul proclaims become active in the lives of those who receive this Word. The risen Jesus, who is "Son of God with power" (v. 4), exercises his divine power in those who receive the gospel: to cause faith in them, to strengthen and transform them. The gospel is "the power of God for salvation to everyone who has faith" (v. 16), for through the apostolic proclamation of the Word, the risen Jesus exercises his power in the lives of those who receive this Word.

By way of a coda, some of Paul's remarks in the dense argument that is Romans 9–11 can be read as suggesting the Word proclaimed and received in faith to be a kind of presence. More specifically, in Romans 10, Paul intimates that faith involves a kind of indwelling, or presencing, of the Word of God, in the believer.

In his discussion of faith as the means of receiving God's gift in Christ, Paul states, "Faith comes from what is heard, and what is heard [is] through the word of Christ" (10:17).[31] The "what is heard" refers to the gospel that the apostles proclaim. Paul has set up this statement in verse 17 by quoting the Septuagint version of Isaiah 52:7, which speaks of those "who bring good news" (Rom. 10:15) and the requirement that one be "sent [*apostellein*] to

30. This proclamation would include the fulfillment of God's promises in Scripture; the free gift of salvation made available to all through the death and resurrection of Jesus; the necessity of obediential faith and baptism for the reception of this gift; the role of the Holy Spirit in Christian life; and so on.
31. NRSV translation slightly amended.

proclaim him" (v. 15). At the same time, the gospel proclaimed by the apostles is "through the word of Christ" (v. 17). This association of the proclaimed Word and the word that Christ speaks can be taken to suggest Christ himself speaks his Word through the apostolic proclamation: "Christ would be speaking his message through the mouths of his authorized heralds."[32]

These associations of "the word of Christ" and "the good news" in 10:15–17 dovetail with Paul's earlier remarks about "the word of faith that we proclaim" (10:8). Paul introduces this mention of "the word of faith" with a quotation of Deuteronomy 30:14: "The word is near you, on your lips and in your heart" (Rom. 10:8). The alignment of the quotation of Deuteronomy 30:14 with Paul's parenthetical remark in Romans 10:8 has the effect of identifying the Word that is "in your heart" with "the word of faith that we proclaim" (10:8). This identification can be extended to include "the word of Christ" (v. 17). So understood, "the word of Christ," proclaimed by the apostles, comes to dwell "in [the] heart" of those who receive it in faith.

Through the apostolic proclamation of the gospel, the Word of Christ comes to indwell believers through faith. This reading of faith as involving the indwelling of the Word of God in believers sheds light on Paul's ensuing statement: "If you confess with your lips that Jesus is Lord and believe in your heart that God raised him from the dead, you will be saved" (Rom. 10:9). Thus, to "believe in your heart" (v. 9) cannot be separated from the "word of faith" (or "word of Christ"; v. 17) that is "in your heart" (v. 8). Faith, in this sense, is not simply a subjective disposition but rather a kind of objective indwelling of the realities of faith in the believer.[33] By so indwelling believers through faith, Christ exercises his divine power to transform believers and cause their salvation.

## 1 Peter: "Born Anew . . . through the Living and Enduring Word of God" (1:23)

First Peter 1:23 contributes to our study of the Word of God as having power and mediating divine reality with this declaration: "You have been born anew, not of perishable but of imperishable seed, through the living and enduring Word of God."[34] Very important for understanding this statement about the power of God's Word are the many points of contact that this statement has

32. Fitzmyer, *Romans*, 598.
33. Cf. Pope Benedict XVI, *Spe Salvi*, §7.
34. This statement resembles that in James 1:18: "In fulfillment of his own purpose he gave us birth by the word of truth, so that we would become a kind of first fruits of his creatures."

with the risen Jesus. In particular, the Word of God comes to light in 1 Peter not simply as a statement about Jesus but as a mode of his presence and a conduit for the spiritually transforming power that flows from him.

### The Word of God and the Risen Jesus: A Basic Alignment

Peter aligns the Word of God and the risen Jesus through a series of verbal and thematic links between his statements about the Word of God in 1:23–25 and the opening benediction in verses 3–12. First, these two passages are the only instances in 1 Peter that employ the Greek verb *anagennan* to talk about Christians' "new birth." In verse 23, Peter tells his new Christian audience, "You have been born anew [*anagegennēmenoi*], not of perishable but of imperishable seed." These words recall the opening of the benediction, where Peter specifies that God is the one who gave them "new birth [*anagennēsas*]" (v. 3). Second, these same two verses (vv. 3, 23) align the Word of God and the risen Jesus by specifying both of them as the cause of God's giving Christians new birth. In both cases, Peter uses the Greek preposition *dia* ("through") to articulate this point: God "has given us a new birth into a living hope through [*dia*] the resurrection of Jesus Christ from the dead" (v. 3); and later he writes that the Christians' new birth from imperishable seed comes "through [*dia*] the living and enduring word of God" (v. 23).[35]

A third, more thematic connection stands in that both the risen Jesus and the Word of God are similarly aligned within the larger conceptual contrast running throughout 1 Peter between the heavenly/imperishable and the earthly/perishable. The benediction begins by declaring that Christians have received new birth to "a living hope" (1:3), which is later described as "an inheritance that is imperishable, undefiled, and unfading, kept in heaven for you" (v. 4). The permanence and the imperishability of believers' heavenly salvation are then contrasted with the temporariness of their present trials (v. 6). The audience's faith, by which they lay claim to this heavenly inheritance, is valued much greater than (and thus contrasted with) the value of "perishable" gold (v. 7). The imperishability of Christians' hope and heavenly inheritance derives from the imperishability of the risen Jesus in heavenly glory (and ultimately from God). As God "raised [Jesus] from the dead and gave him glory" (v. 21), so too does God call Christians "to his eternal glory in Christ" (5:10). When the heavenly glory of the risen Jesus is "revealed" at the parousia (4:13), so too will the glory of Christians, including Peter, be "revealed" (5:1; cf. 5:4).

---

35. John H. Elliott writes, "*Dia* is employed in 1 Peter to express the *means* of rebirth . . . as well as the *means* of proclaiming the good news (1:12)." *1 Peter*, Anchor Yale Bible 37B (New Haven: Yale University Press, 2000), 389.

Peter places the Word of God within the same conceptual contrast of imperishable versus perishable. In 1:23, Peter leads into his comments about the Word of God with the distinction between perishable and imperishable seed, thus aligning the Word with imperishability. Peter then speaks of the Word of God as "living and enduring." The imperishability and permanence of the Word of God is underscored by the quotation from the Septuagint version of Isaiah 40:6–8. Here the Word of the Lord, which "endures forever" (1 Pet. 1:25), is contrasted with "all flesh," which fades away like the grass and the flowers. In these ways, Peter places the Word of God on the heavenly and imperishable side of the conceptual register, along with the Christians' heavenly inheritance of salvation and the risen Jesus himself.

Through these points of contact between 1 Peter 1:23–25 and the benediction, Peter invites his audience to see the risen Jesus and the Word of God as closely connected to each other. Further insight into this relationship can be obtained from the author's remarks about the biblical prophets and Christian evangelists in verses 10–12.

### Prophets and Evangelists (1 Pet. 1:10–12)

The dense remarks in 1 Peter 1:10–12 elaborate on the imperishable, heavenly salvation of Christians as introduced in 1:10. This elaboration brings to light a relationship between the biblical prophets of Israel's past and the Christian evangelists of the author's present. The two groups—the prophets and evangelists—are connected to each other by virtue of their participation in the same divine economy of salvation in Christ.

Peter expounds the relationship between these groups by having them mirror each other, with subtle differences worked in as well. First, Peter speaks of the biblical prophets as inspired by "the Spirit of Christ," who moved and "testified in advance" in them (1:11). Through the Spirit's action, the prophets were given to know things in the divine economy, things that lay in their future. Peter singles out two things: (1) the death and resurrection of Jesus ("the sufferings destined for Christ and the subsequent glory," v. 11), and (2) the gift of "salvation" to be received by Christians (v. 10). Both of these are elsewhere in the letter explicitly connected to the foreknowledge of God.[36]

Peter goes on to speak of Christian evangelists in terms similar to those he used for the biblical prophets. First, like the biblical prophets, the Christian evangelists speak "by the Holy Spirit sent from heaven" (1:12). That is, both the prophets and evangelists utter divinely inspired speech. Second,

---

36. Peter associates God's foreknowledge with Jesus's death in 1:20 and with the sanctification of Christians in 1:2.

the biblical prophets and the Christian evangelists deliver the same content, although under different temporal aspects. Peter says of the biblical prophets in 1:12, "It was revealed to them that they were serving not themselves but you, in regard to the things [*auta*] that have now been announced to you through those who brought you the good news [*tōn euangelisamenōn*] by the Holy Spirit." The use of *auta* in 1:12 identifies the content spoken of by the biblical prophets (as future to them) with the content proclaimed by the Christian evangelists as present.

The prophets and evangelists participate in the same economy of salvation. They both speak under the inspiration of the Holy Spirit. They proclaim the same reality, though under different temporal aspects (i.e., as future or as present). This reality, given in inspired speech by both the biblical prophets and the Christian evangelists, is the death and resurrection of Jesus and the salvation that flows from it.[37]

Significant for present purposes is that the same Greek verb—*euangelizein*—that designates the Christian proclamation of this reality (salvation by Christ's death and resurrection) is later used by Peter in 1:25 with reference to the quotation of Isaiah 40:8 about the living Word of God. There, the author follows up the end of the Isaiah quotation ("but the word of the Lord endures forever") with his interpretive commentary: "That word is the good news that was announced [*euangelisthen*] to you" (1 Pet. 1:25). This lexical link suggests that the Word announced by the biblical prophets, given in Scripture, and proclaimed by Christian evangelists is one and the same. It is the same reality: the death and resurrection of Jesus and the salvation that flows from it. The Word is not simply about the reality; in some manner, it *is* the reality, or rather the Word makes the reality (the crucified and risen Jesus) present in his power to those who hear it. This Word of God is a kind of presencing of the risen Jesus.

The Word of God has causal power because it communicates the reality of the risen Jesus and his life-giving power. The only other instance of *euangelizein* in 1 Peter corroborates this point. In 4:6, the author writes, "For this is the reason the gospel was proclaimed [*euēngelisthē*] even to the dead, so that, though they had been judged in the flesh as everyone is judged, they might live in the spirit as God does." Irrespective of whoever "the dead" referred to in this verse might be, the result of the proclamation of the good news remains the same. It imparts or enables them to have "life in [or by] the spirit" before

37. Cf. Lewis R. Donelson, *I & II Peter and Jude*, New Testament Library (Louisville: Westminster John Knox, 2010), 38; David L. Bartlett, "The First Letter of Peter," in *The New Interpreter's Bible*, ed. Leander E. Keck, 12 vols. (Nashville: Abingdon, 1994–2004), 12:253.

God. The Word of God has the power to give new life. It has this capacity because, as evidenced in Peter's adjustment to Isaiah 40:8, it is "the word of the Lord," that is, of the Lord Jesus.

Commenting on the description of the Word of God as "living" (1:23), David Bartlett writes, "Like the living hope [mentioned in 1:3], the living word is itself alive, lively, and life-giving."[38] As the living hope comes from God through the death and resurrection of Jesus (1:3), the same applies for the life-giving power of the Word. That is, the heavenly life associated with the Word flows from the death and resurrection of Jesus through the Word given in Scripture, uttered by the prophets, and in the apostolic proclamation of the gospel (cf. 4:11). The Word proclaimed in inspired speech, being both "imperishable" and of the Lord, communicates the life-giving and life-transforming power of the risen Jesus.[39] These points find further illustration and support from Peter's comments in 2:1–3.

### "Tasting the Lord" (1 Pet. 2:1–3)

Peter's exposition in 1 Peter 2:1–3 follows immediately on his statements in 1:23–25 about the living Word of God proclaimed to Christians. It focuses on the new life that Christians now possess. Similar to the exhortations in 1:13–16 and also in 1:22, 1 Peter 2:1 instructs Christians that the new life given them entails a new form of moral conduct.[40] Peter develops this topic of the Christians' new life by likening them to "newborn infants" (2:2). This simile easily recalls the language of "new birth" (*anagennan*), which, as discussed previously, is said to come through both the resurrection of Jesus and the Word of God. Like infants, who have recently experienced "new birth," Christians are to "hunger for the guileless milk of the word [*to logikon adolon gala*] so that by it, [they] may grow up towards salvation" (2:2).[41]

The description of this milk that nourishes the spiritually newborn Christians subtly associates it with the Word of God, and with Jesus in particular. First, the description of this milk as "pure" or "guileless" (*adolon*) connects it to Peter's identification of Jesus as Isaiah's Suffering Servant. Within the household code, Peter quotes the Septuagint version of Isaiah 53:9 with reference to Jesus, thus saying of him: "No deceit [*dolos*] was found in his mouth" (1 Pet. 2:22). Both this "milk of the word" and Jesus are without any *dolos*.

---

38. Bartlett, "First Letter of Peter," 260.

39. Cf. Elliott, *1 Peter*, 392.

40. See Joel B. Green, *1 Peter*, Two Horizons New Testament Commentary (Grand Rapids: Eerdmans, 2007), 48–52.

41. We use here the very apt translation in Elliott, *1 Peter*, 399.

Moreover, the modifier *adolon* serves to contrast the nourishment of Christians with the sort of vicious behavior that they need to cease in their new life: "Rid yourselves, therefore, of all malice, and all guile [*panta dolon*]" (2:1; cf. 3:10).

Second, the description of the milk as *logikon* resonates with the previous mention of the Word (*logos*) of God in 1:23. Peter follows up these comments about "the milk of the word" with a quotation of Scripture that features the language of "tasting." Christians should hunger for this "milk of the word," because, as Peter writes, "you . . . tasted that the Lord is good" (2:3). This quotation of the Septuagint version of Psalm 33:9 (EV 34:8) accomplishes several things. It aligns the spiritual milk, which Christians should long for (i.e., desire to consume), with the Lord, whom Peter's Christian audience has "tasted." Throughout the letter, Peter employs *kyrios* to refer to Jesus proper (1:3, 25; 2:3, 13; 3:15), and the implication is that the Christians have already tasted the sweetness of Jesus and want more—that is, they long for the pure "milk of the word." Paul Achtemeier writes, "It would furthermore be appropriate for Christians who were rebegotten by the word of God to yearn for that word so that they may experience further growth leading to salvation."[42]

Seen within this setting, the pure milk that nourishes Christians and helps them grow in salvation is the Lord Jesus himself, whom Christians taste (i.e., experience) through the inspired Word proclaimed by apostolic evangelists and given in Scripture—a point perhaps obliquely hinted at by the fact that this claim is made by using the words of Scripture. Because of its connection with the reality of the risen Jesus, the Word has causal power not only for imparting "new birth" but also for sustaining and facilitating the development of Christian life (as "the milk"). John Elliott writes, "For positive growth to take place (vv. 2–3), it is urgent that the reborn readers nurse constantly on the *guileless* (contrast v. 1) milk of the word, drawing nourishment from the same word through which they were brought to new life (vv. 23–25)."[43] The inspired Word, whether given in Scripture or in the evangelists' proclamation, puts Christians in contact with the reality of the risen Jesus and thus in contact with the life-giving and life-transforming power that flows from his death and resurrection.

## Looking Back and Looking Forward

Like the Old Testament witnesses, New Testament writers affirm that the Word of God can be given through inspired human discourse. In Acts, Luke

42. Paul J. Achtemeier, *1 Peter: A Commentary on First Peter*, Hermeneia (Minneapolis: Fortress, 1996), 147.
43. Elliott, *1 Peter*, 405.

presents the apostolic proclamation of the Word of God in terms similar to those of Jesus in the Gospel. The apostles proclaim "the word of God" as essential to their ministry as "witnesses." The risen Jesus sends the Holy Spirit to guide the apostles' ministry and empower their proclamation of the Word. As the apostles proclaim the gospel in the power of the Holy Spirit, many are brought to faith in Jesus, and the spiritual enemies of God's people are defeated. Paul presents the apostolic proclamation of the gospel as mediating the power and reality of Jesus Christ, who comes to dwell in Christians by faith. The apostolic proclamation of the Word bears the reality and power of God, which works in the lives of those who receive this Word in faith. In 1 Peter, the "living and enduring word of God" is a means by which the reality of the risen Jesus and his divine power are communicated to Christians. The Word has causal life-giving and life-sustaining power because it communicates the reality of the risen Jesus and the power of his death and resurrection.

Having thus established that the Word of God, whether spoken directly by God or through inspired human beings, has both divine causal power and associations with modes of presence, we can now extend our reflections one step further and consider the Word of God as given in inspired written discourse. This component fills out the theological picture for conceiving of Scripture as putting people in living and life-giving contact with the divine realities of which it speaks.

# 4

# The Word of God
# in Inspired Written Discourse

We conclude our examination of biblical witness concerning the Word of God and its associations with power and presence by considering the Word of God as given in inspired written discourse. The biblical writings do not offer much explicit reflection on the theological nature of Scripture as inspired written discourse. There are biblical teachings about this topic, but they tend to be more subtle and implicit. Making them explicit requires more detailed exegetical analysis. In this chapter, therefore, we will look at evidence from two biblical writings—the Letter to the Hebrews and the Gospel according to John—that attribute to inspired written discourse these associations of the Word of God with power and presence. Namely, the Word of God, given in Scripture, mediates divine reality and God's causal power to Scripture's audience.

## The Letter to the Hebrews: "The Word of God Is Living and Active" (4:12)

### Hebrews 4:12 in Context

From its numerous biblical quotations and allusions to its larger argumentative strategy, the anonymous early Christian writing known as the Letter to the Hebrews is saturated with Scripture.[1] Hebrews also contains one of the

---

1. For general discussion of the use of Scripture in Hebrews, see Craig R. Koester, *Hebrews: A New Translation with Introduction and Commentary*, Anchor Yale Bible 36 (New Haven:

most famous descriptions of the Word of God in the Christian Bible: "The word of God is living and active, sharper than any two-edged sword, piercing until it divides soul from spirit, joints from marrow; it is able to judge the thoughts and intentions of the heart" (Heb. 4:12). While much can be said about the role and function of Scripture in Hebrews, we will focus more narrowly on these remarks about the Word of God, which penetrates and works within human beings.

Hebrews refers to itself as a "word of exhortation" (13:22), and an important goal of Hebrews is to encourage Christians who are tempted to abandon Christianity (i.e., to commit apostasy). One way Hebrews works toward this goal is by demonstrating the superlative character of Christ and the salvation that he offers. Literarily, Hebrews integrates sections of theological exposition and moral exhortation, and in doing so, it argues that certain forms of conduct and practice follow upon certain truths about who Jesus is and what he has accomplished.

The remarks about the Word of God as "living and active" (Heb. 4:12) appear at the close of a subsection that features an interpretive meditation on the narrative of the Israelites' time in the wilderness and the implications of that episode for Christian life (3:7–4:13). This argumentative section sheds important light on the author's remarks about the Word of God in 4:12–13. And so it is helpful to have a general sense of the preceding argument that these remarks about the Word of God in 4:12 presuppose.

The practical purpose of the exegetical meditation on the wilderness generation is to encourage Christians to persevere in faith and obedience by avoiding the vices and failures of the Israelites in the wilderness. Integral to the author's reflection on the wilderness generation is Psalm 95, which he quotes at length in Hebrews 3:7–11 and employs throughout this subsection.[2] The author meditates on the fate of the exodus generation, who rebelled against God by their "disobedience" (4:6) and "unbelief" (3:19). As a consequence, God would not allow them to enter the promised land, and instead, they were to wander the wilderness for forty years until their "bodies fell in the wilderness" (v. 17; cf. Num. 14:29, 32). The author views these events in light of Psalm 95, which he understands to contain the direct discourse of God: "As in my anger I swore, 'They will not enter my rest'" (Heb. 3:11, quoting Ps. 95:11).

---

Yale University Press, 2001), 115–18; for Hebrews' use of *qal wahomer* argumentation (meaning "light and heavy," referring to a Jewish form of an argument made a fortiori), see Luke Timothy Johnson, *Hebrews: A Commentary*, New Testament Library (Louisville: Westminster John Knox, 2006), 31–32.

2. The author of Hebrews quotes Ps. 95 on several occasions in this unit of argument (Heb. 3:15; 4:3, 7).

The author of Hebrews maintains that his Christian audience and the wilderness generation of Israelites are deeply connected to each other in the divine economy. Both of them received "the good news," albeit in different ways and with different responses: "The good news came to us [*euēngelismenoi*] just as to them" (Heb. 4:2). The author also refers to this "good news" that came to the Israelites in the wilderness as "the word of hearing [*ho logos tēs akoēs*]" (4:2, translation ours). However, the wilderness generation, "those who formerly received the good news" (v. 6), did not profit from it because they were wanting in faith (4:2) and "because of disobedience" (v. 6).[3] By contrast, the author states that his Christian contemporaries, on account of their faith, can enter into "that rest" promised by God (v. 11).[4] However, the possibility remains that Christians can fail to enter the promised (heavenly) "rest" through their own apostasy and disobedience. Since such a fate is possible for Christian believers, the author holds up the wilderness generation—who also received "the good news" but who did not benefit from it because of their faithlessness and disobedience—as an example to be avoided lest Christians share a fate like theirs: "Let us therefore make every effort to enter that rest, so that no one may fall through such disobedience as theirs" (v. 11).

The author follows up this exhortation with a series of remarks about the Word of God (4:12–13). As Luke Johnson points out, the account of God's Word in these verses is "both powerful and ambiguous," for it is not clear whether the author understands the Word as "merely speech, or *a* living being [i.e., the personified Word], or *the* living being [i.e., God]."[5] We first will attend to those aspects of 4:12–13 that concern the association between the Word of God and power.

### God's Living and Active Word

The author opens by describing the Word of God as "living and active" (Heb. 4:12). By describing the Word as "living," the author articulates a profound relationship between the Word and God himself. For just as the author speaks of the Word of God as "living," so too does he identify God as "the living God" (3:12; cf. 10:31; 12:22). The expression "the living God" appears throughout the biblical tradition, often to emphasize the absolute

---

3. As Koester (*Hebrews*, 269) succinctly puts it, "Physical hearing does not automatically produce faith; Moses' generation heard the word but did not heed it."

4. The notion of "rest" here is complex and turns on multiple, interrelated topics, such as the promised land of Canaan, the place of God's dwelling (both on earth and in heaven), and the Sabbath. See Koester, *Hebrews*, 257–58, 268–69, 278–80.

5. Johnson, *Hebrews*, 131, 132 (emphasis added).

reality of the God of Israel, who is the Creator and Lord of all.[6] By speaking of God's Word as "living," the author "applies the same quality of *life* that is normally associated with God's being to God's word."[7] As we have seen, the psalms similarly speak of God's Word as life giving or a means by which God gives life (Ps. 119:25, 107). The author of Hebrews also speaks of God's Word as "active" (*energēs*). Often (though not always) in the New Testament, this language of "energy" is used with respect to God's actions in the world, such as in the resurrection of Jesus and his active presence in the church.[8] Paul also uses the same "energy" language in his statement about God's Word, "which is also at work [*energeitai*] in you believers" (1 Thess. 2:13). Taken in this light, the descriptors "living and active" allow us to understand the Word of God as deeply related to God's own being and powerful activity in the world. These associations invite the audience to think of the Word as a special means by which God is powerfully present and active in people's lives.

The author then elaborates on the power or "energy" of God's Word by setting forth a series of *actions* that the Word does *within people* (Heb. 4:12bc). Drawing on the biblical imagery that likens a word to a sword, the author speaks of the Word's capacity to cut deeply into people: "piercing until it divides soul from spirit, joints from marrow" (v. 12b).[9] The Word of God has the divine power to penetrate and act powerfully at the deepest dimensions of the human being—both spiritual ("soul from spirit") and material ("joints from marrow").[10] In this respect, there is a measure of conceptual convergence between this capacity of the Word and the reaction of the Pentecost crowd to Peter's Spirit-anointed preaching: "they were cut to the heart" (Acts 2:37). Another action of the Word within people is "to judge the thoughts and intentions of the heart" (Heb. 4:12c). The Greek term translated as "judge" is the adjective *kritikos*, which has the sense of being able to discern.[11] So understood, God's Word has total and perfect access to the inner life of

6. E.g., Deut. 5:26; Josh. 3:10; Dan. 6:26; Acts 14:15; 2 Cor. 3:3.

7. Johnson, *Hebrews*, 133.

8. For instance, the Father's power at work in Jesus's resurrection and ascension (Eph. 1:19–20); God's working in the apostleship of Peter and Paul (Gal. 2:8; Col. 1:29); God's activity in the lives of the baptized (Phil. 2:13; Col. 2:12); the Spirit's working of charismatic gifts within the church (1 Cor. 12:6, 11); and especially his working of "mighty deeds" (1 Cor. 12:10; Gal. 3:5). See Johnson, *Hebrews*, 133.

9. The biblical background for the identification of the word as a sword comes from the speech of the Servant of the Lord in Isa. 49:2: "He made my mouth like a sharp sword." The same word-as-sword imagery appears in Eph. 6:17 and Rev. 1:16.

10. Cf. Harold W. Attridge, *The Epistle to the Hebrews: A Commentary on the Epistle to the Hebrews*, Hermeneia (Philadelphia: Fortress, 1989), 134–35.

11. So Attridge, *Hebrews*, 135–36.

human beings. All aspects of human existence are wide open and accessible to the Word of God, who can also work within them. Therefore, all human beings are subject to judgment by the Word of God: "Before him no creature is hidden, but all are naked and laid bare to the eyes of the one to whom we must render an account" (v. 13).[12]

Having considered some elements of the author's description of the Word of God in Hebrews 4:12–13, we now turn to fill out our analysis by considering this passage in light of the preceding meditation on the wilderness generation and the place of Psalm 95 in particular.[13]

### God Speaks in Scripture

To begin with, the author of Hebrews affirms here (and elsewhere) that *God speaks through Scripture*. This is evident in the author's use of Psalm 95 in Hebrews 3:7–4:13. The author understands the first-person language in the psalm to be the direct discourse of God himself. Thus, the declaration in Psalm 95:11—"As in my anger I swore, 'They shall not enter my rest'" (Heb. 3:11; 4:3)—is a statement spoken directly by God about the wilderness generation. The author of Hebrews also recognizes that God's speech is mediated through human authors of the scriptural texts. For instance, the author reads the mention of "today" in Psalm 95:7 as speaking to another kind of "rest," which the wilderness generation did not enter but which remains open for later believers. In Hebrews 4:7, the author introduces his quotation of Psalm 95:7 with an interpretive statement: God "sets a certain day—'today'—saying through David much later, in the words already quoted, 'Today, if you hear his voice, do not harden your hearts'" (Heb. 4:7, paraphrasing Ps. 95:7–8). The author of Hebrews understands such third-person statements about God to be David's own words by which God himself also speaks.

The mediation of God's Word through human speech finds further attestation elsewhere in the letter. Hebrews begins by affirming that God speaks through human mediation: "Long ago God spoke to our ancestors in many and various ways by the prophets, but in these last days he has spoken to us by a Son" (Heb. 1:1–2). Near the end of the letter, the author speaks in comparable terms of the church's faithful leadership as those "who spoke to

---

12. On the judgment motif in this passage, see Johnson, *Hebrews*, 135–37; Koester, *Hebrews*, 280–81.

13. As Johnson (*Hebrews*, 131) points out, "It is important to read Heb. 4:12–13, not as a separate discussion, but as part of the author's argument, indicated by the explanatory connective *gar* ('for'): this is the reason why we should be eager and avoid disobedience of the past generation."

you the word of God" (13:7). Hebrews therefore presents God as speaking his Word through the biblical prophets and in Jesus, and his Word comes to people in Scripture and in the church.

Even more significant for present purposes is the author's subtle claim that *God is speaking through Scripture* to the audience of Hebrews *in their present moment*. This subtle claim comes to light in the ways in which the author brings Scripture, especially Psalm 95, to bear directly on his audience in their present situation.

The author opens his exhortation with the words of Psalm 95:7–8, "Today, if you hear his voice, do not harden your hearts," and he identifies the scriptural words as the speech of the Holy Spirit (Heb. 3:7–8). The placement of these words at the beginning of the exhortation positions the audience of Hebrews as those being addressed by the psalm. They are to understand themselves as the "you" mentioned in the psalm, and the wilderness generation as "your ancestors" (v. 9, quoting Ps. 95:9). Subsequent uses of Psalm 95 in this unit amplify the author's invitation for the audience to understand themselves as addressed by God in the scriptural text. The author quotes these same words from Psalm 95:7–8 and puts them directly to his audience later in the exhortation: "For we have become partners with Christ, if only we hold our first confidence firm to the end. As it is said, 'Today, if you hear his voice, do not harden your hearts'" (Heb. 3:14–15). Similarly, the author directs the psalm's language to his audience when he encourages them by saying, "Exhort one another every day, as long as it is called 'today,' so that none of you may be hardened by the deceitfulness of sin" (v. 13). As mentioned previously, the author interprets the mentions of "today" and "rest" in the psalm as speaking to an open invitation for Hebrews' audience to enter into God's heavenly rest (4:9–11). The cumulative effect of these uses of Psalm 95 is for the audience of Hebrews to understand themselves as being addressed in the present time by the Word of the Lord.

The rhetorical function of the author's exegetical meditation on the wilderness generation is exhortative. It is meant to encourage the Christian audience of Hebrews to think and act in a certain way (i.e., to avoid the fate of the wilderness generation by not imitating their faithlessness and disobedience). Accordingly, the exhortation of Psalm 95, "Today, if you hear his voice, do not harden your hearts," comes to light as God's direct address to the Christian audience of Hebrews in the present moment. The "today" mentioned in Psalm 95 includes the audience's present moment. By so appropriating the psalm's language throughout this argumentative unit, the author puts his readers in the position to "hear" God's "voice," in their present moment ("today"), and invites them not to "harden [their] hearts."

By hearing the words and examples of Scripture as addressed to them in their present moment, the audience of Hebrews thus encounters the "living and active" Word of God (Heb. 4:12).

Through the scriptural language and examples, God speaks to the audience of Hebrews, directs their conduct, warns them of possible condemnation, and offers them the hope of heavenly rest. Moreover, just as the author begins the argumentative unit by mentioning "hearts" (Heb. 3:7), so too at the end of the unit does he speak of the Word's ability to "judge the thoughts and intentions of the heart" (4:12). The Word's discerning judgment of human hearts is displayed throughout the exegetical meditation. The psalm reports God's perception and exposition of the inner life of the wilderness generation's hearts: "They always go astray in their hearts, and they have not known my ways" (3:10, quoting Ps. 95:10). So too, implicitly, does God know the inner depths of the audience's hearts, and it is to God, according to his Word, that "we must render an account" (Heb. 4:13).

The "living God" thus speaks to people in their present moment through his "living" Word, given in Scripture. He invites them to receive this Word and respond with faith and obedience. Thus Craig Koester writes, "God's voice places the listeners in a position where they will respond in some way; the crucial question is whether the response will be one of faith or rejection."[14]

## The Gospel according to John as a Vehicle of Divine Presence

The Gospel according to John contributes significantly to this study of God's Word given through inspired written discourse. When considered in light of its own internal categories, the Gospel can be seen as a vehicle that mediates the reality of the risen Jesus to later generations of people. The words of the Gospel put its audience in living contact with the Word of God himself. The Gospel has this capacity because of its being testimony inspired by the Holy Spirit.[15]

### Encountering the Risen Lord in John 20

To grasp how the Fourth Gospel presents itself as a vehicle by which its audience can encounter the reality of Jesus himself, we begin with the

14. Koester, *Hebrews*, 255.

15. A previous version of the remaining material in this chapter (except the conclusion) originally appeared in William M. Wright IV, "Inspired Scripture as a Sacramental Vehicle of Divine Presence in the Gospel of John and *Dei Verbum*," *Nova et Vetera*, English edition 13 (2015): 156–72. It has been revised in the present text, and all biblical quotations have been adjusted to match the text of the NRSV.

resurrection narrative in John 20, a sequence of four scenes depicting the movement of several disciples to faith in the reality of Jesus as the risen Lord.[16] The chapter first narrates the discovery of the empty tomb (vv. 1–10) and then resurrection appearances to Mary Magdalene (vv. 11–18) and to the disciples on Easter Sunday night without Thomas (vv. 19–25), and then a second appearance to the disciples, a week later, with Thomas present (vv. 26–29). After this resurrection appearance to the disciples with Thomas, John provides valuable (and famous) commentary about his purposes in writing: "Now Jesus did many other signs in the presence of his disciples, which are not written in this book. But these are written so that you may come to believe that Jesus is the Messiah, the Son of God, and that through believing you may have life in his name" (vv. 30–31).

Most Johannine scholars regard John 20:30–31 as the original ending to the Gospel narrative, with chapter 21 subsequently added in the Gospel's composition history as an epilogue. However, this exegetical position de-emphasizes the many connections that verses 30–31 have with the preceding narrative material in 20:1–29. Accordingly, as Paul Minear and others have argued, these verses should be regarded primarily as the conclusion to the narrative sequence in John 20 and not to the Gospel as a whole.[17] One such connection between verses 30–31 and the preceding narrative sequence con-cerns the cause of faith in Jesus as the risen Lord. The narrator claims in verses 30–31 that the written Gospel has a causal function vis-à-vis people's faith in Jesus as the Son of God. If we take verses 30–31 as the conclusion to the narrative sequence in John 20, we then can more readily view its claim in light of what the preceding narrative presents as the only thing that brings about the disciples' faith in the resurrection: a personal encounter with Jesus as the risen Lord.

In brief, our exegetical argument is the following. The narrative sequence in John 20 presents a personal encounter with the risen Jesus as necessary for arriving at full, resurrection faith in him as the Lord. John himself claims in 20:30–31 that the Gospel has been written to bring about in its audience

16. We follow the four-scene division of John 20 proposed by Ignace de la Potterie, SJ, *The Hour of Jesus: The Passion and Resurrection of Jesus according to John*, trans. Dom G. Murray, OSB (Staten Island, NY: Alba House, 1989), 159–90. Compare with the two-scene division of John 20 in Raymond E. Brown, SS, *The Gospel according to John: Introduction, Translation, and Notes*, 2 vols., Anchor Bible 29, 29A (New York: Doubleday, 1966, 1970), 2:965.

17. For argumentation on this point, see Paul S. Minear, "The Original Functions of John 21," *Journal of Biblical Literature* 102 (1983): 85–98; Edwyn Clement Hoskyns, *The Fourth Gospel*, ed. Francis Noel Davey (London: Faber & Faber, 1947), 550; Gail R. O'Day, "The Gospel of John," in *The New Interpreter's Bible*, ed. Leander E. Keck, 12 vols. (Nashville: Abingdon, 1994–2004), 9:851–52, 854–55.

faith in Jesus as the Son of God. This narrative logic indicates that the Gospel presents itself as mediating for its audience a genuine encounter with Jesus as the risen Lord—an encounter as genuine as that of those first disciples who saw the risen Jesus in his glorified humanity.

We can appreciate John's claim that faith in Jesus as the risen Lord requires a personal encounter with him when we examine each of the four scenes in John 20 and consider all those things that do *not* cause, or are insufficient to cause, people to believe in the reality of the risen Jesus.[18]

The first of the four scenes in John 20 centers on the discovery of the empty tomb (vv. 1–10). The scene opens with Mary Magdalene arriving at Jesus's tomb in the predawn darkness, which, in view of John's use of light-and-dark symbolism, indicates her being bereft of Jesus, who is the Light of the World (8:12; 9:5). John reports that Mary "saw that the stone had been removed from the tomb" (20:1). Mary sees the opened tomb, and presumably does so at a distance, because the text does not indicate that she looked into or entered the tomb (cf. vv. 11–12). Simply seeing Jesus's open tomb from the outside is insufficient to cause faith in him, for, as the narrative itself indicates, the open tomb can be variously interpreted. Hence, Mary's conclusion that Jesus's tomb has been the object of grave robbery: "They have taken the Lord [or 'the master'] out of the tomb, and we do not know where they have laid him" (v. 2).

Through Mary Magdalene, John provides his audience with an external view of the empty tomb from a distance. Then, through Peter and the Beloved Disciple, he takes his audience right up to and inside Jesus's tomb. After hearing Mary's claim about grave robbery, Peter and the Beloved Disciple run out toward Jesus's tomb (John 20:3–4). The Beloved Disciple arrives at the tomb first, but he remains outside at the tomb's entrance. From the entrance, he stoops to look in and sees Jesus's graveclothes (v. 5). When Peter arrives, he actually goes in, and the Gospel's audience is given to see the empty tomb from the inside. As the Beloved Disciple did from the entrance, Peter sees Jesus's graveclothes. John adds that Peter also saw the facial covering, which had been on Jesus's corpse, now folded up and in a separate place (vv. 6–7).

Throughout this scene, John repeatedly uses verbs in the passive voice for actions performed with respect to Jesus's tomb: the stone "had been removed [*ērmenon*]" (John 20:1); the graveclothes were "lying there [*keimena*]" (v. 5); the face covering was "rolled up [*entetyligmenon*]" (v. 7). This use of the divine

---

18. Many of these points are likewise discussed in Minear, "Original Functions of John 21," 88–89.

passive indicates syntactically that God has acted in connection with Jesus's empty tomb.[19] This general notion of divine activity probably underlies John's claim that the Beloved Disciple, upon entering the tomb, "saw and started to believe [*kai eiden kai episteusen*]" (v. 8, translation ours).

Many commentators interpret this remark to indicate that the Beloved Disciple was the first to arrive at full faith in the risen Jesus.[20] These commentators take the Greek *kai eiden kai episteusen* to mean simply, "He saw and believed." This interpretation certainly is in keeping with the privilege and priority accorded to the Beloved Disciple in the Fourth Gospel. For instance, the Beloved Disciple rests on Jesus's chest, or heart (*en tō kolpō*), at the Last Supper (13:23), in a manner analogous to the Son's position "close to the Father's heart [*eis ton kolpon tou patros*]" (1:18); the identity of Jesus's betrayer is revealed only to the Beloved Disciple (13:25–26); he is the disciple who witnesses the blood and water flowing from Jesus's pierced side (19:34–36); he outruns Peter and arrives first at Jesus's tomb (20:4); in John 21, he is the first to realize that the risen Jesus speaks from the seashore to the embarked disciples (21:7).

Two factors, however, work against this interpretation. First, when John uses the verb *pisteuein* in the aorist, it is often an ingressive aorist, with the sense of "began to believe."[21] For example, Jesus's disciples "began to believe in him [*episteusan eis auton*]" (2:11, translation ours) after the miracle at the wedding at Cana. But as especially evidenced in the Farewell Discourses, Jesus's disciples, although positively disposed to him, have little grasp of the significance of Jesus's words and deeds during his ministry (e.g., 13:16–14:9; 14:22–24; 16:16–33). Even more stark is John's claim that a group of Jews "began to believe in him [*episteusan eis auton*]" (8:30, translation ours) during Jesus's teaching in Jerusalem at the Festival of Tabernacles. It is this same group of incipient believers whom Jesus engages in an increasingly sharp

19. Donatien Mollat, "La découverte du tombeau vide," in *Études johanniques* (Paris: Editions du Seuil, 1979), 518; referenced by Francis J. Moloney, SDB, *The Gospel of John*, Sacra Pagina 4 (Collegeville, MN: Liturgical Press, 1998), 518–20.

20. E.g., C. K. Barrett, *The Gospel according to St. John: An Introduction with Commentary and Notes on the Greek Text*, 2nd ed. (Philadelphia: Westminster, 1978), 561, 564, 573; Richard Bauckham, *The Testimony of the Beloved Disciple: Narrative, History, and Theology in the Gospel of John* (Grand Rapids: Baker Academic, 2007), 86; Brown, *Gospel according to John*, 2:987, 1001; Hoskyns, *Fourth Gospel*, 540; Craig S. Keener, *The Gospel of John: A Commentary*, 2 vols. (Peabody, MA: Hendrickson, 2003), 2:1184; Moloney, *Gospel of John*, 520–21, 523; Rudolf Schnackenburg, *The Gospel according to St. John*, trans. Kevin Smyth et al., 3 vols. (New York: Crossroad, 1968–82), 3:312.

21. John 2:11, 22–23; 4:39, 41, 53; 7:31; 8:30; 10:42; 11:45. So too Schnackenburg, *Gospel according to St. John*, 3:312; see F. Blass and A. Debrunner, *A Greek Grammar of the New Testament*, ed. Robert W. Funk (Chicago: University of Chicago Press, 1961), §331 (p. 171).

debate, in which each says that the other is associated with the demonic (vv. 44, 48) and which culminates in the former's attempt to kill Jesus (v. 59). In these cases, the kind of faith that is spoken of has some legitimacy, but it is very imperfect.

The second major factor is the narrator's commentary in John 20:9, which interprets the activity of Peter and the Beloved Disciple at the tomb: "As yet they did not understand the scripture, that he must rise from the dead." The evangelist explicitly claims that at that time, when they saw the empty tomb and graveclothes, both Peter and the Beloved Disciple did not have a grasp of the scriptural (and thus providential) necessity of Jesus's resurrection. It is because "they did not understand" (v. 9) the scriptural necessity of the resurrection that these two disciples left the tomb and went back home (v. 10). The Beloved Disciple may have been the first to arrive at some general notion that God was involved in Jesus's tomb being empty. But this incipient belief should not be confused with a full, robust faith in the reality of Jesus as the risen Lord. As Gail O'Day puts it, "What the beloved disciple believes . . . is the evidence of the empty tomb. . . . [His] faith is as complete as faith in the evidence of the empty tomb can be."[22]

In the first scene in John 20, therefore, the evangelist presents three things, which, although related to Jesus's resurrection, do not of their own accord cause faith in him as the risen Lord: (1) the open and empty tomb (whether seen from afar, up close, or inside), (2) Jesus's graveclothes, and (3) the facial covering that had been on Jesus's corpse but now lay separately.

The second of the four scenes, John 20:11–18, centers on Mary Magdalene, who remains at the empty tomb after Peter and the Beloved Disciple have left. In this scene, John presents Mary's movement from hopelessness and unbelief to full faith in Jesus as the risen Lord. The scene opens with Mary "weeping [*klaiousa*]" (v. 11) outside the empty tomb, a detail that recalls Jesus's prediction in the Farewell Discourse that his disciples will "weep" (*klausete*) when they no longer see him (16:20). Like the Beloved Disciple, Mary looks inside the tomb from its threshold. Unlike the Beloved Disciple and even more dramatically, Mary sees two angels seated on the slab where Jesus's corpse had been (20:13). Astonishingly, Mary is totally unmoved by this angelophany. When the angels ask about her weeping, Mary gives basically the same response she had previously given to Peter and the Beloved Disciple: "They have taken away my Lord [or 'master'], and I do not know where they

22. O'Day, *Gospel of John*, 841. Similarly, Minear ("Original Functions," 88–89) interprets the various things in John 20 that are insufficient to cause faith in the risen Jesus (e.g., the empty tomb, the graveclothes, the angels in the tomb) as the "many other signs [which Jesus did] in the presence of his disciples," spoken of in 20:30.

have laid him" (v. 13; cf. v. 2).[23] Mary remains fixed in her belief that Jesus's corpse has been stolen, and not even the appearance of two angels in the empty tomb can shake this belief.

After speaking to the angels, Mary turns around to see the risen Jesus, whom she does not recognize, mistaking him for the gardener (John 20:14–15). Jesus puts the same question to Mary as the angels did—"Woman, why are you weeping?"—and his address to her as "woman [*gynai*]" is significant. There are three other occasions in John (2:4; 4:21; 19:26) in which Jesus uses "woman" in the vocative (the Greek grammatical case used to address someone or something), and all three uses appear in situations wherein Jesus is establishing a new relationship between a specific female (his mother and the Samaritan woman) and another individual, either himself or the Beloved Disciple.[24] Jesus adds, "Whom are you looking for?"—a question that both recalls his first words to his disciples in 1:38 and picks up on Mary's present search for Jesus. Mary responds by reiterating her belief that Jesus's corpse has been stolen and then offers to take custody of it (20:15). The key point here is that Mary's attention remains fixed in the past: she believes that Jesus is still dead and his corpse is missing.

It is only when Jesus calls her name, "Mary" (John 20:16), as the Good Shepherd calls his own sheep by name (10:3), that she becomes alerted to his presence. But even this new awareness that Jesus is now alive does not constitute full faith in his resurrection. Mary responds to Jesus by calling him "Rabbouni" (20:16), a title appropriate to his earthly ministry when he was her teacher and master (cf. 13:13–14), and the text implies that Mary also embraces Jesus as such (cf. Matt. 28:9). Mary now believes that Jesus is alive, but she continues to relate to him as she did previously—that is, as her teacher and master.

This way of relating to Jesus, however, is no longer possible after the resurrection. Hence, Jesus tells Mary to stop touching him, and he then provides

---

23. Mary's use of pronouns shifts from the first-person plural in 20:2 ("*we* don't know where they put him") to the first-person singular in 20:13 ("*I* don't know where they put him"). This shift reinforces that 20:11–18 concerns Mary Magdalene's personal relationship with Jesus.

24. Jesus's first address to his mother as "woman" (2:4) occurs within a narrative dynamic wherein, as Francis Martin puts it, "the relation between Jesus and his mother is founded, not on the ties of human birth, but on the nature of Jesus' mission as determined by the Father." Francis Martin, "Mary in Sacred Scripture: An Ecumenical Reflection," *The Thomist* 72 (2008): 538. For further argumentation, see B. F. Westcott, *The Gospel according to St. John* (Grand Rapids: Eerdmans, 1954), 36–37; Albert Vanhoye, "Interrogation johannique et exégèse de Cana (John 2, 4)," *Biblica* 55 (1974): 163–67. In 4:21, Jesus moves the relationship between himself and the Samaritan woman from within the horizon of extant Jewish-Samaritan relations (4:7–10) to the community of the messianic age, which he establishes (4:21–26). In 19:26–27, Jesus reveals the bonds of spiritual maternity and childhood between his mother and the Beloved Disciple by referring to the former as "mother" of the latter, her "son."

the reason: "I have not yet ascended to the Father" (John 20:17). Throughout the Gospel, Jesus teaches that he has been sent by the Father and offers the gift of eternal life to those who believe in him (3:15–16, 36; 6:40, 47). The prologue articulates this anthropological aspect to salvation in the language of family relations: he gave them "power to become children of God" (1:12). For John, eternal life consists in becoming a child of God. This is a participatory share in Jesus's own relationship to the Father as the Son. Through his death, resurrection, and entrance into the Father's glory, Jesus establishes this new relationship between the disciples and the Father. This point is articulated in 20:17 through the use of family language in the words of the risen Jesus to Mary Magdalene. For the first time in the Gospel, Jesus refers to his disciples as his "brothers," implying that Jesus and his disciples now relate to the same Father as sons. This point is even clearer in the message that the risen Jesus entrusts to Mary to deliver to his brothers: "I am ascending to my Father and your Father, to my God and your God" (v. 17).

The risen Jesus thus teaches that he opens up the divine communion to his disciples, who can now relate to the Father in a new way by participating in Jesus's own life and identity as the Son. As Ignace de la Potterie observes, with the recognition of this new relationship with the Father and the Son, Mary Magdalene makes the characteristic declaration of having arrived at full faith in the reality of the risen Jesus: "I have seen the Lord" (20:18).[25] Mary no longer relates to Jesus simply as teacher or master, but now as "Lord," as sharing the identity of YHWH himself.[26]

Over the course of this second scene, we see Mary's movement in faith from being fixated on the past—either her belief that Jesus is dead or her relating to him as she previously did—to a present encounter with him as the risen Lord. A knowledge of and relationship with Jesus during his mortal life is insufficient to cause faith in him as the Son of God. It is only when Mary personally encounters risen Jesus as the one who has opened up the divine communion to believers that she can confess him as "the Lord."

The last two scenes in the sequence of John 20 concern the appearances of the risen Jesus to his disciples on Easter Sunday evening without Thomas (vv. 19–25) and then to the disciples on the following Sunday evening with Thomas present (vv. 26–29). The numerous points of contact between these two scenes (not least of which is the presence or absence of Thomas) suggest that John invites his audience to read these scenes in light of each other.

---

25. De la Potterie, *Hour of Jesus*, 162–65, 174–75.

26. Drawing here on the divine-identity Christology set forth in Richard Bauckham, *Jesus and the God of Israel: God Crucified and Other Studies on the New Testament's Christology of Divine Identity* (Grand Rapids: Eerdmans, 2008).

Two points emerging from these scenes are especially germane to this study. First, these two scenes reinforce the claim that only a personal encounter with the risen Jesus brings about faith in him as the Lord. Second, a personal encounter with Jesus as the risen Lord is not limited to seeing him in his glorified humanity.

Several narrative indicators further support the theological claim already articulated in the previous scene with Mary Magdalene: only a personal encounter with the risen Jesus causes faith in him as Lord. We can appreciate these by comparing the states of the disciples before and after they encountered the risen Jesus. The third scene opens with the narrator stating, "The doors of the house where the disciples had met were locked for fear of the Jews" (20:19). John uses the same language to open the fourth scene, but with a significant omission. The narrator says, "The doors were shut" (v. 26), but does not mention the disciples being afraid. The disciples' encounter with the risen Jesus on Easter Sunday evening has caused a definite change in them: it has removed their fear. This change in their status comes to light in other ways. When the risen Jesus appears to them and shows them his pierced hands and side, the narrator reports that they "rejoiced when they saw the Lord" (v. 20). The mention of "rejoicing" (*chairein*) recalls the words of Jesus in the Farewell Discourse: "So you have pain now; but I will see you again, and your hearts will rejoice [*charēsetai*], and no one will take your joy from you" (16:22). As Jesus predicted in 16:20, the disciples' "pain [has turned] into joy." After their encounter with the risen Jesus, the disciples declare their resurrection faith to the now-present Thomas with the same language that Mary Magdalene had used in 20:18: "We have seen the Lord" (20:25)—with the verb *horan* used in the perfect tense. In the fourth scene, when Thomas encounters the risen Jesus, he confesses him as "My Lord and my God" (20:28), perhaps echoing the scriptural name YHWH *ʾĕlōhîm* ("Lord God"). Once again, this confession of Easter faith is articulated with the verb *horan* in the perfect tense, although in Thomas's case it appears in the words of Jesus to Thomas: "You have believed because you have seen me [*heōrakas*]" (v. 29, translation ours). In both cases, the disciples' personal encounter with the risen Jesus has led them to confess Jesus as the Lord, as *kyrios*.

However, John is also quick to affirm that such a personal encounter with Jesus as the risen Lord is not limited to a direct, tangible encounter with his glorified humanity as in a resurrection appearance. This point especially comes to light in the fourth scene, where the risen Jesus appears to Thomas, a scene that segues into the narrator's remarks about his purposes in writing the Gospel in 20:30–31.

When Thomas protests the disciples' confession "We have seen the Lord" (20:25), he sets up a direct, tangible encounter with the risen Jesus as a necessary condition for his belief. John underscores this point by extensively using both somatic and sensory language in the condition of Thomas's protest: "Unless I see the mark of the nails in his hands, and put my finger in the mark of the nails and my hand in his side . . ." (v. 25). To reinforce his insistence on a direct, tangible encounter with the glorified humanity of the risen Jesus as a prerequisite for faith, he uses an emphatic negative in the apodosis: *ou mē pisteusō*, "I will never believe" (v. 25).[27]

When the risen Jesus appears to the disciples with Thomas present, Jesus grants Thomas what he has requested: a direct, tangible encounter. Jesus's invitation to Thomas repeats much of the same somatic and sensory language from Thomas's initial protest (John 20:25): "Put your finger here and see my hands. Reach out your hand and put it into my side. Do not doubt but believe." However, there is no indication (either stated or implied) that Thomas ever touches Jesus's glorified body. The personal encounter with the risen Jesus and his direct address to Thomas prove sufficient for Thomas to confess, "My Lord and my God" (v. 28). Thomas has come to believe in Jesus as the risen Lord on account of his personal encounter with him, but a tangible experience of Jesus's glorified humanity has also shown itself to be unnecessary for this faith. Jesus makes this point clear in his concluding beatitude: "Blessed are those who have not seen and yet have come to believe" (v. 29).

This beatitude opens up the narrative's scope beyond itself and looks toward future generations of believers, who will believe in Jesus as the risen Lord without literally seeing him in his glorified humanity. By pronouncing them "blessed," the risen Jesus indicates that the faith of these future believers is no less genuine than that of those first disciples who literally "have seen the Lord" (John 20:25). With the scope having been so opened and the genuineness of future believers' faith affirmed, the narrative sequence comes to rest by specifying the means by which later generations of believers will encounter the reality of the risen Jesus and come to believe in him as the Lord: through "these things [that] are written" (v. 31).

This notice in John 20:31 has been prepared for by previous statements in the Gospel, which look beyond the narrative's own horizon to future generations of believers. During the Good Shepherd Discourse, Jesus declares that he has sheep that "do not belong to this fold" (likely an allusion to future, gentile believers), and these sheep "will listen to [his] voice" (10:16). Similarly

---

27. Translation ours. Thomas articulates his protest in 20:25 as a future-more-vivid condition, which provides additional, syntactical emphasis.

in his prayer of intercession in John 17, Jesus prays for all his disciples both present and future, specifically designating the latter as those "who will believe in [him] through their [i.e., his disciples'] word" (v. 20). When taken together with the preceding analysis of John 20, these statements suggest that the principal means by which future generations of believers will encounter the reality of the risen Lord and "listen to [his] voice" is through the disciples' word, or, to use John's preferred term, their "testimony." The Fourth Gospel itself claims to preserve the testimony of the Beloved Disciple, whom it identifies as "the disciple who is testifying to these things and has written them" (21:24).

The disciples' testimony, either in oral or written form, is, therefore, a key component in the Fourth Gospel's understanding of itself as a vehicle of the risen Jesus's presence to later generations of believers. In the next section, we will argue that the disciples' testimony (which includes the written Gospel) has this capacity to genuinely mediate Jesus's presence to later generations of believers because of the action of the Paraclete. In other words, divine inspiration gives the written Gospel this unique capacity to mediate the reality of Jesus to later generations of believers.

### Inspired Testimony

Ignace de la Potterie rightly observes that the Johannine writings often use the language of testimony to refer to divine revelation.[28] This applies to Jesus's revelation of the Father and divine truth (John 3:32–33; 7:7; 8:14, 18; 18:37). Jesus "testifies to what he has seen and heard" (3:32), for he, the only one who has "seen" the Father (1:18; 6:46), speaks "what [he has] seen in the Father's presence" (8:38). As the Father's perfect emissary, who is himself "the truth" (14:6), Jesus alone is able to give valid testimony about himself (8:13–14).[29] More frequently, the Gospel speaks of other entities giving testimony to Jesus, such as John the Baptist (1:7–8, 15, 19; 3:28; 5:36), Jesus's works (5:36; 10:25), and the Scriptures (5:39); and behind all of these is the testimony of the Father

---

28. For a survey discussion, see Ignace de la Potterie, SJ, *La vérité dans Saint Jean*, 2 vols., Analecta biblica 73–74 (Rome: Pontificio Istituto Biblico, 1999), 1:80–88; George Johnston, *The Spirit-Paraclete in the Gospel of John*, Society for New Testament Studies Monograph Series 12 (Cambridge: Cambridge University Press, 1970), 135–37.

29. So Schnackenburg, *Gospel according to St. John*, 2:120–21, 192–93. On Jesus as the Father's emissary, see Peder Borgen, "God's Agent in the Fourth Gospel," in *Religions in Antiquity: Essays in Memory of Erwin Ramsdell Goodenough*, ed. Jacob Neusner, Studies in the History of Religions 14 (Leiden: Brill, 1968), 137–48; repr. in *The Interpretation of John*, ed. John Ashton, 2nd ed., Studies in New Testament Interpretation (Edinburgh: T&T Clark, 1997), 83–95.

(5:32; cf. 8:18). All these witnesses testify, de la Potterie writes, "directly to the secret of [Jesus's] being, to the mystery of his person."[30]

In only three instances does the Gospel speak of Jesus's disciples giving testimony about him.[31] Two of the three pertain specifically to the testimony given by the Beloved Disciple. The first is the Beloved Disciple's eyewitness testimony about the flow of blood and water from the side of Jesus's corpse (19:35). The second occurs in 21:24, where the narrator states that the Beloved Disciple's testimony has been written in the Gospel. Between these two cases (19:35; 21:24), the narrator describes the Beloved Disciple's testimony as "true" three times. At the crucifixion, the narrator says of the Beloved Disciple, "His testimony is true [*alēthinē*], and he knows that he tells the truth [*alēthē*]" (19:35). Likewise, at the very conclusion of the Gospel, the narrator says of the Beloved Disciple, "We know that his testimony is true [*alēthēs*]" (21:24). These statements in 19:35 and 21:24 combine three elements: (1) a disciple, (2) giving testimony, which is (3) the truth. This three-part combination appears only one other time in the Gospel, and it is the third instance where the disciples are said to give testimony: the Paraclete promise in 15:26–27.

Three things in this Paraclete text (John 15:26–27) stand out for present purposes. First, Jesus says that the Paraclete himself "will testify" (v. 26). Insight into where, how, and to whom the Paraclete testifies can be obtained from the first Paraclete promise (14:16–17). When Jesus first announces that the Paraclete will come to the disciples, he declares that the Paraclete will dwell within his disciples: "He abides with you, and he will be in you [*en hymin estai*]" (v. 17). The activity of the Paraclete is an interior activity that he works in Jesus's disciples only. The latter point is underscored by the sharp contrast that Jesus draws between his disciples and the world: "The world cannot receive [the Paraclete], because it neither sees him nor knows him" (v. 17).[32] Since the world, at whose core lies the willful rejection of God's Word, does not "receive" (*lambanein*) Jesus (1:11; 5:43, translation ours), it is incapable of receiving the Paraclete whom Jesus will send. Stanislas Lyonnet writes, "Since the world has shown it was incapable of 'perceiving' the Spirit

---

30. De la Potterie, *La vérité*, 1:82.

31. An exception is the Samaritan woman, who testified to her fellow townspeople about what Jesus told her (4:39). This case reinforces the basic point that "testimony" is effectively a synonym for "evangelization" in John (so de la Potterie, *La vérité*, 1:80), for on the basis of her testimony, the Samaritans came to Jesus directly and believed in him.

32. As de la Potterie (*Hour of Jesus*, 117–20) observes, the Fourth Gospel often uses *lambanein* to designate the human reception of heavenly realities. For instance, people can receive (or not receive) Jesus himself (1:11–12; 5:43; 13:20), his words (12:48; 17:8), testimony about Jesus (3:11, 32–33); the Holy Spirit (7:39; 14:17; 20:22); and heavenly gifts (3:27; 16:24).

at work during Jesus' life, it is also unable to 'know' him."[33] What fundamentally distinguishes the disciples from the world is their own "receiving" of Jesus in faith and discipleship (1:12; 3:33; 17:8). The Spirit has been present with Jesus throughout his ministry (1:32–34), and the disciples, "despite their intellectual simplicity, had attached themselves to Jesus, and believed and knew that he was the Holy One of God."[34] The disciples' relationship with Jesus opens them up to receive the Paraclete and disposes them to his action upon their hearts. When Jesus says that the Paraclete "will testify" (15:26), it is understood that the Paraclete gives testimony only to the disciples and does so within them.

Second, John 15:26 specifies Jesus as the content of the Paraclete's testimony: "He will testify on my behalf." Significant in this regard is the title "the Spirit of truth," by which Jesus refers to the Paraclete in 15:26. This title, given to the Paraclete three times in the Farewell Discourses (14:16–17; 15:26; 16:13), emphasizes the "christological dependence" of the Paraclete, his essential relationship with Jesus and thus with the Father.[35] The Gospel consistently identifies the divine revelation of Jesus as "the truth."[36] As the divine Word, who reveals the Father and himself as the Son, Jesus is himself "the truth" (14:6; 17:17), and he has spoken "the truth that [he] heard from God" (8:40; cf. 18:37). As the Spirit of truth, the Paraclete is the Spirit of Jesus, and his activity within the disciples—he speaks and announces (16:13–14), teaches and reminds (14:26), and testifies—pertains to Jesus's divine revelation, namely, the truth. The richest expression of this activity appears in the fourth Paraclete promise: "The Spirit of truth . . . will guide you into all the truth" (16:13). De la Potterie thus describes this activity of the Spirit: the Paraclete "will cause [the disciples] to understand the true significance and bearing of the words of Jesus. . . . His task will be to interpret, through the Church, the revelation of Jesus, still not fully understood."[37] He later adds,

33. Stanislas Lyonnet, SJ, "The Paraclete," in *The Christian Lives by the Spirit*, ed. Ignace de la Potterie, SJ, and Stanislas Lyonnet, SJ, trans. John Morriss (Staten Island, NY: Alba House, 1971), 60.

34. Lyonnet, "Paraclete," 60. This connection between the Paraclete's indwelling and the disciples' faith is further supported by other texts that speak of the Spirit as "living water," which "will become in them a spring of water" (4:14) and flow "out of the believer's heart" (7:37–38). The narrator's commentary in 7:39 similarly identifies faith as the prerequisite disposition for receiving the Spirit: "He said this about the Spirit, which believers [*hoi pisteusantes*] in him were to receive [*lambanein*]" (7:39).

35. Johnston, *Spirit-Paraclete*, 37.

36. As de la Potterie summarizes, "The truth is the revelation which comes to us from the Father and is passed on to us in the actual word of Jesus." Ignace de la Potterie, SJ, "The Truth in Saint John," *Rivista biblica italiana* 11 (1963): 3–24, repr. in Ashton, *Interpretation of John*, 71.

37. De la Potterie, "Truth in Saint John," in Ashton, *Interpretation of John*, 77.

"The task of the Spirit will be to cause the message of Jesus to penetrate into the hearts of the faithful, to give them the understanding of faith."[38]

The testimony that the Spirit of truth gives about Jesus is not a generic expression of his pedagogy. Rather, it has a distinctly forensic dimension, related to the context in which the third Paraclete saying (John 15:26–27) occurs.[39] This promise appears within a unit of discourse where Jesus announces to his disciples that they will receive the same hatred and persecution from the world as he did (15:18–16:4a). A prophetic saying about the Spirit assisting Jesus's disciples in a future time of persecution resembles similar units of discourse in the Synoptic Gospels (Matt. 10:16–25; Mark 13:9–13; Luke 12:2, 10–12). These synoptic counterparts envision a forensic setting in which the Spirit serves as a legal advocate (or Paraclete) for the disciples, providing them with what to say or speaking on their behalf (Matt. 10:19–20; Mark 13:11; Luke 12:11–12). Within the Johannine articulation, the Paraclete's testimony similarly consoles and assists the disciples as they confront the world. As Jesus indicates in the words following the third Paraclete promise, the primary threat to the disciples will be apostasy: "I have said these things to you to keep you from stumbling" (John 16:1; cf. 6:61–66). This inner activity of the Paraclete, therefore, "is not only a teaching. . . . It is called 'testimony'; it will consist in making the disciples' faith unshakable, which the opposition of the world could imperil."[40] The Paraclete will convince the disciples of the reality of Jesus so that they will be able to stand firm against the assaults of the world.

Third, John 15:26–27 establishes a connection between the Paraclete's inner testimony and the disciples' own testimony: "He will testify on my behalf. [And] you also are to testify." The inner testimony of Paraclete about Jesus enables the disciples to give testimony about Jesus outwardly to the unbelieving world.[41] As Augustine puts it, "He will bear witness and you will also bear witness: he in your hearts, you in your voices; he by inspiring, you by speaking out loud."[42] The disciples' testimony is thus part of their mission to the world. In his intercessory prayer to the Father, Jesus thus prays for his disciples, "As you have sent me into the world, so I have sent them into the world" (17:18). Later, when the risen Jesus appears to the disciples on Easter Sunday evening, he commissions them: "As the Father has sent me, so I send you" (20:21). The risen Jesus then equips the disciples for their mission by breathing the Holy

---

38. De la Potterie, "Truth in Saint John," in Ashton, *Interpretation of John*, 78.
39. Following in this paragraph de la Potterie, *La vérité*, 1:391–96.
40. De la Potterie, *La vérité*, 1:398.
41. So Brown, *Gospel according to John*, 2:700; de la Potterie, "Truth in Saint John," in Ashton, *Interpretation of John*, 75; Schnackenburg, *Gospel according to St. John*, 3:119.
42. Augustine, *Tractates on the Gospel of John* 93.1 (PL 35:1864), translation ours.

Spirit into them (v. 22). The Father sent Jesus into the world to reveal him and do his work (4:34; 5:23; 8:29; 12:44–50; 18:37), and Jesus extends his mission through his disciples. Jesus was sent to make the Father known to the world for its salvation, and accordingly, the disciples' mission and testimony has an evangelizing and missionary character. Through their word and example of visible unity (17:21, 23) and faithful, loving practice (13:35), the disciples give testimony to the truth of Jesus's revelation (17:23). The purpose of the disciples' testimony is "so that the world may believe" that the Father has sent Jesus (v. 21) and may, by believing in Jesus, receive the gift of participating in the divine communion of life between the Father and Son (v. 23).

The disciples give testimony about Jesus to the world because the Paraclete has first given testimony about Jesus within the disciples. The indwelling Paraclete guides the disciples into the depths of Jesus's revelation, causing its truth to penetrate into their hearts. This inner activity of the Paraclete enables the disciples to give testimony to the world about Jesus through evangeliza- tion and to stand firm in the confrontation that it will necessarily provoke. Similarly, the narrator's claim that the Beloved Disciple's "testimony is true" (John 21:24) connects that disciple's testimony to the activity of the Spirit of truth, who guides the disciples "into all the truth" (16:13). The Beloved Dis- ciple's testimony is "true" because it flows from the testimony of the "Spirit of truth" (15:26) within him about Jesus, who is himself "the truth" (14:6). It is appropriate to say that the Beloved Disciple's testimony—and the written Gospel containing it—claims to be inspired by the Paraclete.[43]

### The Gospel Mediates the Reality of the Risen Jesus

We are now in position to draw together the various threads of this analysis of John's Gospel. The resurrection narrative in John 20 indicates that the only thing sufficient to cause genuine faith in Jesus as the risen Lord is a personal encounter with him. Such an encounter with the risen Jesus is not limited to those who literally saw him in his glorified humanity, for it can be had through the Gospel itself, which contains the testimony of the Beloved Disciple. When considered in light of the Paraclete promises in the Farewell Discourse, the Beloved Disciple's testimony comes to light as proceeding from the Spirit's

---

43. The Gospel also gives evidence of having been composed in alignment with the activ- ity of the Paraclete, as described in its narrative. See the discussion in chap. 10 of this book; William M. Wright IV, "The Theology of Disclosure and Biblical Exegesis," *The Thomist* 70 (2006): 405–11; Marinus de Jonge, *Jesus, Stranger from Heaven and Son of God: Jesus Christ and the Christians in Johannine Perspective*, ed. and trans. John E. Steely, Sources for Biblical Study 11 (Missoula, MT: Scholars Press, 1977), 7–12.

inner activity. The Paraclete comes to dwell within Jesus's disciples after his glorification and teaches them the spiritual depths of Jesus's revelation. The Paraclete's inner testimony enables the disciples to give testimony about Jesus externally to the world and, by doing so, to bring people to believe in him.

If the inspired testimony of the disciples enables later generations to believe in Jesus as Lord, and if true faith in Jesus requires a genuine encounter with him as the risen Lord, then the disciples' inspired testimony, including its written form in the Gospel, mediates the reality of the risen Jesus to later generations, who can personally encounter him and thus believe in him. The Paraclete, who makes the risen Jesus present to the disciples (John 14:18, 23–26), has inspired the Beloved Disciple's testimony and so enabled his Gospel to serve as a vehicle by which later generations can encounter the reality of the risen Jesus.

## Looking Back and Looking Forward

In this chapter, we have focused on two case studies from the New Testament that speak to the Word of God as given through inspired written discourse. Hebrews teaches that "the word of God is living and active" (Heb. 4:12). This remark appears within a larger compositional unit that extensively uses Psalm 95 and examples from the Old Testament. Hebrews presents the words of the psalm and the scriptural examples as speaking directly to the audience of Hebrews. The upshot, we suggest, is that God speaks to people through Scripture in their present moment, and through Scripture, God works powerfully within them at the deepest levels of their being. The Gospel according to John subtly presents itself as mediating the reality of the risen Jesus. Only a personal encounter with the risen Lord can cause faith in him as "the Messiah, the Son of God" (John 20:31). As the inspired testimony of the Beloved Disciple, the Gospel is a way by which future generations of readers can encounter the reality of the risen Jesus and "may have life in his name" (20:31).

These two cases cohere with what we have seen in the previous chapters pertaining to the Word of God, its associations with power and presence, and the capacity of inspired human discourse to mediate the Word. Taken together, these teachings invite us see that Scripture, as a form of inspired human discourse, can put people in living and life-giving contact with the divine realities that it mediates.

# Conclusion to Part 1

We have surveyed a number of biblical passages from both Testaments of the Christian Bible that concern the Word of God. We have examined texts that speak of the Word as spoken directly by God and as given through inspired human discourse, both spoken and written. Acknowledging that the biblical texts give different perspectives on the Word of God, we will summarize some of the major findings of part 1 under four headings.

*First, the Word of God has divine causal power.* The survey of biblical material provides different examples of this. The Word of God is an enacting of God's will. By his Word, God creates (Gen. 1; Ps. 33), providentially governs the world (Ps. 147; Sir. 42), guides human conduct (Pss. 103; 119), and acts in salvation history (Pss. 105; 107; Sir. 39; Wis. 16). Proclaiming the Word of God—the gospel of the kingdom—is central to the messianic ministry of Jesus, who makes the kingdom present in his person, words, and deeds. God also exercises the power of his Word when it is given in inspired human discourse. We see this in the miracles that God performs through the prophets Elijah and Elisha and through the apostles in Acts. Paul similarly speaks of his proclamation of the gospel as charged with the power of God (Rom. 1:16) and as accompanied by mighty deeds "of the Spirit and of power" (1 Cor. 2:4; cf. 1 Thess. 1:5). Through his Word given in inspired discourse, God brings many people to faith and conquers the spiritual powers of evil (Acts), and God's Word continues to work its transforming power in people (Hebrews; 1 Corinthians; 1 Peter).

Remember that the power of the Word is *God's* power. As Paul argues, the power of God's Word is not the power associated with human eloquence, persuasiveness, and "words of wisdom" (1 Cor. 2:4). While human discourse does have a certain power (such as in certain speech-acts), the power of God's Word is fundamentally of a different nature. Through his Word, God produces a divinely caused effect in the world, and he may produce this effect in and through a created reality (e.g., human discourse).

Biblical witnesses also speak of the divine empowering and commissioning of certain individuals by whose discourse God communicates his Word and its power. We see this, for instance, in the call of the biblical prophets, the commissioning of the apostles as Jesus's witnesses and their being gifted with the Holy Spirit in Acts, and the Paraclete-guided testimony of the disciples in John. In such cases, God communicates his Word and causal power through human discourse without effacing its nature as human discourse.[1] The Spirit-touched discourse of the prophets and apostles remains human discourse, but God has elevated it so as to make it apt to mediate his Word and its power. The Word of God, proclaimed in inspired human discourse, has power because it stems from God and not because of the natural abilities of the human beings involved (e.g., their literary or rhetorical skill).

Moreover, Scripture is concerned, especially in Acts, to distinguish the power of God's Word given in inspired discourse from magic words. We see this, for example, in the failures of Simon Magus (Acts 8) and the Jewish exorcists (Acts 19) who attempt to manipulate this power and bring it under their control. Acts stresses the role of the Holy Spirit in empowering the proclamation of the Word by select individuals and the role of faith as a precondition for such powerful proclamation. The power and the Word are properly God's, and he communicates his Word and its power through the inspired discourse of those whom he chooses.

*Second, the biblical witnesses variously associate the Word of God and forms of presence.* This point is more difficult to articulate succinctly, and it includes several different teachings. For instance, biblical witnesses of both Testaments present God revealing divine truths and realities by his Word. We might think of God and these revealed truths and realities as becoming present to people in the modality of being known. Through his Word, God reveals himself, his righteousness, and his faithfulness (Pss. 33; 119; 147). Psalm 147 identifies the Word by which God providentially governs the world as the Torah revealed to Israel (vv. 15–20). By his Word, God reveals his designs and intentions for created realities (Gen. 1), the course of human events and

---

1. In so framing the matter, we draw on the standard Roman Catholic belief, implied by the Chalcedonian definition of the incarnation, that "grace perfects nature." So Thomas Aquinas: "The gifts of grace are added to nature in such a way that they do not destroy it, but rather perfect it." *Super Boethium de Trinitate* q. 2, a. 3, in Thomas Aquinas, *On Faith and Reason*, ed. Stephen F. Brown (Indianapolis: Hackett, 1999), 36.

things to come (e.g., the prophecy-fulfillment dynamic in the Deuteronomic history; the announcement of coming salvation in Second Isaiah), and the inner, theological meaning of things in the divine economy (2 Kings 17). Through his Word given in Scripture, God continues to speak to those who hear or read Scripture in their present moment (Hebrews).

An even stronger association between the Word of God and presence comes to light in texts that present the Word as reality or an acting subject in its own right. Jeremiah speaks of the Word of God as a reality within him that has a power of its own (Jer. 20). In the new-covenant oracle (31:31–34), God promises to make his Word dwell within the hearts of his redeemed people. Other texts present God sending his Word or Wisdom on a mission in the world (Isa. 55; Wis. 9; Sir. 24), and in some cases, the Word of God is a fully personified agent (Wis. 9; 18). The New Testament identifies Jesus as the incarnation of God's Word or Wisdom, who is divine and intrinsic to God's very identity (John 1:1, 14; 1 Cor. 8:6; Col. 1:15–20; Heb. 1:1–3).

*Third, the personal identification of Jesus as the incarnate Word of God has far-reaching effects for Christian theological thinking about the Word of God.* The incarnation reveals the Word to be a divine person, inseparable from God the Father (for the Word is God's and is always presented in relation to him). When the Word is seen in this light, to proclaim the Word of God is to proclaim the reality of Jesus Christ and the divine work of salvation, which is fully accomplished in him. This is the heart of the apostolic proclamation given in Acts and "the mystery of God" that Paul proclaims (1 Cor. 2:1). Moreover, New Testament epistolary literature at times speaks of the apostolic proclamation of the Word as mediating both the reality of the risen Jesus, who indwells believers by faith, and the power that flows from his passion and resurrection (1 Corinthians; 1 Thessalonians; 1 Peter). The Fourth Gospel, as containing the inspired testimony of the Beloved Disciple, presents itself as mediating an encounter with the risen Jesus that is as genuine as the encounters experienced by those who were witnesses to his resurrection. So understood, the Word proclaimed by the apostles in the power of the Holy Spirit mediates the presence of the risen Jesus and its life-giving power. Their inspired words make present to people the Word of God himself.

Jesus presents himself as the promised Messiah, the one in whom God makes good on his saving promises given in Scripture: "Today this scripture has been fulfilled in your hearing" (Luke 4:21). As the incarnate Word and the fulfillment of God's promises of salvation, Jesus causes other biblical realities to appear in a new light: they come to be seen in relation to him. For instance, the manna in the wilderness, the miracles wrought through Elijah and Elisha, the promise of the eschatological banquet (Isa. 55), and Wisdom's invitation to come to her dinner all come to appear as having aspects whereby they anticipate the life of Jesus. First Peter 1:10–12 presents the biblical prophets and Christian evangelists as participating in the same economy of salvation, although in different modes and temporal aspects. The author of Hebrews presents the wilderness generations of Israelites as participating in the same economy as his own contemporaries. They are the spiritual "ancestors" (Heb. 1:1; 3:7–9) of Hebrews' audience, and they are caught up the same economy of salvation.

*Fourth, a number of passages about the Word of God also accent people's interiority.* Jeremiah speaks of the Word of God as a reality within him (Jer. 20:9). In the new-covenant oracle, God promises to place his Word, his Torah, in his redeemed people: "I will put my law within them, and I will write it on their hearts" (31:33). Similarly, the apostolic proclamation described by Paul and Peter seems to be a way by which Jesus himself comes to dwell in believers by faith. The Word of God, Paul writes, is "at work in you believers" (1 Thess. 2:13).

The imagery of eating and food is often used to denote this "taking in" of the Word whereby it comes to have a kind of interior presence in people. The prophet Ezekiel receives the Word of God in his symbolic vision by eating a scroll (Ezek. 3:1–3). The prophet Jeremiah similarly declares, "Your words were found, and I ate them, and your words became to me a joy and the delight of my heart" (Jer. 15:16). The psalmist similarly speaks of tasting the "sweetness" of God's Word: "How sweet are your words to my taste, sweeter than honey to my mouth" (Ps. 119:103). While many other examples can be adduced, such expressions of the "delight" and "sweetness" of the Word suggest a kind of spiritual faith-experience of the Word of God, enjoyed by those who take in its reality. Recalling Wisdom's invitation to take in her teaching, Jesus invites people to believe in him, to take in his reality in faith, with the language of eating: "Whoever comes to me will never be hungry, and whoever believes in me will never be thirsty" (John 6:35).

These teachings about the Word of God and its associations with power and presence appear throughout both Testaments of the Christian Bible. They do so in multiple compositions from different authors, literary genres, and historical moments. We regard them as important components of the revelation of God, given in Scripture, and as providing sacred teaching.

Taken together, these various elements provide the substance and warrant for understanding Scripture as putting people in living and life-giving contact with the divine realities that it mediates. The words of Scripture mediate the Word of God to people, such that people can encounter and experience the Word and his life-giving power in the faith-filled reading of Scripture.

This is the understanding of Scripture that we will reflect on in part 2, where we explicate basic theological and philosophical principles that display the intelligibility of this understanding of Scripture and help us to grasp it better. By leading readers to a better grasp of this biblically grounded understanding of Scripture, we hope to provide a path for people to share the same kind of faith experience attested to by the psalmist, who finds delight, sweetness, and refreshment in the Word of God.

# PART 2

*Quaerens*
*Intellectum*

# 5

# God and the World

## *The Distinction*

As mentioned in the introduction, the exposition in part 2 can be compared to a ladder or staircase, with each chapter as a step presupposing the previous one. Since this chapter is the first step in our theological and philosophical reflections on how Scripture puts people into living and life-giving contact with God, we begin with the most fundamental of issues. Given that this understanding of Scripture involves God's mysterious presence and action in and through created realities, this understanding of Scripture requires us to reflect on the relationship between Creator and creation.

The ways in which one understands the Bible, the world, and God are deeply interconnected. One line of thinking in Christian tradition conceives of Scripture and the created world as "two books" written by God.[1] It is through these two books, Scripture and creation, that God teaches human beings. For instance, Augustine likens creation to a divinely authored book in this way: "Others, in order to find God, will read a book. Well, as a matter of fact there is a certain great big book, the book of created nature. Look carefully at it

---

1. See Francis Martin, "Revelation as Disclosure: Creation," in *Wisdom and Holiness, Science and Scholarship: Essays in Honor of Matthew L. Lamb*, ed. Michael Dauphinais and Matthew Levering (Naples, FL: Sapientia Press, 2007), 205. This chapter develops elements from this essay by Martin. See also Constant J. Mews, "The World as Text: The Bible and the Book of Nature in Twelfth-Century Theology," in *Scripture and Pluralism: Reading the Bible in the Religiously Plural Worlds of the Middle Ages and Renaissance*, ed. Thomas J. Heffernan and Thomas E. Burman, Studies in the History of Christian Traditions 123 (Leiden: Brill, 2005), 95–122.

top and bottom, observe it, read it. God did not make letters of ink for you to recognize him in; he set before your eyes all these things he has made. Why look for a louder voice? Heaven and earth cries out to you, 'God made me.'"[2]

Although creation and Scripture are not equivalents, Augustine holds that both are divinely given means by which human beings can come to know God. In the prologue to book 2 of *On the Trinity*, Augustine prays for assistance in "seeking out the substance of God, either through his scriptures or his creatures."[3] He then adds the following about Scripture and creation: "Both of these are offered us for our observation and scrutiny in order that in them he may be sought, he may be loved, who inspired the one and created the other."[4] God inspired the Scriptures and created the world as two means by which human beings can come to know something of him.

Among the Greek fathers, this basic tradition appears, albeit with different terminology, in Maximus the Confessor and his exegesis of the transfiguration.[5] In his *Ambiguum* 10, Maximus interprets the irradiated garments of Jesus in terms of Scripture and creation. Both Scripture and creation speak in a hidden manner of divine Word. Maximus writes, "In both cases He has been rightly covered with obscurity for our sake, so that we should not dare to approach unworthily what is beyond our comprehension, namely the words of Scripture, for He is the Word; or creation, for He is the creator, fashioner, and artisan."[6] Maximus continues, "Whoever wishes blamelessly to walk the straight road to God, stands in need of both the inherent spiritual knowledge of Scripture, and the natural contemplation of beings according to the spirit."[7]

Writing in the thirteenth century, Saint Bonaventure similarly speaks of the two books of creation and Scripture in his *The Journey of the Mind to God*. Commenting on the intellectual and spiritual ascent through the

2. Augustine, *Sermon* 68.6, in Augustine, *Sermons 51–94*, trans. Edmund Hill, OP, Works of Saint Augustine III/3 (Hyde Park, NY: New City, 1991), 225–26.

3. Augustine, *On the Trinity* 2 (prologue), in Augustine, *The Trinity*, trans. Edmund Hill, OP (Hyde Park, NY: New City, 1991), 97. Reference mentioned by Mews, "World as Text," 95.

4. Augustine, *On the Trinity* 2 (prologue) (Hill, 97).

5. We acknowledge Dr. Bogdan Bucur for his assistance with this text. On the important role of the transfiguration in Maximus's biblical interpretation, see Paul M. Blowers, *Maximus the Confessor: Jesus Christ and the Transfiguration of the World* (New York: Oxford University Press, 2016), 77–86; Blowers, "Exegesis of Scripture," in *The Oxford Handbook of Maximus the Confessor*, ed. Pauline Allen and Bronwen Neil (New York: Oxford University Press, 2015), 253–73, esp. 257–62.

6. Maximus the Confessor, *Ambiguum* 10.17.31, in Maximus the Confessor, *On Difficulties in the Church Fathers—The Ambigua*, trans. Nicholas Constas, 2 vols., Dumbarton Oaks Medieval Library (Cambridge, MA: Harvard University Press, 2014), 1:193.

7. Maximus the Confessor, *Ambiguum* 10.17.31 (Constas, 1:193, 195).

contemplation of order, Bonaventure writes that human beings learn "in the book of creation, the primacy, sublimity, and dignity of the First Principle . . . [and] in the book of the Scriptures, the order of divine laws, commands, and judgments."[8] Likewise, in his *Collations on the Six Days*, Bonaventure speaks of creation as a book, which human beings, because of sin, have lost the ability to read properly: "This book, the world, became as dead and deleted. And it was necessary that there be another book through which this one would be lighted up, so that it could receive the symbols of things. Such a book is Scripture."[9] For Bonaventure, the created world is like a book, which inspired Scripture enables us to read and interpret properly.

This conceiving of the book of Scripture as a kind of lens that enables the proper reading of the book of creation also appears in John Calvin's *Institutes of the Christian Religion*. Like Romans 1:18–19, Calvin speaks of God teaching humanity through creation, but also of human perception of this teaching becoming obscured by sin.[10] Calvin later relates the knowledge of God through creation to the knowledge of God that comes by Scripture. Specifically, Calvin likens creation to a book, which an individual with weak eyes can read only with the assistance of glasses (i.e., Scripture): "Just as old or bleary-eyed men and those with weak vision, if you thrust before them a most beautiful volume, even if they recognize it to be some sort of writing, yet can scarcely construe two words, but with the aid of spectacles will begin to read distinctly; so Scripture, gathering up the otherwise confused knowledge of God in our minds, having dispersed our dullness, clearly shows us the true God."[11] For Calvin as for Bonaventure, the book of Scripture provides the proper lens for reading the teaching of God in the book of creation.[12]

The same tradition of the two books is voiced (albeit with a different twist) by Galileo in his "Letter to the Grand Duchess Christina," written in 1615. Galileo appeals to this tradition in order to dissociate the study of natural

8. Bonaventure, *The Journey of the Mind to God* 1.15, ed. Stephen F. Brown, trans. Philotheus Boehner, OFM (Indianapolis: Hackett, 1993), 10.

9. Bonaventure, *Collations on the Six Days* 13.12, in *The Works of Bonaventure*, vol. 5, trans. José de Vinck (Paterson, NJ: St. Anthony Guild Press, 170), 190–91; also noted in Martin, "Revelation as Disclosure," 206n3.

10. John Calvin, *Institutes of the Christian Religion* 1.5.1–12, in Calvin, *Calvin: Institutes of the Christian Religion*, ed. John T. McNeill, trans. Ford Lewis Battles, Library of Christian Classics (Louisville: Westminster John Knox, 1960), 1:51–66.

11. Calvin, *Institutes* 1.6.1 (Battles, 70).

12. In this way, there is some affinity between this identification of Scripture as a lens by which to view the world rightly and George Lindbeck's famous expression that Scripture "absorbs the world"—that is, it provides the master horizon into which all other discourses are to be integrated. Quotation from George A. Lindbeck, *The Nature of Doctrine: Religion and Theology in a Postliberal Age* (Philadelphia: Westminster, 1984), 118.

phenomena from theological and scriptural considerations, famously remarking, "The intention of the Holy Ghost is to teach us how one goes to heaven, not how heaven goes."[13] And elsewhere: "I think that in discussions of physical problems we ought to begin not from the authority of scriptural passages but from sense-experiences and necessary demonstrations; for the holy Bible and the phenomena of nature proceed alike from the divine Word, the former as the dictate of the Holy Ghost and the latter as the observant executrix of God's commands."[14] While he does not use the language of "books," Galileo goes on to speak of nature and Scripture as two means by which human beings learn about God: "Nor is God any less excellently revealed in Nature's actions than in the sacred statements of the Bible."[15]

A key insight in this line of thinking is that the ways in which one understands the world and the Bible with respect to God are closely interrelated. How one conceives of the relationship between God and the world will necessarily impact the ways in which one understands the world and the Bible in relation to God and each other. Accordingly, our reflections on Scripture as putting people in contact with God must attend to the relationship between God and the world.

In this chapter and the next, we reflect (theologically and philosophically) on the relationship between Creator and creation as the basic setting in which this understanding of Scripture needs to be situated. The doctrine of creation is the indispensable basis for all Christian theological thinking, because, as Robert Sokolowski writes, it "defines how we are to understand God, how we are to understand the world, and how we are to understand the relationship between the world and God."[16] Therefore, all theologically related topics, such as the Bible's capacity to put people in contact with divine realities, must be understood within the horizon provided by the doctrine of creation. The need for a theologically sound grasp of the Creator-creation relationship becomes all the more pressing because of aberrant understandings of this relationship that arose in the early modern period. Such aberrant accounts

---

13. Galileo Galilei, "Letter to the Grand Duchess Christina," in *Discoveries and Opinions of Galileo*, trans. Stillman Drake (Garden City, NY: Doubleday, 1957), 186.

14. Galilei, "Letter to the Grand Duchess Christina," in Drake, *Discoveries and Opinions*, 182.

15. Galilei, "Letter to the Grand Duchess Christina," in Drake, *Discoveries and Opinions*, 183. For support, Galileo quotes Tertullian: "We conclude that God is known first through Nature, and then again, more particularly, by doctrine; by Nature in His works, and by doctrine in His revealed word." Drake, *Discoveries and Opinions*, 183, quoting Tertullian, *Against Marcion* 2.18.

16. Robert Sokolowski, "Creation and Christian Understanding," in *Christian Faith and Human Understanding: Studies on the Eucharist, Trinity, and the Human Person* (Washington, DC: Catholic University of America Press, 2006), 38.

of the Creator-creation relationship can skew how we think about God's activity in and through Scripture.

## The Distinction between God and the World

### The Distinction

An essential element in the biblical witness concerning God as the Creator of all things is that God and the world (i.e., "everything that is not divine") are radically distinct.[17] The Creator neither is part of the creation nor can be thought of as any kind of thing. The importance of "the distinction between God and the world" has been variously explored by an ecumenical range of authors such as Kathryn Tanner, David Bentley Hart, and Robert Sokolowski.[18] Given the significance of Sokolowski's contributions for this project as a whole, we will focus primarily on his exposition and refer to this understanding of the relationship between God and the world simply as "the Distinction."

Sokolowski argues that biblical revelation conveys a particular understanding of the relationship between the divine and the world, which is not identical with how other religions and philosophical systems understand it.[19] Sokolowski articulates the Distinction through a series of contrasts as to how the divine is understood in biblical and nonbiblical religions.[20] In philosophies or religions that do not develop out of the biblical tradition, the gods or the divine are reckoned among things in the world or are defined in relation to the world. Whether in a religious register (e.g., Zeus, Hera, and Apollo) or a philosophical register (e.g., Plato's the One or Aristotle's Prime Mover), the divine is considered the best or highest part of the whole of things, or it is defined by its relation to the world. In nonbiblical religion, Sokolowski writes,

17. Sokolowski, "Creation and Christian Understanding," 40.

18. See Kathryn Tanner, *God and Creation in Christian Theology: Tyranny or Empowerment* (Minneapolis: Augsburg Fortress, 1988); David Bentley Hart, *The Experience of God: Being, Consciousness, Bliss* (New Haven: Yale University Press, 2013); Hart, *The Hidden and the Manifest: Essays in Theology and Metaphysics* (Grand Rapids: Eerdmans, 2017); Robert Sokolowski, *The God of Faith and Reason: Foundations of Christian Theology* (Notre Dame, IN: University of Notre Dame Press, 1982), 1–30; Sokolowski, *Eucharistic Presence: A Study in the Theology of Disclosure* (Washington, DC: Catholic University of America Press, 1993), 34–54; Sokolowski, "Creation and Christian Understanding," 38–50.

19. The remainder of this paragraph first appeared in William M. Wright IV, "The Doctrine of God and the Liturgical *Res* in John's Gospel: Reading John 8:12–20 with the Theology of Disclosure," *Nova et Vetera*, English edition 12 (2014): 951. The present text has been adjusted slightly.

20. Sokolowski, *God of Faith and Reason*, 12–19.

"the divine, even in its most ultimate form, is never conceived as capable of being without the world. It is divine by being differentiated from what is not divine and by having an influence on what is not divine."[21]

To elaborate on Sokolowski's example, consider the gods and goddesses in Greek and Roman mythology.[22] The gods are understood to be the most powerful beings within the world. They are the immortals, who are more powerful and more intelligent than human beings. What makes the gods different from the mortals is that the gods have more of any given quality (e.g., more life, more strength, more wisdom) than the mortals do. The key point is that the difference between humans and the gods is a *matter of degree*—the gods have to a greater degree the same qualities that human beings have.

The biblical doctrine of creation, by contrast, entails a different under-standing of God and the world. The difference between human beings and God, for example, is *not* that God is the smartest and strongest of all things, as if the difference were a matter of degree. Rather, the difference between God and creation is a matter of radical distinction and otherness. God is totally independent of the world. The Creator is not part of the creation, and creation owes its entire existence to its Creator.

Even though we are speaking in philosophical terms, this basic premise—the distinction between God and the world—informs a variety of biblical texts. For instance, when God gives the Ten Commandments to the people Israel at Mount Sinai, he instructs them, "You shall not make for yourself an idol, whether in the form of anything that is in heaven above, or that is on the earth beneath, or that is in the water under the earth. You shall not bow down to them or worship them" (Exod. 20:4–5). The Israelites are not to make idols or depict the Lord in the image of any created thing. The reason for this is that to depict God in the form of some created thing (e.g., the golden calf; cf. Exod. 32:4) would be to identify the Creator with some part of the creation. It obscures the radical distinction between God and the world. Unlike the gods of the gentile nations, who often are closely associated or identified with natural forces and realities, the God of Israel is not to be confused in any way with things in the world. Thus, the Wisdom of Solomon cites as the principal error of idolatry this confusion of Creator and creation (Wis. 13:1–2). Paul likewise sees gentile idolatry as a critical consequence of gentiles' fundamental denial of the Creator, some knowledge of whom is

21. Sokolowski, *God of Faith and Reason*, 18.
22. Hart (*Experience of God*, 28–41) does something similar in contrasting "God" and "the gods."

available to them in creation: "They exchanged the truth about God for a lie and worshiped and served the creature rather than the Creator" (Rom. 1:25).

The distinction between God and the world also informs the biblical understanding of "holiness." Ingredient to the biblical notion of holiness is being set apart. The people Israel are called to be "a priestly kingdom and a holy nation" (Exod. 19:6), who are to live according to God's covenantal instructions, the Torah, and not like the nations (Lev. 18:2–5). The Lord thus instructs Israel, "You shall be holy, for I the LORD your God am holy" (Lev. 19:2). By living according to the Torah (and not like the nations), the people Israel will be a "holy people," a people set apart, and in doing so, they will show forth the holiness of the radically transcendent God to the world.

The incarnation of God in Jesus of Nazareth modifies our understanding of the Distinction.[23] Sokolowski observes that the basic understanding of God and the world set forth across the Old Testament seems to rule out the possibility that God could become human.[24] Such a notion would seem to run afoul of the "otherness" of God and the imperative not to confuse God with creatures. The Christian belief in the incarnation presupposes the biblical understanding of God and creation and at the same time modifies it. Sokolowski writes that in the incarnation, "God is revealed to be so transcendent that he can enter into his creation without suffering limitation in his divinity. His divinity is such that he can become man without ceasing to be God."[25] The distinction between God and the world, revealed in the Old Testament, undergoes an "intensification" in the New Testament.[26] Accordingly, Sokolowski tends to speak of "the Christian distinction between God and the world" so as to distinguish it from the similar, though not identical, understanding of God in the Old Testament.[27]

### Implications of the Distinction

The Distinction, and especially as it is modified by the incarnation, has far-reaching implications for Christian theological thinking. For present purposes, we will highlight four of them.

First, the Distinction entails that God "is not a 'kind' of thing at all."[28] God is neither a kind of being among other beings in the world nor a being

23. Sokolowski, *Eucharistic Presence*, 52–54.
24. Sokolowski, *Eucharistic Presence*, 53.
25. Sokolowski, *Eucharistic Presence*, 54.
26. Sokolowski, *Eucharistic Presence*, 54.
27. So Sokolowski, *God of Faith and Reason*, 24.
28. Sokolowski, *God of Faith and Reason*, 42.

external to the world. To think of God in such a way would be to misconceive of the God of biblical revelation in terms of a natural understanding of the divine. Rather, biblical revelation presents us with God as radically distinct from and independent of the world, and accordingly, he cannot be conceived of as any kind of "thing." Furthermore, since God is not a thing, we should not conceive of God's distinction from the world as a matter of distance (even infinite distance) between two things. Indeed, the complementary flip side of God's radical transcendence is God's immanence, or intimate presence, to all things. Since God is not a thing, God does not take up space, exist in time, or rival things in any respect. God is everywhere, entirely, and at all times according to his unique mode of presence. As we will discuss in the next chapter, God is the pure, unlimited act of existing from which all things derive their own existence, and accordingly, the transcendent God can be most intimately present to his creation: "Quite literally nothing stands between [God] and that which he makes."[29]

A second implication of the Distinction is that God's relationship to the world is one of "noncompetitiveness"—an aspect very much thematized by Sokolowski's student Robert Barron.[30] We can appreciate this noncompetiveness through a consideration of the doctrine of the incarnation. Sokolowski calls attention to the dogmatic formula of the Council of Chalcedon, which defines the mystery of the incarnation: "One and the same Lord Jesus Christ, the only begotten Son, must be acknowledged in two natures, without confusion or change, without division or separation. The distinction between the natures was never abolished by their union but rather the character proper to each of the two natures was preserved as they came together in one Person and one hypostasis."[31] The formula speaks of the union of the divine and human natures of the incarnate Son of God as being "without confusion or change, without division of separation." In the incarnation, the divinity of Christ does not blend with his human nature into a divine-human hybrid (as in monophysitism) or exist as a separate thing from his humanity (as in Nestorianism). Rather, the human and divine natures each retain their respective integrities when united together in the divine person of the Son of God.

29. Robert Barron, *Exploring Catholic Theology: Essays on God, Liturgy, and Evangelization* (Grand Rapids: Baker Academic, 2015), 111.

30. Robert Barron, *Thomas Aquinas: Spiritual Master* (New York: Crossroad, 1996, 2008), 57. See also Barron, *The Priority of Christ: Toward a Postliberal Catholicism* (Grand Rapids: Brazos, 2007), 17, 204–7, 226–29; Barron, "To See according to the Icon of Jesus Christ: Reflections on the Catholic Intellectual Tradition," in *Exploring Catholic Theology*, 65–67.

31. Heinrich Denzinger, *Compendium of Creeds, Definitions, and Declarations on Matters of Faith and Morals*, ed. Peter Hünermann, Robert Fastiggi, and Anne Englund Nash, 43rd ed. (San Francisco: Ignatius, 2012 [2010]), §302. See Sokolowski, *God of Faith and Reason*, 35–36.

Hence, the formula's articulation that the "distinction between the natures was never abolished by their union but rather the character proper to each of the two natures was preserved as they came together in one Person."

Sokolowski argues that the mystery of the incarnation as defined by Chalcedon is intelligible only within the horizon provided by the Distinction. Sokolowski writes, "If the Incarnation is to be possible, the divine nature must be taken as not a worldly nature, as not one of the kinds of beings that are encompassed by the whole."[32] If Christ's Godhood were "a thing" in the world, like his human nature, it would have to exist in some kind of rivalry with his human nature. As Barron explains the matter, "A creature can enter into the reality of another creature only in an aggressive and domineering sense, the former forcing the latter as it were to cede something of itself."[33] If construed as a kind of thing, Christ's divinity would lead to such a "domineering" of his human nature and thus compromise its dignity and integrity. But since the Godhood of Christ, rightly understood, is not "a competing part of nature or a part of the world," it can be united to a human nature without any compromising of the integrity of either his humanity or his divinity.[34]

A critical point revealed by the incarnation, Sokolowski argues, is that "God does not destroy the natural necessities of things he becomes involved with."[35] God does not compete with created realities for anything, as if God were one "thing" exercising power over against another thing, like two competitors or rivals. God is not like one of the Greek gods, who forces his or her will on people or who overpowers them with greater strength. Rather, just as Christ's human nature retains all of its integrity and loses nothing when united to his divinity, so too do the realities of creation retain all of their integrity when God exercises causal power vis-à-vis the world.

Accordingly, this noncompetitive relationship between God and the world, which the Distinction implies, is fundamentally one of nonviolence.[36] God is so transcendent that he can act in creation, be present to it, and even become united to it in the incarnation without impinging on the integrity or freedom of created realities.

A third implication of the Distinction is the incomprehensibility, or mysteriousness, of God. As the Creator radically transcends creation, so does he radically transcend the abilities and categories of finite creatures. God's

---

32. Sokolowski, *Eucharistic Presence*, 53.
33. Barron, *Thomas Aquinas*, 57.
34. Sokolowski, *God of Faith and Reason*, 36.
35. Sokolowski, *God of Faith and Reason*, 36.
36. So Robert Barron, "The Metaphysics of Coinherence: A Meditation on the Essence of the Christian Message," in *Exploring Catholic Theology*, 31–37; Barron, *Thomas Aquinas*, 57–58.

nature or essence is such that creatures can never comprehend or exhaustively grasp it. Affirmations of the mysteriousness and incomprehensibility of God appear throughout the creedal Christian tradition. For instance, in his *Letter to Ablabius*, Gregory of Nyssa teaches that "the divine nature is unnameable and unutterable," and what humans can know or say about God pertains to the divine power (which is itself founded on the divine nature) by way of observing the divine power's effects produced in the world.[37] Comparably, Thomas Aquinas later writes, "We cannot know in what consists the essence of God, nevertheless in [theology] we make use of His effects, either of nature or of grace."[38]

Human thinking and speaking is primarily ordered toward the world and the things within it—and God is not one of them. Since the Creator is not part of the creation, human beings cannot think or speak about God in the same manner that we do about things in the world. Accordingly, the Distinction requires that all human thinking and speaking about God be highly qualified. Our discourse about God needs to be adjusted from its ordinary use and provenance within the world and transposed into the setting of the Distinction.[39] We need to be highly nuanced and flexible in our thinking and speaking about God (i.e., we speak analogously of God) and ever attentive to the uniqueness of the Distinction and the ineffable nature of God.

These modifications in thinking and speaking that the Distinction necessitates allow for the mysteries of faith to be received as such: "The Christian distinction between God and the world serves to permit the other mysteries to be thought as mysteries and not as incoherences. The Christian understanding of God is necessary to open the space within which the other Christian mysteries can be believed."[40] As suggested previously, the union of two natures in the single person of the Son of God is intelligible only within the horizon of the Distinction and the understanding of God that it entails. Proper consideration of the realities of faith requires attentiveness to the Distinction and the conceptual and linguistic shifts that it requires. The

37. Gregory of Nyssa, "Concerning We Should Think of Saying That There Are Not Three Gods to Ablabius," in *The Trinitarian Controversy*, ed. and trans. William G. Rusch (Philadelphia: Fortress, 1980), 152–53, quotation from 152. For secondary discussion, see Lewis Ayres, *Nicaea and Its Legacy: An Approach to Fourth-Century Trinitarian Theology* (Oxford: Oxford University Press, 2004), 351–56.

38. Thomas Aquinas, *Summa Theologica* I, q. 1, a. 7, ad. 1, in Thomas Aquinas, *Summa Theologica*, trans. Fathers of the English Dominican Province, 3 vols. (New York: Benziger, 1947–48).

39. Sokolowski, *God of Faith and Reason*, 31; Sokolowski, "Creation and Christian Understanding," 45–46; Sokolowski, *Eucharistic Presence*, 48–51.

40. Sokolowski, *God of Faith and Reason*, 37.

failure to attend properly to the Distinction can result in misunderstanding or even heresy.[41]

A fourth implication of the Distinction concerns the giftedness of creation. If God exists independently of creation and has done so from all eternity in absolute perfection and goodness, then God does not need the world. Sokolowski writes, "In Christian belief we understand the world as that which might not have been, and correlatively we understand God as capable of existing, in undiminished goodness and greatness, even if the world had not been."[42] Creation is a totally free act of God's will. God is under no necessity to create, and the whole of things does not have to exist. Moreover, since God exists in total perfection apart from the world, the existence of the world does not add anything to God's perfection and greatness (since, by definition, if something is perfect, it lacks nothing). Thus, God does not profit or benefit from the world in any way.

If God does not have to create and he does not gain anything from creation, then the fact that God brought the world into existence in the first place means that creation is a pure *gift* of God's selfless goodness. Creation, at its deepest levels, is a unique kind of gift, and accordingly, giftedness is ingredient to the very nature of created reality.

## A Point of Contrast: A Supreme Being and a Closed System

The importance of the Distinction for theological thinking today becomes even more important in light of aberrant construals of the relationship between God and the world that came to prominence in seventeenth-to-eighteenth-century thought and continue to the present day. Historically, a complex set of shifts in late medieval and early modern thinking about God resulted in what William Placher has called the "Domestication of Transcendence."[43] A key feature of this "domestication" has been the tendency to think of God as a kind of thing within or outside the world. Put differently, there came to be in modernity the theologically aberrant trend to conceive of God, as David Bentley Hart puts it, as one of "the gods."[44]

These changes resulted from a variety of intellectual, cultural, political, and social factors, and we make no attempt here to map their development.[45]

41. Sokolowski, *God of Faith and Reason*, 34–37.
42. Sokolowski, *God of Faith and Reason*, 19.
43. William C. Placher, *The Domestication of Transcendence: How Modern Thinking about God Went Wrong* (Louisville: Westminster John Knox, 1996).
44. See Hart, *Experience of God*, 28–41.
45. In addition to the works cited in this section, we have found the following especially helpful and illuminating: Louis Dupré, *Passage to Modernity: An Essay in the Hermeneutics*

At the risk of oversimplification, however, we will sketch very basically some factors contributing to this aberrant understanding of God as a thing within or outside the world. This understanding of God deviates from the biblical and classic Christian tradition, and accordingly, we mark it out as a conceptual road better not taken.

A helpful point from which to consider this shift is the development of the mechanical view of the cosmos, which emerged in connection with the "new science" of Galileo (1564–1642), Kepler (1571–1630), and Newton (1642–1726). On this account, the cosmos was likened to a giant, self-contained machine. It is composed of bits of matter that act on and react to one another, and they do so according to blind, impersonal forces of nature.[46] As Galileo and Newton demonstrated, these forces of nature can be observed experimentally and expressed mathematically, and they apply universally.[47] The world came to be conceived of as a closed system that operates according to its own internal and impersonal material components and laws.[48]

This mechanical view of the cosmos, which displaced the Ptolemaic model of the heavenly spheres, went hand in glove with the successes and appeal of inductive, empirical method. Important in this regard is the work of Francis Bacon (1561–1626). Bacon opens his *New Organon* by foregrounding the place of empirical observation: "Man . . . can do and understand so much and so much only as he has observed in fact or in thought of the course of nature; beyond this he neither knows anything nor can do anything."[49] Significant is the association that Bacon makes between knowing and doing. For

---

of *Nature and Culture* (New Haven: Yale University Press, 1993); Dupré, *The Enlightenment and the Intellectual Foundations of Modern Culture* (New Haven: Yale University Press, 2004); Dupré, *The Quest of the Absolute: Birth and Decline of European Romanticism* (Notre Dame, IN: University of Notre Dame Press, 2013). Dupré offers a succinct overview of his larger case in his *Religion and the Rise of Modern Culture* (Notre Dame, IN: University of Notre Dame Press, 2008). See also Michael J. Buckley, SJ, *At the Origins of Modern Atheism* (New Haven: Yale University Press, 1987); Buckley, *Denying and Disclosing God: The Ambiguous Progress of Modern Atheism* (New Haven: Yale University Press, 2004). Also very helpful is the analysis given in Michael Maria Waldstein, "The Self-Critique of the Historical-Critical Method in Cardinal Ratzinger's Erasmus Lecture," *Modern Theology* 28 (2012): 732–47.

46. See Edward Feser, *The Last Superstition: A Refutation of the New Atheism* (South Bend, IN: St. Augustine's Press, 2008), 178–79.

47. Frederick Copleston, SJ, *A History of Philosophy*, vol. 3, *Late Medieval and Renaissance Philosophy* (New York: Image, 1993), 287–91; Joyce Appleby, Lynn Hunt, and Margaret Jacob, *Telling the Truth about History* (New York: Norton, 1994), 19–22.

48. See Francis Martin, "Historical Criticism and New Testament Teaching on the Imitation of Christ," in *Sacred Scripture: The Disclosure of the Word* (Naples, FL: Sapientia Press, 2006), 55–63; Martin, "Some Aspects of Biblical Studies since Vatican II: The Contribution and Challenge of *Dei Verbum*," in *Sacred Scripture*, 237–42; Martin, "Revelation as Disclosure," 233–37.

49. Francis Bacon, *The New Organon* 1.1, in *Francis Bacon: A Selection of His Works*, ed. Sidney Warhaft (Toronto: Macmillan, 1965), 331.

Bacon, the purpose of the inductive study of the world is to acquire control over nature and so manipulate it. Knowledge, in other words, is for power: "Human knowledge and human power meet in one, for where the cause is not known the effect cannot be produced. Nature to be commanded must be obeyed."[50] By learning how nature works, human beings are able to acquire power over it, and the progressive acquisition of such power leads to practical applications and the improvement of life in the world.[51] Knowledge, on this account, becomes instrumental: humans seek to know the world in order to bring about some practical effect.

This practical end also marks a shift away from classic philosophical inquiry, wherein the contemplation of the truth was reckoned as an end in itself.[52] The interest in instrumental reasoning had its own conceptual forebears, including the so-called *via moderna* associated with William of Ockham (ca. 1290–1349) and the nominalist movement, which deliberately distinguished itself from classical philosophical inquiry, the *via antiqua*.[53] To illustrate this shift away from classical thought, both Edward Feser and David Bentley Hart reference Aristotle's four causes.[54] Aristotle famously identified four causes that give an account of a thing's being.[55] The four causes are the following: the material cause (the stuff—or potentiality—out of which a thing can be composed), the formal cause (a thing's intelligible nature or principle of identity, which accounts for its being *this kind* of thing), the efficient cause (that which brings a thing to exist in a certain way), and the final cause (those effects that a thing tends to produce by virtue of the kind of thing it is).[56] Both Feser and Hart point out that the modern interest in inductive method and applied science led to a preoccupation with (and reconceiving of) material

---

50. Bacon, *New Organon* 1.3 (Warhaft, 331).

51. Technological progress can also, on the other hand, lead to the destruction of human beings and their world. See Pope Francis, *Laudato Si*, §§101–36; Pope Benedict XVI, *Caritas in Veritate*, §§68–77; William M. Wright IV, "Echoes of Biblical Apocalyptic in the Encyclical Teaching of Benedict XVI," *Gregorianum* 95 (2014): 548–51.

52. See Josef Pieper, *Leisure: The Basis of Culture*, trans. Gerald Malsbary (South Bend, IN: St. Augustine's Press, 1998), 8–26.

53. Copleston, *History of Philosophy*, 3:10–23.

54. See Feser, *Last Superstition*, 174–80; Feser, *Aquinas: A Beginner's Guide* (Oxford: Oneworld, 2009), 38–42; Hart, *Experience of God*, 54–55. Their accounts are very similar, and we follow them in what follows above.

55. For "cause," we offer the succinct definition given by D. Q. McInerny: "One thing is said to be the cause of another thing because (a) it explains the very existence of that thing, or (b) it explains why the thing exists in this or that particular way, the 'mode' of its existence." McInerny, *Being Logical: A Guide to Good Thinking* (New York: Random House, 2004), 27.

56. Cf. Aristotle, *Physics* 2.3.194b–195b; Aristotle, *Metaphysics* 4 (Δ).2.1013a–1014a. For a helpful summary treatment of Aristotle's four causes that informs our presentation, see Feser, *Aquinas*, 16–23.

and efficient causes.[57] By attending to what things are made of (material causality) as well as how they are assembled and operate (efficient causality), human beings can better understand things in order to manipulate them for desired ends. Since formal and final causes cannot be empirically observed or analyzed, they fall outside the purview of the dominant mode of inductive scientific inquiry. As the natural sciences became the model and standard for "what counts" as human knowing, formal and final causality fell into further disrepute. But as Feser and Hart both argue, modern thought has not so much disproven the reality of formal and final causes as chosen to ignore them and rule out their rational consideration by methodological (and political) fiat.[58]

As a scientific theory, a mechanical conception of the cosmos is neither incompatible with the understanding of God entailed by the Distinction nor an intrinsic impediment to theism—although quantum mechanics has shown on scientific grounds that the mechanical model of the cosmos is inadequate and flawed.[59] For our purposes, problems come to the fore with inadequate *theological* responses of how to situate God vis-à-vis the mechanical account of nature. As a result of many factors, such as the construal of the world as a closed mechanical system as well as the disregard of formal and final causality, God came to be seen solely as an external, efficient cause who creates the great cosmic machine, puts it in motion, and remains external to its internal workings. Isaac Newton, for example, articulates this conception of God as an external cause that is responsible for the local motion of the planets: "The Motions which the Planets now have could not spring from any natural Cause alone, but were impressed by an intelligent Agent."[60] This reconfiguration of God as the external, efficient cause of the cosmos segued into deism and eventually into modern atheism. Louis Dupré summarizes the matter: "Seventeenth-century thinkers, following the systems of Descartes and Newton, replaced traditional ways of symbolizing the relation between the finite and its transcendent source by a type of causality conceived on a mechanistic model. God became, once again, a remote Prime Mover responsible for the motion of the universe. Deism was the inevitable outcome of this distant

57. Feser, *Last Superstition*, 178; Hart, *Experience of God*, 55–58.

58. See Feser, *Last Superstition*, 71–72, 175–77; Hart, *Experience of God*, 55–57.

59. Copleston, *History of Philosophy*, 3:288. Very helpful here is the work of distinguished particle physicist Stephen Barr. Barr has argued that scientific materialism has developed in concert with this model, but it is not a necessary part of it—materialism is a philosophical idea, not a scientific one. Moreover, Barr notes how discoveries in quantum mechanics have indicated the need to revise this mechanical conception. See Stephen M. Barr, *Modern Physics and Ancient Faith* (Notre Dame, IN: University of Notre Dame Press, 2003), 1–37.

60. Isaac Newton, "Letter to Rev. Dr. Richard Bentley," in *The Portable Enlightenment Reader*, ed. Isaac Kramnick (New York: Penguin, 1995), 98.

relation to God. Atheism was to follow soon as the need for an external source of mechanical motion ceased to exist."[61]

Instead of being conceived of as the transcendent, yet intimately present, source for the world's ongoing existence (a point to be discussed further in the next chapter), God came to be seen as extrinsic to the workings of the world. Like the proverbial clockmaker who creates his clock and leaves it to run on its own, God fashions the cosmos and puts it in motion, but he remains outside the closed system. God's causal activity with respect to the world comes by way of starting it up and (possibly) by miraculous intervention from its outside. On this account, Hart writes, "The cosmos did not live and move and have its being in him [as it did in traditional theism]; he lived and moved and had his being in it, as a discrete entity among other entities, a separate and definite thing, a mere paltry Supreme Being."[62]

This modern understanding of God stands in striking contrast with the understanding of God entailed by the Distinction. For instance, the Distinction holds that God, the Creator, is not part of the creation, nor is God some kind of thing beside the world. Since the Creator is not a thing, he is both radically other to creation and yet most intimately present to it. Moreover, as discussed above, the distinction between God and the world is unlike distinctions between things in the world, because God is not a kind of thing to be distinguished from the world as another kind of thing (like the craftsman and his artifact are distinguished as two separate things). But when God comes to be seen solely as the external efficient cause who creates the closed cosmic system, God comes to be understood as a being and a cause in contradistinction to the being and causality of the world. As Placher points out, this account involves what Kathryn Tanner calls a "contrastive" view of God's transcendence:[63] "Divinity characterized in terms of a direct contrast with certain sorts of being or with the world of non-divine being as a whole is brought down to the level of the world and the beings within it in virtue of that very opposition: God becomes one being among others within a single order."[64] When God so comes to be understood in contrast to the world, God inevitably comes to be understood as one kind of thing in contrast to another kind of thing.

The Distinction also entails a noncompetitive relation between God and creation. Since God exists in total perfection apart from the world, it is not true either that God needs the world or that the world adds anything to God's

61. Dupré, *Enlightenment*, 243.
62. Hart, *Experience of God*, 62.
63. So Placher, *Domestication*, 111n1.
64. Tanner, *God and Creation*, 45.

perfection or that God rivals things for time, space, or causal power. Moreover, as the Chalcedonian definition of the incarnation entails, God does not destroy the natural integrity and powers of those things with which he becomes involved. Not only is God intimately present to all created things, but also his presence and causal activity to his creatures is nonviolent. However, in what Tanner calls the contrastive view of transcendence, God is a kind of thing, who is external to the closed system as another kind of thing. God's activity in the world comes to be seen as interventions into a closed system by a being who is external to the workings of the world. Such interventions from without can only be reckoned as a violent act. Thus, for instance, David Hume defines a miracle as "a violation of the laws of nature."[65] So understood, God's causality and the causality of the things within the world rival each other—they are situated over against each other and are thus enmeshed in a cosmic power play.

Last, when God and the world are understood contrastively, as two kinds of competing things, faith and reason likewise come to be seen as rivals. Sokolowski observes that for the ancient Greeks, philosophy and religion were competitors, for each gave a rival account of the whole of things, which included the divine.[66] However, the understanding of God that the Distinction entails allows for revealed faith and human reason to be fundamentally compatible, while each retains its respective integrities. But when the Distinction came to be obscured in modern thinking about God, the divine came to be seen as a part of the whole of things, and a modern version of the ancient Greek rivalry between theology and philosophy arose in the so-called modern conflict between science and religion. Indeed, as many have pointed out, this aberrant understanding of God in modern thought ends up being the center point in much contemporary debate between theism and atheism.[67] But such framing of this debate turns on an understanding of God that the classic Christian tradition would itself reject! As Herbert McCabe bluntly puts the matter: if to be an atheist is to deny "that there is some grand architect of the universe who designed it . . . that there is a Top Person in the universe who issues arbitrary decrees for the rest of the persons and enforces them because he is the most powerful being around . . . then I and Thomas Aquinas and a whole Christian tradition are atheistic too."[68] This construal of the world

65. David Hume, "Essays and Treatises on Several Subjects," in Kramnick, *Portable Enlightenment Reader*, 109. Cf. Placher, *Domestication*, 135–38.
66. Robert Sokolowski, "Autonomy of Philosophy," in *Christian Faith and Human Understanding*, 13–15, 17–18.
67. So Hart, *Experience of God*, 13–45; Robert Barron, "Thomas Aquinas and Why the Atheists Are Right," in *Exploring Catholic Theology*, 17–29.
68. Herbert McCabe, OP, *God Matters* (London: Continuum, 2005), 7.

as a closed system and the aberrant understanding of God in relation to the closed system can also affect how one understands the Bible and God's active presence in and through it. But to discuss adequately the implications of the world as a closed system for understanding Scripture, we must first introduce some other principles and will do so in the next chapter. Accordingly, we will defer our discussion of the implications of the Creator-creation relationship for the understanding of Scripture until chapter 7.

## Looking Back and Looking Forward

The belief that Scripture can put people in living and life-giving contact with God needs to be situated within the horizon of the distinction between God and the world. Implicit in the doctrine of a free creation, the Distinction holds that God, as the Creator, radically transcends creation, while also being immanently present to it. The Creator is radically "other" to creation and exists independently of it in total perfection. Continuing to follow Sokolowski, we identified four key implications of the Distinction. First, the radically transcendent and ever-immanent God is not any kind of thing or being—the Creator of all things is not himself a thing. Second, the relationship between God and the world is one of noncompetition. Since the radically transcendent yet immanent Creator is not a thing, the Creator does not rival created realities in any way, nor does his action or presence compromise the natural integrity of the created things. Third, since God is not any kind of thing, human beings cannot think and talk about God like we think and talk about things in the world. Accordingly, all of our thinking and speaking about God needs to be flexible and highly qualified. Fourth, since God does not need the world to be God, the very existence of the world is a pure, selfless gift of God's goodness.

We can further appreciate the Distinction by distinguishing it from an understanding of the world as a closed system. A confluence of factors in the early modern period, including new scientific discoveries, the successes of inductive scientific method, and the disregard for formal and final causality, contributed to the thinking of the cosmos as a giant, self-enclosed machine. God came to be seen a kind of supreme being, existing over against the world solely as an external, efficient cause. On such a "contrastive understanding" (Tanner's expression) of God's transcendence, God is reckoned as a kind of being whose existence and causal activity compete with that of creatures. This understanding of God in relation to the world as a closed, mechanical system is inadequate. Scientifically, the inadequacy of the mechanistic model has been revealed by quantum mechanics, and theologically, this construal of the Creator-creation relationship deviates from that understood in classical biblical theism. For a variety of reasons, therefore, we do best to avoid approaching Scripture within the understanding of the world as a closed system and its attendant understanding of God.

Thus far, we have considered the Creator-creation relationship in largely theological terms. In the next chapter, we will fill out this picture by reflecting philosophically on created reality with some teachings of Saint Thomas Aquinas. Aquinas firmly believed that what human beings know by divine revelation and what we know by human reason cannot ever contradict each other (when both are properly understood). The reason for this is that all truth, whether divinely revealed or discovered by intellectual reflection on the world, is from God. Or, to return to the motif of "the two books" of the Bible and creation, what God teaches in one book cannot contradict what God teaches in his other book.

# 6

# The Metaphysics of the Created World

We have argued for the need to understand Scripture in light of the distinction between God and the world, an understanding that comes to light in biblical revelation. We have also appealed to the traditional theme of Scripture and creation as God's "two books." God teaches not only through divine revelation given in the book of Scripture but also in the book that is creation. Accordingly, our understanding of the world as created can be enhanced by philosophical reflection on the nature of created reality and its relationship to the Creator.

As mentioned in the introduction, all understandings of Scripture and its interpretation presuppose theological and philosophical ideas of one sort or another, and not all ideas are equally truthful. One such area of intellectual presupposition is what an interpreter holds, consciously or unconsciously, about the nature of the real world and its relationship (if any) to a deity. In other words, all biblical interpretation presupposes some sort of metaphysics.

A classic philosophical discipline, metaphysics is the study of the nature and basic structures of being qua being. It "seeks to understand all reality, all beings, in terms of the universal properties, laws, and ultimate causes of *being* as such."[1] Conventional topics in classic metaphysical inquiry are causes and effects, change, and the one and the many (i.e., how and why are things both similar and dissimilar to one another).

Metaphysics explores such topics with a distinctive mode of reasoning, and we need to have a sense of what metaphysical reasoning is (and is not) so as

1. W. Norris Clarke, SJ, introduction to *An Introduction to the Metaphysics of St. Thomas Aquinas*, trans. and ed. James F. Anderson (1953; repr., Washington, DC: Regnery, 1997), x.

not to fundamentally misconstrue things. Edward Feser helpfully elucidates the nature of metaphysical reasoning by comparing and contrasting it with mathematical reasoning and the kind of empirical reasoning employed in the natural sciences.[2] As Feser writes, scientific reasoning begins "from empirical premises and [draws] merely probabilistic conclusions," and mathematical reasoning begins "from purely conceptual premises and [draws] necessary conclusions."[3] Metaphysical reasoning incorporates aspects of each. Like the natural sciences, metaphysics will "take obvious, though empirical, starting points," and like mathematical reasoning, metaphysics will "try to show that from these starting points, together with certain conceptual premises, certain metaphysical conclusions follow necessarily."[4] In a sense, it is more helpful to think of metaphysical reasoning as being more like geometry (which deals with abstract objects and employs various axioms and postulates) than it is like the natural sciences, which proceed by empirical observation, hypothesis, and experiment (although, like the natural sciences, metaphysics begins from simple empirical observations).[5]

For a variety of reasons, metaphysical thinking is not popular in many intellectual circles today.[6] Some dismiss metaphysics because it does not proceed like the natural sciences or conform to its criteria of truthfulness. On this account, only the methods of empirical science (e.g., empirical observation, repeated experimentation, quantification) provide access to truth. Since metaphysical inquiry does not proceed by these methods, it cannot provide access to truth about reality. Others dismiss metaphysical inquiry in tandem with widespread intellectual and cultural trends that deny the very existence of "the truth" or the capacity of human beings to know reality on its own terms. One of the strongest influences on the contemporary distrust of any notion of "the truth" is nineteenth-century German classicist and philosopher Friedrich Nietzsche. According to Nietzsche, the notions of things such as objective truth, justice, or natural moral laws are all "idols"—they are human

2. Edward Feser, *The Last Superstition: A Refutation of the New Atheism* (South Bend, IN: St. Augustine's Press, 2008), 80–85. See also W. Norris Clarke, SJ, *The One and the Many: A Contemporary Thomistic Metaphysics* (Notre Dame, IN: University of Notre Dame Press, 2001), 14–23.

3. Feser, *Last Superstition*, 82–83.

4. Feser, *Last Superstition*, 83.

5. Feser, *Last Superstition*, 81–82.

6. See Clarke, *The One and the Many*, 8–14; Matthew Levering, *Proofs of God: Classical Arguments from Tertullian to Barth* (Grand Rapids: Baker Academic, 2016), 8–12, 167–99. As we do below, Thomas Joseph White likewise singles out postmodernism and positivism as sources of two contemporary objections to metaphysical thinking. See Thomas Joseph White, *Thomism for the New Evangelization*, 4–5, website of The Dominican Friars—England & Scotland, http://english.op.org/latest-news/free-book-on-the-new-evangelisation.

constructions that are as much an illusion as the very idea of God to which they relate.[7] According to this Nietzschean trajectory, things such as *the* truth and *the* good are not discovered by intellectual inquiry; rather, such notions are constructed by individuals and groups to serve their own interests. And if such notions are arbitrarily constructed in one way, they can be broken down and constructed in another way so as to suit a particular individual's or group's interests.

Against these trends, we hold that metaphysics not only is a legitimate philosophical project that can yield genuine knowledge about the world but also is, in a very real respect, unavoidable.[8] All intellectual and practical life necessarily involves some account of the nature of reality, of "how things are." Even the natural sciences presume certain metaphysical tenets (e.g., the existence and intrinsic intelligibility of an extramental world and its know-ability by the human mind) that are indispensable for their inquiry and that the natural sciences cannot prove by their own methods.[9] Indeed, the very denial of the possibility of metaphysics is itself a metaphysical claim of sorts; it is a claim about the whole of reality and our understanding of it—that is, "this is how it really is." While metaphysical inquiry may be informed by a classical system, such as Platonism or Aristotelianism, very often today it appears in the form of some kind of materialism (e.g., Marxism or scientific materialism) or in an au courant form of nominalism (e.g., some species of postmodernism).[10]

To reiterate, all readers of Scripture presuppose metaphysical ideas of one sort or another. Not all metaphysical ideas are equally true or conducive

7. For discussion, see Henri de Lubac, *The Drama of Atheist Humanism*, trans. Edith M. Riley, Anne Englund Nash, and Mark Sebanc (San Francisco: Ignatius, 1995), 42–72.

8. Cf. Thomas Joseph White, OP, *The Incarnate Lord: A Thomistic Study in Christology* (Washington, DC: Catholic University of America Press, 2015), 467–509. White (*Incarnate Lord*, 497) writes, "Every narration—including that of the materialist—makes an implicit appeal not only to human ontology and teleology but also to a deeper or more primal concern with the metaphysics of the real and the hierarchy of goods."

9. Given the historical patterning of the historical-critical method on the methods of the natural sciences (i.e., as a "scientific" discipline), it is worth mentioning the recognition that the natural sciences themselves depend on philosophical premises (such as causation and the know-ability of an intelligible world) "both to justify [their] presuppositions and to interpret [their] results." Citation from Edward Feser, *Scholastic Metaphysics: A Contemporary Introduction* (Heusenstamm: Editiones Scholasticae, 2014), 11.

10. Nominalism is a philosophical belief that denies that things have essential principles of being by nature (i.e., formal causes). Rather, the "nature" of things is conventional—that is, created by the human knower. The nominalist character of much postmodernism is noted by Louis Dupré, *Passage to Modernity: An Essay in the Hermeneutics of Nature and Culture* (New Haven: Yale University Press, 1993), 104–5; Aidan Nichols, OP, *Christendom Awake: On Re-energising the Church in Culture* (Edinburgh: T&T Clark, 1999), 55.

to understanding Scripture as putting people in living contact with divine reality. The metaphysical doctrines that an interpreter may (consciously or unconsciously) hold can have far-reaching effects on how he or she deals with other intellectual matters pertinent to understanding Scripture (e.g., human knowing, language, historical reality). For such reasons, interpreters of Scripture need to be mindful of the deeper philosophical ideas that inform their work.

In this chapter, we will take another "step" on the ladder of exposition in part 2 and examine certain metaphysical ideas of Thomas Aquinas and some of his expositors.[11] These metaphysical ideas, we contend, are both intellectually defensible on their own terms and helpful for grasping important aspects of how Scripture can put people in living contact with divine reality. We focus here on two important aspects of Aquinas's metaphysical analysis of the world as created: participation and relationality. These two metaphysical notions will be of great importance in our subsequent discussions of human knowing, language, and the realities of the divine economy.

## Participation

### Essence and the Act of Existing

When Thomas Aquinas was in his twenties and a student at the University of Paris, he wrote a philosophical treatise called *On Being and Essence*.[12] In chapter 4 of this work, he sets forth an important philosophical doctrine: the "real distinction" between essence and existence (or the act of existing). That is, there is a real distinction between what a thing is (its essence or *essentia*) and the power whereby it is (its act of existing or *esse*). Aquinas's argument is very subtle and involves some precise philosophical concepts. Here, we articulate the major contours of his argument as they pertain to our larger case.[13]

Aquinas holds that when we know something, we grasp its intelligibility (or essence) to some extent. But in that act of knowing something of a thing's

11. We emphasize that the discussion provided here will of necessity be a basic sketch. Given the aims of this book, we cannot provide an in-depth discussion of these metaphysical principles, every aspect or implication, or the historical mapping of these ideas, nor can we address objections to them. We look to provide an informed introduction to these principles, and for readers wishing to learn more, we recommend the secondary works cited in the notes.

12. See Thomas Aquinas, *On Being and Essence*, in *Thomas Aquinas: Selected Writings*, ed. and trans. Ralph McInerny (New York: Penguin, 1998), 30–49.

13. For a more in-depth analysis of Aquinas's work, see Joseph Bobik, *Aquinas on Being and Essence: A Translation and Interpretation* (Notre Dame, IN: University of Notre Dame Press, 1965).

essence, we do not grasp the thing's actually existing in the real world:[14] "Every essence or quiddity can be understood without its existence being understood: for I can understand what a man or a phoenix is and yet not know whether they exist in reality."[15] Aquinas's point here is that knowing *what* a thing is does not provide us with any information as to *whether* or not the thing actually exists. Consider this helpful illustration given by Edward Feser:

> Suppose a person had never before heard of lions, velociraptors, or unicorns, and you give him a thorough description of the natures of each. You then tell him that of these three creatures, one exists, one used to exist but is now extinct, and the third never existed; and you ask him to tell you which is which given what he now knows about their essences. He would, of course, be unable to do so. But then the existence of the creatures that exist must be really distinct from their essences, otherwise one *could* know of their existence merely from knowing their essences.[16]

A person can know something of what a thing is (i.e., its essence), but this, of itself, does not mean knowing that a thing exists in the real world (i.e., its act of existing). Accordingly, Aquinas concludes, "Therefore, it is clear that to exist is other than the essence or quiddity."[17] Aquinas, though, does leave open the possibility that there be a single reality wherein essence and the act of existing are identical.

Given Aquinas's identity theory of knowledge, wherein the same intelligibility in things known comes to exist cognitively in the mind of the knower, this distinction between essence and the act of existing obtains not just conceptually but also in reality.[18] A thing's essence and its act of existing are two distinct, constitutive coprinciples. Essence and the act of existing are not individually existing "things," like two parts of a puzzle. Rather, they are inner coprinciples of things that exist only in relation to each other.[19] To

14. So Bobik, *Aquinas on Being and Essence*, 163–64. Bobik explains Aquinas's point: "What is being said is that the one who knows *what a man is* does not *in and by that very knowing* know that men exist, although he most certainly does know it *in another way*, namely, by means of sense observation" (164).

15. Aquinas, *On Being and Essence* 4 (McInerny, 42).

16. Feser, *Scholastic Metaphysics*, 243.

17. Aquinas, *On Being and Essence* 4 (McInerny, 42).

18. So Bobik, *Aquinas on Being and Essence*, 167–68.

19. Frederick Copleston explains existence and essence as coprinciples in this way: "The two principles are not two physical things united together, but they are two constitutive principles which are concreated as principles of a particular being. There is no essence without existence and no existence without essence; the two are created together, and if its existence ceases, the concrete essence ceases to be." Copleston, *A History of Philosophy*, vol. 2, *From Augustine to Duns Scotus* (New York: Image, 1993), 333–34.

illustrate this point, David Oderberg adduces the example of the radius and circumference of a circle:[20] "The radius of a circle is really distinct from its circumference, as proved by the fact that the latter is twice the former multiplied by *pi*. Since the radius is *part* of the property *having a radius* and the circumference is part of the property *having a circumference*, the properties themselves are really distinct through inseparable."[21] A radius and a circumference are both essential properties of a circle—a circle cannot be a circle without having a radius and a circumference—and they are really distinct from each other. And yet they are inseparable from each other and are understood in terms of each other. A radius is the distance from the center of a circle to any point on its circumference, and the circumference (as distance around the circle's edge) is the value of $2\pi r$. As a radius and a circumference are real, though inseparable, principles of a circle, so are metaphysical coprinciples real, though inseparable, principles of a being.

Significantly, Aquinas's Latin expression, which is often translated into English as "existence," is not a noun but a verb. It is the word *esse* (the present active infinitive of the Latin verb *sum*, "to be.").[22] This grammatical point is significant. For when we conceive of "existence" in this register, we should think of it as an action (as "be-ing"), rather than a static noun. For Aquinas, existence is fundamentally something dynamic and active, not static and inert. Hence, we will refer to this coprinciple as the act of existing.[23]

Given that a thing's essence and its act of existing are distinct coprinciples, Aquinas asks how they come to be conjoined. He states, "Whatever belongs to a thing is either caused by the principles of its nature . . . or comes to it from some extrinsic principle."[24] Whatever a thing has, it has by one of two ways. Either a thing has a given feature or capacity by virtue of its own essence (i.e., a thing has the feature or capacity on account of what it is) or it has that feature or capacity by receiving it from some source outside itself. As for the former, Aquinas gives the example of the ability to laugh as arising from the

20. David S. Oderberg, "The Non-Identity of the Categorical and the Dispositional," *Analysis* 69 (2009): 677. We thank Edward Feser for his assistance with this example and reference.

21. Oderberg, "Non-Identity," 678 (emphasis original).

22. Aquinas also uses the Latin phrase *actus essendi*, or "act of existing."

23. As we will discuss below, we are very much indebted to W. Norris Clarke's interpretation of Aquinas's metaphysics regarding the active character of being. For previous appeals to Clarke on these matters, see Francis Martin, "Revelation as Disclosure: Creation," in *Wisdom and Holiness, Science and Scholarship: Essays in Honor of Matthew L. Lamb*, ed. Michael Dauphinais and Matthew Levering (Naples, FL: Sapientia Press, 2007), 238–40; Martin, "Joseph Ratzinger, Benedict XVI, on Biblical Interpretation: Two Leading Principles," *Nova et Vetera*, English edition 5, no. 2 (2007): 303–5; Martin, "Reflections on Professor Bockmuehl's 'Bible versus Theology,'" *Nova et Vetera*, English edition 9 (2011): 64–65.

24. Aquinas, *On Being and Essence* 4 (McInerny, 42).

essential makeup of the human being. Human beings have the ability to laugh simply by virtue of being human. As for the latter, Aquinas cites the example of "heat . . . caused in water by fire."[25] Liquid water is not essentially hot (i.e., it could be hot, but it does not *have* to be hot). Fire, however, is essentially hot (i.e., fire cannot but be hot). Thus, when liquid water becomes hot, it must receive heat from a cause outside itself, such as fire.

Aquinas then argues that a finite thing's essence cannot be the source of its own act of existing. He writes, "Existence cannot be caused by the form or quiddity of a thing . . . because in this way a thing would be a cause of itself and produce itself in existence, which is impossible."[26] To claim that a finite thing's act of existing arises from its own essence would be to claim that a thing is the cause of its own existing. It would make something to be "both cause and effect in the same relation . . . [or] to say that the thing depends on itself and at the same time that it does not depend on itself."[27] Given that this is both intellectually nonsensical and ontologically impossible, the other possibility must be the case: a thing in which essence and the act of existing are really distinct must receive its act of existing from a cause outside itself: "It is necessary that each thing whose existence is other than its nature has its existence from another."[28]

Neither artificial things such as books nor natural things such as human beings can be the cause of their own existence. Such things are, therefore, contingent; they do not *have* to exist, and they *depend* on causes for their existence. This contingency is evidenced by the fact that both books and human beings come into and pass out of existence. They do not, in the words of Robert Barron, "contain within themselves the reason [or cause] for their own existence."[29] Thus, according to Aquinas, all things whose essence differs from their act of existing must receive their act of existing from a cause external to themselves.

Feser points out that this bringing together of essence and the act of existing not only applies to the moment of a thing's coming into being but also runs throughout its entire existence.[30] It is primarily a matter not of temporal

25. Aquinas, *Summa Theologica* I, q. 3, a. 4, in Thomas Aquinas, *Summa Theologica*, trans. Fathers of the English Dominican Province, 3 vols. (New York: Benziger, 1947–48). Aquinas gives the example of the human capacity to laugh (or risibility) both in this article of the *Summa Theologica* and in *On Being and Essence* 4.

26. Aquinas, *On Being and Essence* 4 (McInerny, 42).

27. Bobik, *Aquinas on Being and Essence*, 174.

28. Aquinas, *On Being and Essence* 4 (McInerny, 42).

29. Robert Barron, *Catholicism: A Journey to the Heart of the Faith* (New York: Image, 2011), 65.

30. Feser, *Aquinas: A Beginner's Guide* (Oxford: Oneworld, 2009), 85.

dependence (e.g., parents have children at one point in time, and then children can exist temporally apart from their parents), but of ontological dependence. When a thing's essence and its act of existing are distinct, a thing must continually receive its act of existing from outside itself (since it cannot produce its act of existing on its own). Feser writes, "The essence and act of existing must be *kept* together at every point at which the thing exists. Accordingly, such a thing must be caused to exist not once for all, but *continuously*, here and now as well as at the time it first came into being."[31] In other words, the causal sequence does not primarily track backward in time, but downward in the structures of being (in what is called a per se or an "essentially ordered causal series").[32]

Given that such things must receive their act of existing from a cause outside themselves, Aquinas reasons that this per se causal sequence must ultimately be ontologically grounded in a reality whose essence *is* the very act of existing: "There must be some thing which is the cause of the being of all things by the fact that it is existence alone, otherwise there would be an infinite regress in causes, since everything which is not existence alone has a cause of its existence."[33] The ultimate cause of existing in all things, wherein essence and the act of existing are distinct, must be a cause in which the two (essence and the act of existing) are one and the same. Such a reality is responsible for the continual existing of all things and receives the act of existing from none. This, according to Aquinas, is God, whose essence is the very act of existing itself.

Aquinas holds that God is not a thing existing among other things, but rather is the pure, unlimited, subsistent act of existing itself: *ipsum esse subsistens*.[34] In this light, Aquinas sees convergence between this philosophical argument for God as the subsistent act of existing itself and the revelation of God's name to Moses at Mount Sinai (Exod. 3:14). Aquinas interprets the revelation of God's sacred name "He who is" (*qui est*) in this way: it "does not signify form [i.e., a kind of thing], but simply existence itself . . . [and] the existence of God is His essence itself."[35]

We should add an important qualification here. W. Norris Clarke argues that despite our need to use language to talk and think about God in this way, Aquinas's identification of God as the pure act of existing is something that

---

31. Feser, *Aquinas*, 85.
32. So Aquinas, *On Being and Essence* 4 (McInerny, 42). For discussion of a causal series ordered per se, or an "essentially ordered causal series" (Feser's expression), and the vital role it has in Aquinas's philosophical theology, see Feser, *Aquinas*, 69–73; Feser, *Last Superstition*, 91–96.
33. Aquinas, *On Being and Essence* 4 (McInerny, 42).
34. E.g., Aquinas, *Summa Theologica* I, q. 4, a. 2; Aquinas, *Summa contra Gentiles* 3.19.3.
35. Aquinas, *Summa Theologica* I, q. 13, a. 11.

ultimately transcends our language and our concepts.[36] Clarke points out that the most basic of linguistic elements is the distinction between subject and verb. When we form linguistic statements or articulate concepts, we conjoin subject and verb. But when we do so, the distinction between subject and verb never collapses: "Subjects can never function as their own verbs, expressing in identity of form both the subject and its activity or act of presence, nor can verbs function identically as their own subjects."[37]

And yet, Clarke continues, "this is exactly what Saint Thomas is asking us to do in naming God as *Ipsum Esse*."[38] The identification of God's essence as his act of existence is just such an identification of subject and verb. It is something that defies and utterly transcends our thinking and our language. Even though we must use language and conceptual categories to talk about God, we must simultaneously recognize that our language and categories will ultimately fail to capture or do justice to God's transcendent reality. Clarke concludes, "This identity [of God's essence and existence] transcends all linguistic forms and categories, and therefore cannot properly be said in any language, though it can be evocatively suggested by a special use of language and shown forth as something that must be affirmed if reality is to make ultimate sense."[39] While human beings are able to say something about God, we must also be highly attentive to the inadequacies of our thinking and speaking as to God's mysterious, transcendent reality.

### Ontological Participation

Aquinas's identification of God as the pure subsistent act of existing entails that God is the source from which all things continually receive their own act of existing. The metaphysical identification of God as the pure act of existing from which all other things receive their own act of existing is at the heart of Aquinas's doctrine of ontological participation.

Participation is a relationship between things, principles, concepts, and so on that involves some kind of derivation or sharing. At a basic level, "to participate," Aquinas writes, "is to take a part."[40] He continues, "When anything

36. So W. Norris Clarke, "What Cannot Be Said in Saint Thomas's Essence-Existence Doctrine," in *The Creative Retrieval of Saint Thomas Aquinas: Essays in Thomistic Philosophy, New and Old* (New York: Fordham University Press, 2009), 120–23.

37. Clarke, "What Cannot Be Said," 121.

38. Clarke, "What Cannot Be Said," 121.

39. Clarke, "What Cannot Be Said," 121.

40. Aquinas, *Commentary on Boethius' Goodness of Substances* 1.2, in *An Aquinas Reader: Selections from the Writings of Thomas Aquinas*, ed. Mary T. Clark (New York: Fordham University Press, 1972), 51.

receives particularly what belongs to others universally, it is said to participate in it."[41] Participation concerns a thing's limited receiving of some attribute, ability, experience, activity, or the like that is had more fully in something else. Drawing on the work of contemporary Thomistic metaphysician W. Norris Clarke, we will set forth some basic features of this topic in Aquinas's metaphysics.[42]

The philosophical use of the term "participation" goes back to Plato as a way of accounting for the relationship between the one and the many (or unity-in-diversity).[43] It is an answer to the philosophical problem of how *many different* individuals can all share *one common* feature. For example, one might ask, "How is it that all things are alike in that they really exist and that, nevertheless, they do so as different kinds of things and furthermore as individual members of a given kind?" Clarke articulates the basic Platonist doctrine of participation in this way: "Wherever there is a multiplicity of members all of which possess some common attribute there must also be some one superior source possessing the same attribute in unmixed purity and perfection, from which each of the inferior participants derives its own diminished and imperfect participation."[44]

To illustrate, let us develop an example that Aquinas himself provides in his *Commentary on Boethius' Goodness of Substances*. Aquinas writes, "Man is said to participate in animality inasmuch as he does not possess the animal mode of being in the same way as do those who constitute the entire community of animal being, and likewise does Socrates participate in man."[45] A human being is an animal. So too is a giraffe. Both of them share the common genus "animality" without either of them exhausting the entirety of what it is to be an animal. The one mode of being—animality—is shared (or

41. Aquinas, *Commentary on Boethius' Goodness of Substances* 1.2, in Clark, *Aquinas Reader*, 51–52.

42. In what follows, we will summarize key points in W. Norris Clarke, SJ, "The Meaning of Participation in St. Thomas," in *Explorations in Metaphysics: Being—God—Person* (Notre Dame, IN: University of Notre Dame Press, 1994), 89–101, and Clarke, *The One and the Many*, 72–91. Other substantial studies of participation in Aquinas include Cornelio Fabro, *Participation et causalité selon S. Thomas D'Aquin*, Chaire Cardinal Mercier 2 (Leuven: Publications Universitaíres de Louvain; Paris: Éditions Béatrice-Nauwelaerts, 1961); Rudi A. te Velde, *Participation and Substantiality in Thomas Aquinas*, STGM 46 (Leiden: Brill, 1995); John F. Wippel, *The Metaphysical Thought of Thomas Aquinas: From Finite Being to Uncreated Being* (Washington, DC: Catholic University of America Press, 2000), 94–131.

43. Clarke, "Meaning of Participation," 90. Clarke (99) cites this basic principle as given in Plato, *Republic* 507b.

44. Clarke, "Meaning of Participation," 90.

45. Aquinas, *Commentary on Boethius' Goodness of Substances* 1.2, in Clark, *Aquinas Reader*, 51–52.

participated in) by different individuals in diverse ways. Accordingly, animality must in some respect be greater than its particular instantiations, since it cannot be reduced to any one of them.

Aquinas takes over (and modifies somewhat) the notion of participation from the Platonist tradition, which came to him through figures such as Augustine and Pseudo-Dionysius. Clarke writes that, for Aquinas, there are three necessary components in a participatory relationship:

(1) a *source* which possesses the perfection in question in a total and unrestricted manner;
(2) a *participant subject* which possesses the same perfection in some partial or restricted way; and
(3) which has *received this perfection* in some way from, or in dependence on, the higher source.[46]

Let us elaborate on each of these three components. First, there is *a single source* from which others derive a given attribute, ability, or "perfection" (i.e., some real good).[47] According to Clarke, the source is the perfection or attribute in its fullness: "The source is by definition that which is the ultimate font of the perfection in question. . . . It must not merely *have* [the perfection] as part of its essence but must *be* it totally, in perfect purity and simplicity."[48] The source must singularly be the perfection in question because otherwise it would have to derive the perfection from another source (thus kicking the participatory can down the road). The second component is *the participator*: the one or more subjects that share that perfection or attribute in a limited way.[49] Since these participating subjects do not have the perfection or attribute in question essentially, they must derive it from another source. This leads to the third component, which is *the relational, receptive dependence* of the participating subjects on the source. That is to say, the participating subjects do not possess a given "perfection" fully or essentially but rather must derive

46. Clarke, "Meaning of Participation," 93 (arrangement of the text slightly modified and emphasis added).

47. Peter Kreeft offers the following definition(s) of "perfection" as used by Aquinas: "most generally, any definite actuality in a being; more particularly, any definite *good* suitable to a being; most particularly, complete good attained by a being." Kreeft, *A Summa of the Summa: The Essential Philosophical Passages of St. Thomas Aquinas' "Summa theologica"* (San Francisco: Ignatius, 1990), 28.

48. Clarke, "Meaning of Participation," 94.

49. Clarke adds, "Since [the participating subject] does not possess its perfection by essence but as received from another and contracted in some way, it cannot be simple but must be composed of the perfection received and the subject or capacity receiving and limiting it." "Meaning of Participation," 95.

it from a higher source. They *depend* on the source for the participated perfection, which they *receive* from the source.

Participation is key to Aquinas's metaphysics of creation, and it interfaces with the real distinction between essence and the act of existence. In his *Disputed Questions on Truth*, Aquinas provides a crisp summary statement: "The divine nature or essence is itself its act of being [*actus essendi*], but the nature or essence of any created thing is not its own act of being but participates in being from another. So in God the act of being is pure, since God is his own subsistent act of being (*esse*); whereas in the creature the act of being is received or participated."[50] God is the pure, subsistent act of existing itself: *ipsum esse subsistens*. With reference to Clarke's threefold articulation given above, God is *the source*, and the act of existing is *the perfection* that God possesses entirely and in fact is. Everything else, whose essence does not account for its act of existing, must continually receive its act of existing from a single source outside itself and that is the very act of existing itself. Accordingly, created things (in which essence and the act of existing differ) are the *participating subjects* who receive their act of existing (i.e., the participated perfection) from God, who conjoins it continually with the things' essences. All created things, therefore, participate in God's own act of existence at every moment of their own existence.

These considerations lead us to a highly complex and controverted topic, of which, in light of present purposes, we can only scratch the surface: analogy.[51] As we have seen, God's essence is the pure subsistent act of existing (*esse*), whereas in everything-other-than-God, a thing's essence does not account for its existence. Important here is that God's mode of being and everything else's mode of being are radically different. In fact, as we have seen, Aquinas holds that God is not any kind of "being" or "thing" at all.[52] Moreover, Clarke has argued that Aquinas's identification of God's essence as his act of existing transcends our language and categories. And yet, we can truthfully say, "God exists," and "creation exists." But they do not "exist"—and cannot be said to "exist"—in the same way. Therefore, "being," Aquinas maintains, is *analogous*.

Discussions of analogy often distinguish three different modes in which human beings use concepts and language in a literal way.[53] First, humans can literally use terms and concepts in a *univocal* way. That is, we use the same term and with the same meaning for different subjects. For instance, when we

---

50. Aquinas, *Disputed Questions on Truth* q. 21, a. 5, cited in Clark, *Aquinas Reader*, 49.
51. Cornelio Fabro has referred to analogy as "the semantics of participation" in his *Participation et causalité*, 634. A helpful and accessible discussion of Aquinas on analogy is Copleston, *History of Philosophy*, 2:352–58.
52. See Aquinas, *Summa Theologica* I, q. 3, a. 5.
53. See Aquinas, *Summa Theologica* I, q. 13, a. 5.

say "the knife is sharp" and "the axe is sharp," we are using the term "sharp" univocally—we are applying the same term ("sharp") with the same meaning ("capable of cutting") to different subjects (a knife and an axe). A second way of using of terms and concepts in a literal way is to speak *equivocally*. That is, we use the same term, but with completely different meanings, for different subjects. For instance, when we say, "We took a plane to Rome" and "I used a plane to smooth the wood," we are using the term "plane" equivocally—we are applying the same term ("plane") to different subjects and with very different meanings: in the first case, "plane" means a vehicle for air transportation, and in the second case, "plane" means a tool for shaving and smoothing wood. The third way in which we literally use speech and concepts is *analogously*.[54] An analogous use of the word "occurs when the same term is applied to several different subjects according to a meaning that is *partly the same*, *partly different* in each case."[55] For instance (to adapt a favorite example of Aquinas), we can say, "Jones is healthy" and "the apple is healthy."[56] In this case, the same term "healthy" is used in ways that are in some respects similar, but in other respects different. In the first example, "healthy" refers to the state of Jones's constitution, but in the second example, "healthy" refers to the positive contribution of an apple to a person's health. There is some measure of commonality between the two uses, but the two are not identical; they name something different. Aquinas holds that "being" cannot be univocal when it comes to God and the world because God's unique mode of existing (as *ipsum esse subsistens*) and creatures' mode of being (as limited participations in God's *esse* conjoined to an essence) are fundamentally different. Thus, Aquinas writes, "Diversity with respect to act of existing prevents the univocal predication of being [*ens*]."[57] Moreover, "being," along with all other human terms and concepts, cannot be used in a wholly equivocal manner between God and creatures.[58] If this were true, then human beings could not know or say anything about God whatsoever, because all our thoughts and words about God would have *nothing* in common with God. They would be devoid of meaning and be utter nonsense. Accordingly, Aquinas holds that "being" is analogous with respect to God and the world. All the perfections and goods

54. Aquinas also differentiates between different subcategories of analogous speech; see Aquinas, *Commentary on the Sentences* 19.5.2, ad. 1; see Anderson, *Metaphysics of St. Thomas Aquinas*, 37–38.

55. Clarke, *The One and the Many*, 45.

56. Aquinas cites "health" as an example of analogy in *Summa Theologica* I, q. 13, a. 5.

57. Aquinas, *On the Power of God* q. 7, a. 7, cited in Anderson, *Metaphysics of St. Thomas Aquinas*, 44.

58. Aquinas, *Disputed Questions on Truth* q. 2, a. 11, cited in Anderson, *Metaphysics of St. Thomas Aquinas*, 41.

that creatures possess in a limited manner are derived from God's *esse*, in which all goods exist perfectly: "Whatever is said of God and creatures, is said according to the relation of a creature to God as its principle and cause, wherein all perfections of things pre-exist excellently."[59]

Such analogous use of "being" is an example of the analogy of proportionality.[60] This occurs, Aquinas writes, "where there is no equality either with respect to the common concept involved or to actual existence."[61] In these cases, Aquinas continues, "the common term must exist in some way in each of the things of which it is predicated, while different with respect to greater or lesser perfection."[62] Applied to our example, "being" in some respect applies both to God and to creatures—both God and creatures really do exist. But the term applies in radically different ways, since the way in which God exists and the way in which creatures exist are so utterly different. Accordingly, human beings can know and say something about God, but it is very limited and imperfect, and falls far short of his reality. As Robert Barron puts it, "We may say that God exists, but we're not quite sure what we mean when we say it."[63]

According to Aquinas, the notion that God is the pure act of existing itself from which all things derive their limited act of existing (as well as their essence) is a philosophically discoverable and demonstrable truth. It also accords with what is given in Scripture and articulated in the Distinction. Namely, God "created the heavens and the earth" (Gen. 1:1), and the Creator is not to be confused with any created thing (Wis. 13:1–3; Rom. 1:25). Or in the words of the Gospel according to John, "All things came into being through him, and without him not one thing came into being" (John 1:3).

## Relationality

Another important feature of the metaphysics of creation is relationality. By relationality, we mean that created beings always exist in relation to other beings, such that relationality is an essential structure of created being itself. In

---

59. Aquinas, *Summa Theologica* I, q. 13, a. 5. Aquinas sees this notion of analogical relation between creature and Creator present in Paul's claim in Rom. 1:20: "Ever since the creation of the world his eternal power and divine nature, invisible though they are, have been understood and seen through the things he has made."

60. Clarke specifies it as an example of "proper proportionality." *The One and the Many*, 51.

61. Aquinas, *Commentary on the Sentences*, book 1, distinction 10, q. 5, a. 2, ad. 1, cited in Anderson, *Metaphysics of St. Thomas Aquinas*, 38.

62. Aquinas, *Commentary on the Sentences*, book 1, distinction 10, q. 5, a. 2, ad. 1, cited in Anderson, *Metaphysics of St. Thomas Aquinas*, 38.

63. Robert Barron, *The Priority of Christ: Toward a Postliberal Catholicism* (Grand Rapids: Brazos, 2007), 13.

simpler terms, to be a creature is "to be *substance-in-relation*."[64] To explicate these metaphysical insights, we again turn to W. Norris Clarke.[65]

### Being Is Active

We have seen that for Aquinas, all created things are a composite of two coprinciples: essence and the act of existing. As mentioned previously, Aquinas's term for "existence" is the verb *esse* or the phrase "the act of existing" (Latin: *actus essendi*). These grammatical choices are ontologically significant. For Aquinas, existence (*esse*) is not a noun, but a verb. It is an act. Moreover, Aquinas holds that in the ontological composition of created beings, *esse* is more fundamental than essence.[66] It is more ontologically basic in a being "to exist in the first place" than it is "to exist as this kind of thing."[67] Put differently, the deepest level, the most intimate sphere of any created being is its act of existing, which it continuously receives from God.[68] The key point of these two observations—*esse* denotes action; *esse* is the most fundamental aspect of a being—is that being is fundamentally not something static and unchanging, but dynamic and active.

Clarke adduces a number of passages from Aquinas's writings where he articulates this point philosophically.[69] For instance, when discussing the infinite power of God in the *Summa contra Gentiles*, Aquinas writes, "From the fact that something is in act it is active."[70] That is, from the very fact that a thing actually exists, it is also engaged in some sort of activity. Later in the same

---

64. W. Norris Clarke, SJ, *Person and Being* (Milwaukee: Marquette University Press, 1993), 17.

65. While we follow Clarke's analysis of relationality as regards created being, we do not follow his extension of Aquinas's metaphysical insights on relationality to God's *esse*—a move that Clarke acknowledges that Aquinas does not (and would not) make. See W. Norris Clarke, SJ, "To Be Is to Be Substance-in-Relation," in *Explorations in Metaphysics*, 108–9. We are indebted here to the appreciative critique of Clarke on this point given in Matthew Levering, *Scripture and Metaphysics: Aquinas and the Renewal of Trinitarian Theology* (Malden, MA: Blackwell, 2004), 197–235.

66. In technical terms, *esse* is to essence as act is to potency. Act is always preferable and more real since potency is just potential being, not actual being. As Feser writes, "While actuality and potentiality are fully intelligible only in relation to each other, there is an asymmetry between them, with actuality having metaphysical priority. A potential is always a potential *for* a certain kind of actuality. . . . Furthermore, potentiality cannot exist on its own, but only in combination with actuality." *Last Superstition*, 55.

67. We are speaking here of ontological priority, not temporal priority. The one is ontologically more fundamental than the other, but this does not mean that one precedes the other in time as a separate thing, which as a coprinciple, it is not.

68. Clarke, "To Be Is to Be Substance-in-Relation," 107.

69. See Clarke, introduction to Anderson, *Metaphysics of St. Thomas Aquinas*, xviii–xix.

70. Thomas Aquinas, *Summa contra Gentiles* 1.43.2, in Thomas Aquinas, *Summa contra Gentiles*, 5 vols., trans. Anton C. Pegis, FRSC, James F. Anderson, Vernon J. Bourke, and Charles J. O'Neil (Notre Dame, IN: University of Notre Dame Press, 1975), 1:165.

work, Aquinas states, "Active potency follows upon being in act; for a thing acts in consequence of being in act."[71] In other words, the ability of something to act (i.e., its "active potency") proceeds from its having real existence—that is, its participated *esse*. From statements such as these, Clarke discerns that a thing's action naturally flows from its act of existing: "It is proper to every being, insofar as it is in act, to overflow into action, to act according to its nature, whether such action be free or necessitated in its modality."[72] Being is naturally active and dynamic, and it tends to issue forth in further activity.

A few things need to be said about the use of the category "action" in this context. To begin with, action, Clarke notes, is *"essence-structured action."*[73] A created thing acts in a manner delimited by the kind of thing it is (i.e., its essence). For instance, consider a rock in a garden. A rock cannot act consciously or willfully in the way that a human being acts. But the rock can "act" in a manner corresponding to its nature as a rock, its mode of being. A rock may "act" by exerting pressure on the earth beneath it on account of gravity. A rock also appears to those who observe or sense it. A rock may provide support to a bird that lands on it to rest. These are not conscious actions, but they are kinds of actions nonetheless that are proper to what it is to be a rock. Conversely, human beings, who have intellects, wills, and emotions, are capable of a wide range of actions that are beyond the capacities of a rock. The actions of a human being are of a different sort than the actions of a rock, because humans and rocks are fundamentally different kinds of things. They have different natures. Accordingly, we should consider "action" here as an analogous term. Action need not be conscious or deliberate (as it is in much human activity), but can encompass a range of analogous ways in which one thing has influence on another.[74]

### Self-Communication through Action

Clarke then argues that since action flows naturally from the act of existing, action is the means by which creatures naturally communicate themselves. For Aquinas, Clarke notes, every finite being, "insofar as it *is* in act, tends

71. Aquinas, *Summa contra Gentiles* 2.8.3 (Pegis et al., 2:38); reference from W. Norris Clarke, SJ, "Action as the Self-Revelation of Being: A Central Theme in the Thought of St. Thomas," in *Explorations in Metaphysics*, 46.

72. Clarke, "Action as the Self-Revelation of Being," 46.

73. Clarke, "Action as the Self-Revelation of Being," 54 (emphasis original).

74. Thus, Clarke maintains that action can be either *"immanent action,* which terminates within the agent itself, as in the case of knowledge or love," or it may be *"transient action,* which terminates outside the agent by exercising some influence on another." "Action as the Self-Revelation of Being," 46–47.

naturally to overflow into action, and this action is a *self-communication*, a self-giving in some way."[75] Highly indicative of this claim, Clarke points out, is Aquinas's (dense) statement in his treatise *On the Power of God*: "It is in the nature of every act to communicate itself as far as possible. Wherefore every agent acts forasmuch as it is in act: while to act is nothing else than to communicate as far as possible that whereby the agent is in act."[76] Aquinas reiterates the point previously discussed: the act of existing, which comprises the deepest core of a being, naturally tends to issue forth in action. What this quotation from *On the Power of God* adds to the discussion is the notion of communication. That is, for Aquinas, action is a means by which created things naturally communicate themselves to other things. The active nature of being entails that beings tend to communicate and manifest themselves to other beings through activity. As Clarke himself puts it succinctly, "Not only does every being tend, by the inner dynamism of its act of existence, to overflow into action, but this action is both a self-manifestation and a self-communication, a self-sharing, of the being's own inner ontological perfection, with others."[77] Finite beings manifest and share of themselves with other beings through action. This also means that things play "an active role in their being known" by other beings—a point that will be of decisive significance in our reflections on human knowing in chapter 8.[78]

This notion of being as dynamically self-communicative through action goes back to the Platonist belief in the "self-diffusiveness of the Good."[79] The nature of goodness is such that it naturally lends itself to be shared by many. While this claim is put in philosophical terms, it is quite evident in common human experience. For instance, a person who receives some good news immediately wants to share that good news with others. Similarly, a person who has a good experience very often tells others about it so they can experience it for themselves and share in the goodness. Since goodness and being are convertible for Aquinas and goodness is diffusive of itself, so too is it in the nature of being to communicate itself through action. If we apply this principle to finite beings, we can say with Clarke, "The whole point of [every substance's] being is to express itself, to fulfill itself, to share its riches, through action appropriate to its mode of being (its essence)."[80]

75. Clarke, "Action as the Self-Revelation of Being," 47.

76. Thomas Aquinas, *On the Power of God* q. 2, a. 1, as cited in Clarke, "Action as the Self-Revelation of Being," 47.

77. Clarke, "Action as the Self-Revelation of Being," 48.

78. Martin, "Bockmuehl's 'Bible versus Theology,'" 62; cf. Martin, "Benedict XVI, on Biblical Interpretation," 303–5.

79. Clarke, "Action as the Self-Revelation of Being," 48.

80. Clarke, "To Be Is to Be Substance-in-Relation," 106–7.

Action is not only how creatures share themselves with others. It is also the means by which a knowing subject experiences and knows other beings. The dynamism of being includes not only an agent's acting but also its being acted on by others. In the case of human beings, we experience the world and the different things within it through mutual *interaction*. Given what has been said about the nature of being as dynamic and oriented to self-communicating action, the whole sphere of existence comes to light as an interactive network. Clarke writes, "The universe becomes a vast interconnected web of interacting beings, reciprocally acting on and being acted on by others, giving and receiving."[81]

The metaphysics of participation, therefore, is simultaneously a metaphysics of relationality. As limited participants in God's unlimited *esse*, created beings manifest and communicate themselves with others through action. The whole of creation is composed of different creatures acting on and being acted on by others. Relationality is not something tacked on to individual, isolated substances—as, for example, the notion of substance is for Descartes and other modern philosophers.[82] Rather, relationality is part and parcel of what it is to be a creature. To be is to have self-possession of *esse*, which orients a being to self-manifestation to others through action.[83] This is an ontology wherein beings give of themselves and receive from others. It is a metaphysics of gift. And in the modality of personal being, the higher and more intense forms of being, it is a metaphysics of love.

### Looking Back and Looking Forward

In this chapter, we have climbed another step on the expository ladder in part 2. With others, we have argued that creation provides the indispensable context for theological thinking, and more specifically, the understanding of the Creator-creation relationship entailed by the Distinction. We have filled out our reflections on the world as created by reflecting philosophically on the Creator-creation relationship. All readers of Scripture presuppose some metaphysical ideas about reality, and not all metaphysical ideas are equally true—and thus conducive to understanding Scripture as putting people in living contact with God. Though it may seem out of place with contemporary biblical studies, metaphysical thinking is an important, though largely unrecognized, dimension of biblical interpretation.

81. Clarke, "Action as the Self-Revelation of Being," 51.
82. So Clarke, "To Be Is to Be Substance-in-Relation," 109–13.
83. Clarke, "To Be Is to Be Substance-in-Relation," 104–5.

We have focused on two core elements in Thomas Aquinas's metaphysical analysis—participation and relationality—which are congruent with the Distinction. We started our reflections on ontological participation with the "real distinction" between essence and the act of existing (*esse*). Aquinas identifies a real distinction in created things between essence (*what* a thing is) and its act of existing (*that* by which a thing is). Aquinas asks how these two coprinciples are conjoined in a being and reasons that since a thing's essence cannot cause its own act of existing, a thing must receive its act of existing from an external source. This per se (or "essentially ordered") causal series of ontological dependence must ultimately be caused by a reality whose essence is the act of existing. This, according to Aquinas, is God, who is *ipsum esse subsistens* (the subsistent act of existing itself), who radically transcends the cognitive and linguistic capacities of creatures. Within this metaphysics of participation, all created beings depend on the Creator for their very being at every moment. At the depths of every creature's being is its participated *esse*, its limited and derivative sharing in the very life of Creator God.

Aquinas's term for the act of existing, *esse*, is a verb, and as Clarke has argued, *esse* for Aquinas is active and dynamic. Since the act of existing lies at their ontological depths, created beings are naturally active and are given to communicate themselves through activity. That is, creatures manifest and communicate their own being to one another through their various modes of activity. Created being, as Clarke points out, is self-communicative through action. Accordingly, relationality is another aspect of the metaphysics of created being. The whole of creation is an interactive network of creatures acting and being acted on by others.

Having concluded these philosophical and theological reflections on the relationship between God and creation, we are in a position to draw together some key elements and begin to consider how they impact our understanding of Scripture. In the next chapter, we will pause our ascent on the expository ladder in part 2 and consider some ways in which how one understands the world can impact how one understands the Bible.

# 7

# Creation, the Bible, and the Question
# of Transcendence

In the two preceding chapters, we have reflected theologically and philosophically on some basic elements in the Creator-creation relationship, entailed by the Distinction and explicated in the conceptually congruent Thomistic metaphysics of creation. We also contrasted the understanding of the world in the Distinction with models of the world as a closed system. In this chapter, we will bring some of these reflections to bear on the Bible and reflect on ways in which the Creator-creation relationship impacts the understanding of Scripture. While various aspects of this topic can be helpfully explored, here we focus principally on the question of transcendence and how (if at all) it factors into our understanding of the Bible and the realities that it mediates.[1]

## The Bible and the Closed System

In the previous chapter, we contrasted the Distinction with an understanding of the world as a "closed system." To recapitulate: in the early modern period, there arose a trend to conceive of the world as being like a giant machine

1. See Francis Martin, "Spiritual Understanding of Scripture," in *"Verbum Domini" and the Complementarity of Exegesis and Theology*, ed. Scott Carl (Grand Rapids: Eerdmans, 2015), 15–21. We also acknowledge here the work of Matthew Levering, whose contributions very much dovetail with the ones presented here. See Matthew Levering, *Participatory Biblical Exegesis: A Theology of Biblical Interpretation* (Notre Dame, IN: University of Notre Dame Press, 2008).

or self-enclosed box, which operates wholly according to its own internal laws and forces. Anything that happens within this closed system must be explained in terms of its internal forces and causes. These causes, moreover, can only be of an efficient or material sort, for the popularity and successes of inductive scientific inquiry contributed to the dismissal (though not disproving) of formal and final causality. Formal and final causes simply do not have a place in this restrictive account of human reasoning and the corresponding methodological purview. This modern account of rationality effectively predetermines the topics that can be reasonably discussed as well as what "counts" as knowledge and as rational inquiry.[2] But as David Bentley Hart points out, it is one thing to bracket considerations of formal and final causality to concentrate attention on a specific part of the whole (e.g., scientific method), but it is another to make this "new anti-metaphysical method . . . into a metaphysics of its own."[3] The latter is what happened with the development of the conceptual model of the world as a closed system. When the world is construed as a closed system, its relationship to a deity (if any relation is acknowledged) is wholly extrinsic. On this view, God is not immanently present to the world and causing its existence at every moment. Where God's transcendence is acknowledged, it is along the lines of what Kathryn Tanner calls a "contrastive" notion of transcendence. Here, God is one kind of "thing" contrasted from the world as another kind of "thing."

A closed-system model of the world impacted the development of modern understandings of the Bible. Consider, for instance, some elements in Baruch Spinoza's *Tractatus Theologico-Politicus*.[4] Written in 1670, Spinoza's work is a milestone in the development of the modern historical-critical understanding of the Bible. To be sure, not all biblical scholars follow Spinoza's program or share all his presuppositions, but his work, as James Kugel writes, "became the marching orders of biblical scholars for the next three centuries."[5] To give a sense for Spinoza's program, we will identify a few of its key elements.

2. So David Bentley Hart, *The Experience of God: Being, Consciousness, Bliss* (New Haven: Yale University Press, 2013), 65; Edward Feser, *The Last Superstition: A Refutation of the New Atheism* (South Bend, IN: St. Augustine's Press, 2008), 171–78. Cyril O'Regan writes the following of Enlightenment discourse and inquiry: "The Enlightenment frustrates opposition precisely because its determinacy is indeterminate, and induces sputter, since the only game in which it is willing to participate is one in which it is player, referee, and rules committee." O'Regan, *The Anatomy of Misremembering: Von Balthasar's Response to Philosophical Modernity*, vol. 1, *Hegel* (New York: Herder & Herder, 2014), 3.

3. Hart, *Experience of God*, 56–57, 70–71, quotation from 57.

4. Benedict de Spinoza, *A Theologico-Political Treatise*, trans. R. H. M. Elwes (New York: Dove, 1951).

5. James L. Kugel, *How to Read the Bible: A Guide to Scripture Then and Now* (New York: Simon & Schuster, 2007), 31.

To begin with, in a kind of inversing of the tradition of the "two books" of the Bible and creation, Spinoza argues that the Bible should be studied according to the way in which people study the natural world: "The method of interpreting Scripture does not widely differ from the method of interpreting nature—in fact, it is almost the same."[6] Spinoza argues this, in part, because he regards God and nature as identical: "Nature herself is the power of God under another name, and our ignorance of the power of God is co-extensive with our ignorance of Nature."[7] This (pantheistic?) point is very significant for our purposes, because, for Spinoza, there is no transcendent reality beyond nature. Jonathan Israel writes, "Spinoza's God, then, is the creative power of nature, and everything that actually is, conceived as the totality of everything, with nothing lying beyond it and no such thing as supernatural agency, the miraculous, or revelation does or could exist."[8] Spinoza's denial of transcendence and his account of God as the world are thoroughly at odds with the Creator-creation relationship entailed by the Distinction.

Spinoza's program for interpreting Scripture follows upon these naturalistic premises. Like other thinkers of the "radical Enlightenment," Spinoza holds that "there is only one source of truth—science and scientifically based scholarship in the humanities. . . . [It is] 'science' understood as *Wissenschaft*."[9] Given Spinoza's denial of transcendent reality and his restriction of rationality to the scientific, to study the Bible like the natural world means inductive, empirical observation. Moreover, this "scientific" model of inquiry means that the study of the Bible must be separate from any kind of theological considerations or faith-community commitments. Hence, Spinoza argues, "Our knowledge of Scripture must . . . be looked for in Scripture only."[10] This means, as James Kugel notes, that the traditions of biblical interpretation, through which faith communities read their Scriptures, are not hermeneutically relevant in biblical

---

6. Spinoza, *Theologico-Political Treatise*, 99; cf. Levering, *Participatory Biblical Exegesis*, 115.

7. Spinoza, *Theologico-Political Treatise*, 25. On Spinoza's account of the divine, see Scott W. Hahn and Benjamin Wiker, *Politicizing the Bible: The Roots of Historical Criticism and the Secularization of Scripture, 1300–1700* (New York: Herder & Herder, 2013), 357–60.

8. Jonathan I. Israel, "Spinoza and Early Modern Theology," in *The Oxford Handbook of Early Modern Theology, 1600–1800*, ed. Ulrich L. Lehner, Richard A. Muller, and A. G. Roeber (Oxford: Oxford University Press, 2016), 577–93, here 579.

9. Israel, "Spinoza and Early Modern Theology," 579. The descriptor "radical Enlightenment" is that of Leo Strauss, *Spinoza's Critique of Religion*, trans. E. M. Sinclair (New York: Schocken, 1965), 140. See also Joseph Cardinal Ratzinger, "Biblical Interpretation in Conflict: On the Foundations and Itinerary of Exegesis Today," in *Opening Up the Scriptures: Joseph Ratzinger and the Foundations of Biblical Interpretation*, ed. José Granados, Carlos Granados, and Luis Sánchez-Navarro, essay trans. Adrian Walker (Grand Rapids: Eerdmans, 2008), 8, 12–13, 17–19.

10. Spinoza, *Theologico-Political Treatise*, 100.

studies.[11] For Spinoza, neither theology nor tradition determines the meaning of biblical texts, but only history done according to these restricted, modern canons of reason. Hence, Spinoza writes, "The universal rule in interpreting Scripture is to accept nothing as an authoritative Scriptural statement which we do not perceive very clearly when we examine it in the light of its history."[12]

History, therefore, is *the* proper mode for biblical study, and Spinoza lists three principal aspects of what constitutes "history" as regards the Bible.[13] First, historical study of the Bible requires the study of the original languages in which the biblical texts were written and which their authors used. Second, history involves analyzing the books and their contents with a special interest in the human author's intended meaning. Important for Spinoza here is the severing of a text's "truth" and its "meaning."[14] The scholar's interest is to not determine the truth of a text (i.e., its doctrinal truth or divine teaching), but rather the text's meaning, which Spinoza in turn identifies with the human author's intention: "We are at work not on the truth of passages, but solely on their meaning."[15] The author's intended meaning is ascertained by historical analysis of the biblical texts: "In order not to confound the meaning of a passage with its truth, we must examine it solely by means of the signification of the words, or by a reason acknowledging no foundation but Scripture."[16] As Hans Frei reflects on Spinoza's program, the truth of a text "becomes a matter of demonstration in which, presumably, scriptural ideas are measured for their agreement or disagreement with the universal faith by means of general ideas drawn from human nature."[17] Moreover, this quest for the author's intended meaning entails that the interpreter study a text on its own terms and in its own historical context—and not impose his or her own ideas or beliefs on the text.[18] In short, the study of Scripture becomes a secular, historicist endeavor, and any consideration of the truth of a text comes from evaluating its ideas according to some philosophical criteria.[19]

11. Kugel, *How to Read the Bible*, 31.
12. Spinoza, *Theologico-Political Treatise*, 101.
13. Spinoza, *Theologico-Political Treatise*, 100–103.
14. See Louis Dupré, *The Enlightenment and the Intellectual Foundations of Modern Culture* (New Haven: Yale University Press, 2004), 231–32; Hans W. Frei, *The Eclipse of Biblical Narrative: A Study in Eighteenth and Nineteenth Century Hermeneutics* (New Haven: Yale University Press, 1974), 42–46; Hahn and Wiker, *Politicizing the Bible*, 373–75.
15. Spinoza, *Theologico-Political Treatise*, 101.
16. Spinoza, *Theologico-Political Treatise*, 101.
17. Frei, *Eclipse of Biblical Narrative*, 44.
18. Spinoza, *Theologico-Political Treatise*, 103.
19. As Steven Smith remarks of the program of biblical study that Spinoza inaugurates, "This higher criticism aims at nothing less than the historical understanding and reconstruction of the Bible. Spinoza's biblical criticism is, then, historical criticism; its goal is the historicization or

The third aspect of history in Spinoza's program is an extension of the first two points. Namely, we study the historical setting of the author and of the original audience, as well as the book's composition history and the transmission history of a biblical text: the biblical scholar should examine "the life, the conduct, and the studies of the author of each book, who he was, what was the occasion, and the epoch of his writing, whom did he write for, and in what language."[20] For Spinoza, the biblical scholar's task is to determine the text's meaning, which is the same as the human author's intention. The proper means for determining the text's meaning are history and philology, deployed according to modern canons of reason.

Sitting within the trajectory of Cartesian skepticism, Spinoza holds that only when there is clarity on all these historical matters (à la Descartes's "clear and distinct ideas") can a scholar claim to have ascertained an authoritative teaching of Scripture. But given the way that Spinoza sets up the rules of the game, this is a veritably impossible task (and part of Spinoza's political endgame).[21] Consequently, as Jeffrey Morrow observes, "All the exegete is left with are the numerous historical questions and the fruitless investigations to try and answer them."[22]

When we consider the general program that Spinoza bequeaths to modern biblical studies, it is striking that in this program there is neither any place nor consideration for transcendence. The Bible, its contents, and its readers are considered wholly within the closed system, or what Charles Taylor calls "the immanent frame."[23] The study of the Bible is reduced to philology and history and aims at determining a text's meaning, which is identified with the human author's intention. Moreover, historical study must proceed according to specific modern canons of rationality and causality—no considerations from theology or faith traditions are admissible. The historical and temporal realities depicted in the Bible are to be understood only in terms of the closed system's internal causes.[24] Scott Hahn and Benjamin Wiker link Spinoza's account of human reason to the conceptual view of the world as a

secularization of the biblical text." Smith, *Spinoza, Liberalism, and the Question of Jewish Identity* (New Haven: Yale University Press, 1997), 36, quoted in Hahn and Wiker, *Politicizing the Bible*, 374.

20. Smith, *Spinoza, Liberalism*, 103.

21. Hahn and Wiker, *Politicizing the Bible*, 375–88.

22. Jeffrey L. Morrow, *Three Skeptics and the Bible: La Peyrère, Hobbes, Spinoza and the Reception of Modern Biblical Criticism* (Eugene, OR: Pickwick, 2016), 130. He writes, "One of the purposes of all this tedium is to narrow down the point of Scripture to a few general moral principles (love of neighbor and obedience to the state) which in turn served both his religious and political ideals" (128).

23. Charles Taylor, *A Secular Age* (Cambridge, MA: Belknap, 2007), 542.

24. Francis Martin, "Revelation as Disclosure: Creation," in *Wisdom and Holiness, Science and Scholarship: Essays in Honor of Matthew L. Lamb*, ed. Michael Dauphinais and Matthew Levering (Naples, FL: Sapientia Press, 2007), 243.

closed mechanical system: "Spinoza held a severely restricted view of reason, that is, a view of reason restricted to one of its modes, mathematical reason. This restricted account of reason (and hence science) stands or falls on the reductionist mathematical-mechanical account of nature upon which it was built, and this restricted view of nature may itself be unreasonable."[25]

For Spinoza, what the Bible yields to historical study "are concepts strictly embedded in history understood as a linear space-time continuum."[26] There is no place for God or transcendence in the study of the Bible. Such dismissal of God and transcendent causality has led to the labeling of modern biblical criticism as "*methodologically* atheistic."[27] Brian Daley explains the label in this way: "Only 'natural', inner-worldly explanations of why or how things happen, explanations that could be acceptable to believers and unbelievers alike, are taken as historically admissible. So God is not normally understood to count as an actor on the stage of history; God's providence in history, the divine inspiration of Scriptural authors and texts, even the miracles narrated in the Bible, are assumed to be private interpretations of events, interior and non-demonstrable, rather than events or historical forces in themselves."[28] Within this view of things, the existence or nonexistence of God has no bearing on the interpretation and analysis of the Bible. And so, a construal of the world as a closed system with no place for transcendence has no place for understanding Scripture as putting its readers in living contact with divine reality.

If the historical study of the Bible—which, to reiterate, is a legitimate and important endeavor—is to be of service to orthodox Christian theology and help us to grasp how Scripture can put its audience in living contact with God, then it must be refitted to a conceptual context that recognizes the radically transcendent yet immanently present Creator and the continual dependence of all creation upon him. In other words, the study of the Bible should be situated within the horizon of the Distinction and the metaphysics of creation.

### The Bible and the Open System: Creation

The Distinction and the metaphysics of creation impact the understanding of Scripture in a variety of ways. We will focus here on two in particular: first, God's presence to the world; second, God's nonviolent, transcendent causality.

25. Hahn and Wiker, *Politicizing the Bible*, 391.
26. Levering, *Participatory Biblical Exegesis*, 116.
27. Brian E. Daley, SJ, "Is Patristic Exegesis Still Usable?: Reflections on Early Christian Interpretation of the Psalms," *Communio* 29 (2002): 191 (emphasis original).
28. Daley, "Is Patristic Exegesis Still Usable?," 191.

### God's Presence to the World

As Robert Sokolowski has argued, the Distinction provides the most basic context for all theological thinking. We must, therefore, seek to understand the mediation of divine reality and God's causal power through Scripture within the context provided by the Distinction. To begin with, the Distinction and the metaphysics of creation steer us away from conceiving of God as some "thing" external to the world, which is naturally closed off to him. As we have seen, modern thought has tended to conceive of God as a supreme kind of being who exists alongside the world simply as its efficient cause. If God were to act in the closed system, it would only be by way of miraculous interventions, which would themselves be construed as a violation of the system's internal laws. This construal of God and God's action vis-à-vis the world, however, is theologically aberrant and inadequate.

By contrast, the Distinction entails that God is not any kind of thing or being. The Creator radically transcends creation, while being immanently present to it. The radical otherness of the Creator enables him to be so intimately present to all things. The participatory ontology of creation furthermore holds that all contingent things continually receive their act of existing from the Creator, who is the pure, limited act of existing itself. Since a created thing's essence cannot cause its own existing, it must continually receive its act of existing from a source other than itself. This per se causal series must originate in a source that is the pure act of existing itself. In other words, every single thing that exists—from subatomic particles to galaxies, from strawberries to skyscrapers, from ants to angels—is grounded, in the depths of its being and at every moment of its existence, in the very life of the Creator God.[29]

Since the transcendent Creator is present to all creation and at all times as the ground of its existence, there is no such thing as "God-less" space. There is no place where God is not in some respect actively present. Moreover, there is no time that is not present to God. As Matthew Lamb has shown, Augustine had a crucial role in parsing the relationship between God's eternal, creative presence and the temporal existence of creatures.[30] Anticipating theologically what would be discovered scientifically in twentieth-century physics, Augustine argues that time is ingredient to the nature of created reality. As he

29. Similarly noted in Robert Barron, *And Now I See: A Theology of Transformation* (New York: Crossroad, 1998), 5–6.

30. Matthew L. Lamb, "Temporality and History: Reflections from St. Augustine and Bernard Lonergan," *Nova et Vetera*, English edition 4 (2006): 815–50, esp. 828–38. See also Francis Martin, "Some Aspects of Biblical Studies since Vatican II: The Contribution and Challenge of *Dei Verbum*," in *Sacred Scripture: The Disclosure of the Word* (Naples, FL: Sapientia Press, 2006), 239–43.

famously put it in *City of God*, "The world was not created *in* time but *with* time."[31] God's eternity is a fullness of presence, which creates and embraces the whole of created, temporal existence. For Augustine, Lamb writes, "the whole of reality, including all past, present, and future events, [is] present in the Divine Presence as 'totum esse praesens.'"[32]

This account of participatory ontology militates against a construal of the world as a closed system with God solely as an extrinsic efficient cause. Rather, God is present to all things in the depths of their being, and God keeps them in existence at all times. He does so as the very ground from which all things continually receive their very existence. In this way, Aquinas's metaphysics of participation comes to light as deeply spiritual, even mystical. This is also why Augustine can famously say of God, "You were more inward than my most inward part and higher than the highest element within me."[33]

The doctrine and metaphysics of creation thus entail that all things exist continually in relationship with the Creator God. In this light, *we can think of all things as having an inner, vertical dimension to their being.* From the depths of their being, all things exist in continuous relationship with God, and much of this relationship, though real, remains hidden from empirical observation. Particular aspects of this dimension only come to light when they are revealed.

Such thinking of created realities as having an inner, spiritual dimension finds an analogy in interpersonal relationships. Consider the following example. I am sitting in a coffee shop, and I notice two individuals, Smith and Jones, whom I do not know, sit down at another table. At first, both Smith and Jones appear tense, and their facial expressions are stern. But as the two sit and converse, they appear to become more relaxed and comfortable with each other. Eventually, they get up from the table, shake hands, smile, and then go their separate ways.

I can learn a variety of things about these two people from empirical observation of things at a distance. What remain hidden from my outsider's view are the inner, personal dimensions of this interaction. Let us say that I later learn that those two individuals had been lifelong friends but had had a bitter falling-out a few years ago. Their meeting at the coffee shop was the moment of their reconciliation after a long period of feuding. These deeply personal and meaningful aspects of their meeting remain hidden from my

---

31. Augustine, *City of God* 11.6, quoted in Lamb, "Temporality and History," 836.

32. Lamb, "Temporality and History," 830, quoting Augustine, *Confessions* 11.11.

33. Augustine, *Confessions* 3.6.11, in Augustine, *Confessions*, trans. Henry Chadwick (Oxford: Oxford University Press, 1991), 43.

view and come to light only by their being revealed to me by another. My learning of their past history and the significance of their current meeting does not negate those things that I had learned from observation but rather complements them.

As they are created and kept in existence by God at every moment, all created things possess such an inner, vertical dimension wherein they are most deeply grounded in God. This ontological relationship applies to all created realities, including the people who produced the biblical books, the created realities of which the biblical books speak, and all those individuals (past and present) who have read these books. This is a natural aspect of all created realities as they are ontologically participants in God's *esse*. This inner dimension is intensified and elevated when certain realities are caught up into the divine economy of salvation, wherein God reveals himself and unfolds his saving plan—a point to which we shall return in chapter 9.

Methodologically, the fact that created realities have this invisible dimension of their being means that the tools of historical and literary analysis cannot in principle exhaust the meaning and significance of the biblical texts and realities.[34] Just as, in the example cited above, there was more to the encounter between the two people in the coffee shop than what I could observe, so too are there dimensions of biblical realities, authors, and readers that empirical analysis cannot discern. These aspects are what Matthew Levering has called the "participatory dimension[s]" whereby things exist in continual relationship with the immanently present Creator God.[35] Recognition of this aspect of created being opens the conceptual space for other modes of knowing biblical realities and discerning their significance (e.g., liturgy, creeds, prayer, lived faith-experience). As Levering has aptly put it, "To enter into the realities taught in the biblical texts requires not only linear-historical tools (archaeology, philology, and so forth), but also and indeed primarily, participatory tools—doctrines and practices—by which the exegete enters fully into the biblical world."[36]

Historical and literary analysis remains an important element in biblical study. The texts and realities of the Bible have a historical and literary character, and the corresponding mode of study can only increase our understanding

---

34. Cf. the distinction between "critical history" and "real history" made by Maurice Blondel. See Maurice Blondel, "History and Dogma," in *"The Letter on Apologetics" & "History and Dogma,"* trans. Alexander Dru and Illtyd Trethowan (Grand Rapids: Eerdmans, 1994), 236–39; William M. Wright IV, "The Literal Sense of Scripture according to Henri de Lubac: Insights from Patristic Exegesis of the Transfiguration," *Modern Theology* 28 (2012): 267–70.

35. Levering, *Participatory Biblical Exegesis*, 3.

36. Levering, *Participatory Biblical Exegesis*, 1–2.

of the sacred text. But these modes of study are not sufficient for understanding the biblical realities in their fullness. To contemplate the depths of
these biblical realities, historical and literary modes of analysis need to be
situated within the setting of the Distinction and the metaphysics of creation
and be complemented by those "participatory tools—doctrines and practices"
that Levering mentions.

### God's Nonviolent, Transcendent Causality

Scripture's capacity to put people in living and life-giving contact with
divine realities involves God's action in and through created realities. Accordingly, it is important to add some reflections on God's nonviolent, transcendent causality in light of the preceding account of creation.

The Distinction holds that God is not any kind of thing, and he does
not create the world out of any necessity. Accordingly, God neither rivals
created realities in any way nor compromises their natural integrities when
he interacts with them. Creatures do not exist over against God in the way
that two things exist over against each other. Accordingly, God's transcendent activity cannot be conceived of as an intervention or breach of natural
laws—as if God were one thing exerting force against another thing. Rather,
as Sokolowski and Barron have argued, God's causal activity with respect to
creation is essentially nonviolent and noncompetitive. God "causes" creation
by sustaining all things in existence at every moment. Moreover, the immanent
presence of the Creator to all creatures is likewise noninvasive since creatures
are themselves grounded in the Creator's own being. Creatures continually
receive their own act of existing from God's own being, and accordingly, he
is present to all things in the depths of their being.

The intrinsically nonviolent metaphysics of participation also informs how
we might think of God's causal activity vis-à-vis the world. Very helpful here
is the Thomistic distinction between primary and secondary causes.[37] Brian
Davies succinctly sums up Aquinas's understanding of the matter: "God is
the first cause of all being and change. He is, therefore, the *primary* cause
of everything. . . . But Aquinas also thinks that God sometimes brings about
events by arranging for them to be the effects of causes distinct from himself
. . . what Aquinas calls *secondary* causes."[38]

---

37. A very succinct presentation of Aquinas's thought on this matter, to which we are here
indebted, is given in Brian Davies, *The Thought of Thomas Aquinas* (Oxford: Clarendon,
1992), 163–65. Also helpful is Étienne Gilson, *Christian Philosophy of St. Thomas Aquinas*,
trans. L. K. Shook, CSB (Notre Dame, IN: University of Notre Dame Press, 1994), 180–86.
38. Davies, *Thought of Thomas Aquinas*, 163.

As their Creator, God is the primary cause of all things.[39] Aquinas writes in the *Summa Theologica*, "All beings apart from God are not their own being [*esse*], but are beings by participation [*participant esse*]. Therefore it must be that all things which are diversified by the diverse participation of being, so as to be more or less perfect, are caused [*causari*] by one First Being, Who possesses being most perfectly."[40] Put differently, God is the first and most fundamental cause of all things, for he brings into existence and continuously sustains in existence all things. For Aquinas, this is primary causality, and it belongs only to God the Creator.

But God also endows the things that he creates with the power to produce effects of their own accord. As Aquinas writes in his *On the Power of God*, God "gave natural things the powers by which they can act, not only as the producer . . . but also as keeping the power in existence."[41] God creates things with causal powers of their own, such that created things can be real causes of real effects. In the Thomistic vocabulary, these are "secondary causes."[42] We might say that God "sets up" things' natures to have particular causal powers by which they can produce a range of effects correlated with those powers.

This distinction between primary and secondary causes is helpful for thinking about God's causal activity in and through created realities. On the one hand, Aquinas holds that God can exercise his causal power to produce certain effects by using secondary causes: "There are certain intermediaries of God's providence; for He governs things inferior by superior, not on account of any defect in His power, but by reason of the abundance of His goodness; so that the dignity of causality is imparted even to creatures."[43] Since God is the very ground of a creature's being, God can nonviolently move created things to bring about effects that he wants, and without compromising the freedom and integrity of those created things. That is, God can employ things as causes to produce effects that those things can produce by their own powers. For

39. So Aquinas, *Summa Theologica* I, q. 19, a. 4, co.

40. Aquinas, *Summa Theologica* I, q. 44, a. 1, co. He later adds, "From the fact that a thing has being by participation, it follows that it is caused." *Summa Theologica* I, q. 44, a. 1, ad. 1.

41. Aquinas, *On the Power of God* q. 3, a. 7, in Thomas Aquinas, *The Power of God*, trans. Richard J. Regan (Oxford: Oxford University Press, 2012), 56, cited in Davies, *Thought of Thomas Aquinas*, 163–64.

42. See Aquinas, *On the Power of God* q. 3, a. 7 (Regan, 54); references from Davies, *Thought of Thomas Aquinas*, 164. That created realities have their own causal power is evident from sense experience, despite David Hume's famous, yet flawed, construal of cause and effect as two separate events, instead of a single event considered from two different angles. For this critique of Hume, see Feser, *Last Superstition*, 64–67, 102–8; Feser, *Aquinas*, 20–23, 53–55.

43. Aquinas, *Summa Theologica* I, q. 22, a. 3, co, referenced by Davies, *Thought of Thomas Aquinas*, 163.

instance, Aquinas uses the example of a person cutting with a knife.[44] When a person cuts a loaf of bread with a knife, both the person and the knife each cut the bread. The person cuts the bread by using the knife as an instrument (i.e., a secondary cause) to produce an effect (i.e., cut the bread), which the knife has the potential to do by its own causal capabilities.

Given that God is not a "thing" and he is intimately present to all created realties, when God works through secondary causes, he does so noninvasively and without compromising a thing's nature. Accordingly, on a Thomistic account, there is no contradiction or competition between God's providential governing of the world and the various forces, structures, and processes of the natural world.[45]

But on the other hand, Aquinas also holds that God, the ever-present Creator, can exercise causal power in the world without a secondary cause or beyond a secondary cause's capacity. This is, according to Aquinas, a miracle.[46] Davies points out that, for Aquinas, miracles should not be construed as an intervention of God where God was not already present—that is, as an intervention by God into the closed system from without.[47] As we have seen, the metaphysics of creation holds that God is continuously present to all creatures at the deepest part of their being. There is no place where God is not present. Nor should miracles be construed as God violently breaking the laws of nature. Keep in mind that the Distinction teaches that the whole of creation is radically contingent. It does not have to exist, and it owes its entire existence to God. Therefore, Davies writes, "if God miraculously brings about something in the created order, that is no more a violation of the created order than is the fact that this order exists in the first place."[48] Both the providential governance of creation and a miracle are effects of God's will brought about by different ways.[49] The main difference between a miracle and the ordinary workings of divine providence is the presence or absence of a secondary cause. Davies summarizes the matter very well: "Miracles, for [Aquinas], do not occur because of an extra added ingredient (i.e., God).

---

44. See Aquinas, *On the Power of God* q. 7, a. 3 (Regan, 56).

45. For instance, the processes of biological evolution are compatible with the doctrine of creation, when the former are seen as the series of secondary causes by which God, the primary cause of all things, brings about the material origins of things. For an illuminating analysis of these and related issues, see Nicanor Pier Giorgio Austriaco, OP, James Brent, OP, Thomas Davenport, OP, and John Baptist Ku, OP, *Thomistic Evolution: A Catholic Approach to Understanding Evolution in the Light of Faith* (Tacoma: Cluny Media, 2016).

46. Davies, *Thought of Thomas Aquinas*, 172.

47. Davies, *Thought of Thomas Aquinas*, 173.

48. Davies, *Thought of Thomas Aquinas*, 173.

49. Davies, *Thought of Thomas Aquinas*, 173.

They occur because something is *not* present (i.e., a secondary cause or a collection of secondary causes)."[50]

As the grounding for all things' existence, God can act nonviolently in the world by means of secondary causes (i.e., created realities that possess their own causal powers) or without any secondary causes (i.e., the definition of a miracle). Therefore, when considering the mediation of divine reality and power through Scripture, we have some conceptual resources for thinking of God's acting in and through created realities (e.g., human discourse and the realities of the divine economy) without compromising their nature as created realities.

## Looking Back and Looking Forward

We have brought some of our theological and philosophical reflections on creation to bear on the interpretation of Scripture. We discussed the construal of the world as a closed system: a vast cosmic machine with God (if his existence is affirmed) understood only as an external, efficient cause. On this view, God is one kind of thing contrasted with the world as another kind of thing. This closed-system model influenced the program for modern biblical criticism set forth by Baruch Spinoza. Spinoza denies any kind of transcendent reality, and his program for biblical interpretation reflects this belief. Spinoza restricts biblical study to historical and philological analysis and denies any hermeneutical role given to religious beliefs, practices, or participation in the faith community. Without a conceptual overhaul, which opens up the space for transcendence and transcendent causality, his program simply cannot grasp how Scripture puts its audience in living contact with God.

By contrast, the Distinction and the congruent, Thomistic metaphysics of creation identify the world as an open system. As the Creator of all things, God is radically transcendent yet intimately present to all things in the very depths of their being. Since God is not any kind of being, God's presence to the world is noninvasive, and his causal activity is nonviolent. As created participants, ontologically grounded in God's *esse*, all created beings possess an inner dimension wherein they are acutely and intimately related to God. These inner aspects are real, though not apparent to empirical observation. Applied to the topic of Scripture, the historical and literary analysis of the Bible and its contents, while very important, is not all-sufficient. A robust appreciation for creation leads us to recognize the validity and necessity of

---

50. Davies, *Thought of Thomas Aquinas*, 174.

what Levering calls "participatory tools [of scriptural study]" such as the religious beliefs and practices of the faith community, in order to arrive at a deeper understanding of the biblical realities.

As we have seen, an interpreter's metaphysical ideas impact how he or she thinks about God's presence and causal activity with respect to the world. These ideas can also affect how one thinks about other areas pertinent to Scripture, such as how human beings come into cognitive contact with realities other than themselves and do so by way of a written medium. In the next chapter, therefore, we will bring some of these theological and metaphysical ideas about creation to bear on the relationship between the mind, words, and the world. The relationship between these natural realities provides a basis for thinking about how divine reality can be mediated to human knowers through the written biblical text.

# 8

# Creation and the Communion of Mind, Words, and World

The belief that Scripture puts its audience in living and life-giving contact with the divine realities that it mediates entails at a very basic level that in the act of reading or hearing Scripture, a person encounters various things that are external to him- or herself. For instance, we encounter the biblical text itself and its discourse, the voices of those human beings who composed the biblical texts. The biblical discourse is also about something. The Bible speaks of concrete historical realities such as Jesus or the Jerusalem temple, but also of things of other sorts such as prescriptions for moral and liturgical action, spiritual thoughts and insights, and so on. When we read or hear Scripture, therefore, we encounter various things that are independent of ourselves. We are encountering these things, and not inventing or projecting them.

The belief that Scripture puts us in contact with such external things further entails that these things have an intelligibility of their own. By "intelligibility," we mean the "intellectual structure" or intrinsic pattern of things that enables them to "make sense" and be intellectually grasped by a knower.[1] If

---

1. The phrase "intellectual structure" is from Joseph Cardinal Ratzinger, *Introduction to Christianity*, trans. J. R. Foster (San Francisco: Ignatius, 2004), 152. As Robert Sokolowski observes, the term "intelligibility" is a contemporary way of getting at what is called "form" in classical and medieval philosophy. See Robert Sokolowski, *Phenomenology of the Human Person* (Cambridge: Cambridge University Press, 2008), 166–69. This correlation of "intelligibility" and "form" finds warrant in Aquinas's association of a thing's nature or essence with its knowability. See Aquinas, *On Being and Essence* 9, 70.

something were inherently unintelligible, no one could ever comprehend or communicate anything about it.[2] Even though much of what Scripture talks about exceeds human comprehension (e.g., God), this excess does not mean Scripture's contents lack an intelligibility of their own. Rather it may be due, as Aquinas holds, to a defect in the human capabilities to grasp the excessive intelligibility of these biblical realities.[3] The point here is that in Scripture, we encounter intelligible discourse about intelligible things. It provides information that comes to us "preformed," and it is neither intrinsically unintelligible nor the pure projection or creation of Scripture's audience.[4]

When a person hears or reads the words of Scripture and understands them to some extent, he or she comes into cognitive contact with the realities of which Scripture speaks. Just as our study of Scripture's mediating an encounter with God called for reflections on God and his relationship to creation, so too does it call for reflections on human cognition, its relationship to reality, and the ways in which words put people in cognitive contact with reality.

The notion that in the act of knowing, human beings come into genuine contact with intelligible realities other than themselves is called epistemological realism.[5] It holds that human beings can genuinely (even if imperfectly) know the truth about reality that exists independently of the knower. Certain trends in modern philosophy, however, are skeptical of—or deny outright—the notion that human beings can have genuine knowledge of extramental reality. Indeed, such denials of the human ability to know extramental, intelligible reality are a major impediment to a proper reception of the biblical teaching on encountering God through Scripture. For if human beings cannot come into genuine cognitive contact with a reality independent of themselves in the act of knowing, then they cannot come into cognitive contact with the divine realities mediated by the biblical text.

In this chapter, therefore, we provide a basic account, building off our previous reflections on creation, for how people can come into genuine contact with intelligible realities through the medium of language. First, we will bring the topic of creation to bear on the subject of human cognition by reflecting

2. So Josef Pieper, "The Negative Element in the Philosophy of St. Thomas Aquinas," in *The Silence of St. Thomas: Three Essays*, trans. John Murray, SJ, and Daniel O'Connor (South Bend, IN: St. Augustine's Press, 1957), 59–60.

3. Thomas Aquinas, *Summa Theologica* I, q. 1, a. 5, ad. 2.

4. W. Norris Clarke, SJ, "The 'We Are' of Interpersonal Dialogue as the Starting Point of Metaphysics," in *Explorations in Metaphysics: Being—God—Person* (Notre Dame, IN: University of Notre Dame Press, 1994), 34.

5. See Étienne Gilson, *Thomist Realism and the Critique of Knowledge*, trans. Mark W. Wauck (San Francisco: Ignatius, 1986); Gilson, *Methodical Realism: A Handbook for Beginning Realists*, trans. Philip Trower (San Francisco: Ignatius, 1990).

on voices from Scripture and tradition that link the intelligibility of things to their being created by God. Second, we consider the highly influential challenge to this vision in some modern philosophical circles and in particular by Immanuel Kant. Kant's theory of knowledge effectively denies the intrinsic intelligibility of things and makes the individual determinative in the act of knowing. In doing so, Kantianism poses a unique challenge to our understanding of how Scripture mediates an encounter with divine reality. Third, we will respond to the Kantian problem by offering an alternative, realist account of the cognitive union between mind and world. We will again draw on the philosophical contributions of W. Norris Clarke both to identify some flaws in the basic Kantian vision and to offer a constructive alternative based on the relational ontology of creation discussed previously. Fourth, we will reflect on the role of human language in mediating the intelligibility of things to a knowing subject by making use of Robert Sokolowski's phenomenological analyses of human language and intentionality.

## The Intelligibility of Creation and the Wisdom of the Creator

We begin our reflections on human knowing with an experience to which all can relate: no one likes being lied to. As Augustine aptly put it, "I have met with many people who wished to deceive, [but] none who wished to be deceived."[6] Being lied to, being deliberately deceived by another, is an unpleasant, negative experience. Why is this so?

To begin with, we might ask, "What makes a lie to be a lie?" A person who lies to us presents something as being true, and we take it as such. But when the lie is found out, what the other person has presented as being true turns out, first, to be false and, second, as having been deliberately misrepresented by the other person as the truth. We can identify several aspects of wrongness involved in this case, and we highlight two of them here. First, there is a wrongness concerning what is proposed to be the case and what actually is the case.[7] For instance, the liar may say, "Smith took the papers," while knowing that in fact Jones took the papers. The liar says X is true, when in fact X is false (and the liar knows that X is false). But there is also wrongness at the moral and personal level. We initially trust that the other person is being

6. Augustine, *Confessions* 10.23.33, in Augustine, *Confessions*, trans. Henry Chadwick (Oxford: Oxford University Press, 1991), 199. See also Pope John Paul II, *Fides et Ratio* §25, which likewise adduces this text.

7. Our way of framing the matter is indebted to the "disquotational theory of truth" given in Robert Sokolowski, *Introduction to Phenomenology* (Cambridge: Cambridge University Press, 2000), 97–104.

truthful in his or her words to us. But when the lie is found out, we realize that the other person has been deliberately deceptive. It is not simply that the other person has been mistaken in his or her speech but that the person has willfully misled us. We have been betrayed by the person who lied to us, for there has been a breach of personal trust.

And yet the very fact that we feel frustrated, angry, or upset when we realize that we have been lied to reveals something quite positive and profound about us as human beings. Namely, we want to know the truth about the world, about other people, about ourselves. We want to know what and how things really are on their own terms and not just another person's subjective take on them (which may or may not be true to reality). This drive to know what is actually the case is precisely why being lied to or deceived is such a negative experience. We seek to know some truth about the world (what is the case) and also about another person (namely, that he or she is trustworthy). But when we are deceived, both turn out to be false. Hence, we are wronged. This basic point—human beings want to know the world and the things in it truthfully and accurately—was famously made by Aristotle in the very first line of his book *The Metaphysics*: "By nature, all men long to know."[8]

The natural inclination of human beings to know the truth has as its correlative the intrinsic intelligibility of reality. Debates over the intrinsic intelligibility of reality are complex and long-standing in the history of philosophy, and delving into them would lead this project too far afield. Suffice it to say that this belief that the world has an intrinsic intelligibility (or knowability) underlies the whole of the natural sciences.[9] The sciences presuppose (and cannot by themselves prove) that the natural world has an intelligibility that can be discovered, studied, analyzed, and so on by human reason. We also find affirmations of the intelligibility of the world in both Scripture and subsequent Christian thought. Witnesses from both Scripture and Christian tradition ground the intrinsic intelligibility of the world in the doctrine of creation.

### Testimony from Scripture

Scriptural texts that associate the Word of God with creation display this grounding of the world's intelligibility in its being created by God. The seven-day account of creation in Genesis 1:1–2:4a presents the world created by God as good and well ordered. A principal means by which Genesis 1 teaches the

8. Aristotle, *The Metaphysics* 980a, trans. Hugh Lawson-Tancred (New York: Penguin, 1998), 4.
9. Edward Feser, *Scholastic Metaphysics: A Contemporary Introduction* (Heusenstamm: Editiones Scholasticae, 2014), 11.

order, purpose, and intelligibility of the world is through its literary mode (e.g., its repetition, formulaic language, symmetrical literary structure). The Wisdom literature likewise speaks to the created world as being suffused with God's Wisdom. As we discussed in chapter 1, Wisdom literature often depicts God's Word, or Wisdom, as present when God creates the world. Thus, God's personified Wisdom says in Proverbs 8:27, "When he established the heavens, I was there, when he drew a circle on the face of the deep." In the prayer addressed to God in the Wisdom of Solomon (which identifies God's Wisdom with God's Word), we read, "With you is wisdom, she who knows your works and was present when you made the world" (Wis. 9:9). By so associating God's Wisdom with God's creative activity, the Wisdom books present the created world as reflecting God's Wisdom. There are, to use Augustine's expression, "traces" of the Creator in the creation.[10]

That the created world reflects the wisdom of the Creator provides theological warrant for the philosophical project of natural theology, which holds that human beings can by their own natural abilities know something about the Deity and often by way of creation. A basic form of this belief appears in circles of Greek-speaking Judaism prior to the birth of Jesus. For instance, the Wisdom of Solomon voices a conventional Jewish polemic against the worship of created things by gentile pagans. The author indicts the gentiles: "They were unable from the good things that are seen to know the one who exists, nor did they recognize the artisan while paying heed to his works" (Wis. 13:1). The author sees such gentiles as genuinely seeking the divine (13:6–7), but they err in confusing the Creator with creation. Regardless, the author teaches that human beings can in fact know something about the Creator from creation, "for from the greatness and beauty of created things comes a corresponding perception of their Creator" (Wis. 13:5).

The intelligibility of the created world, as stemming from the wisdom of its Creator, is likewise presumed by Paul in Romans 1. In Romans 1:18–3:20, Paul sets forth the fundamental problem of the human race, to which God's saving action in Christ is the solution: the problem of sin (cf. 3:9). Paul begins

---

10. Augustine writes, "Now we are human beings, created in our Creator's image . . . and the constituents of the world which are inferior to us could not exist at all, could not have shape or form, could not aspire to any ordered pattern, or keep that pattern, had they not been created by him who supremely exists, and who is supremely wise and supremely Good. Therefore, let us run over all these things which he created in such wonderful stability, to collect the scattered traces of his being, more distinct in some places than in others." Augustine, *City of God* 11.28, in Augustine, *The City of God*, trans. Henry Bettenson (New York: Penguin, 1984), 463. For this reference and related discussion, see John C. Cavadini, "God's Eternal Knowledge according to Augustine," in *The Cambridge Companion to Augustine*, ed. David Vincent Meconi, SJ, and Eleonore Stump, 2nd ed. (Cambridge: Cambridge University Press, 2014), 45–47.

by explaining how the gentiles, who do not know God by divine revelation as do the Jews, give evidence of being afflicted by the reality of sin and stand guilty before God. Paul's argument turns on the point that some knowledge of God the Creator is available to gentile pagans from created nature. Echoing the Wisdom of Solomon, Paul writes, "Ever since the creation of the world [God's] eternal power and divine nature, invisible though they are, have been understood and seen through the things he has made" (1:20). The gentiles could in principle know something about the Creator from the creation and, on this basis, acknowledge and worship him. Moreover, Paul teaches that something about the Creator's will for human conduct can be known from creation and conscience. Thus, Paul writes that the gentiles, who "do instinctively what the law requires" (i.e., they do good deeds that are likewise prescribed in Torah), give evidence that "what the law requires is written on their hearts, to which their own conscience also bears witness" (2:14–15). Whether from speculative reasoning about the created world or practical moral reasoning, gentile pagans could know something about the Creator by their own natural abilities apart from revelation.

But the gentiles, "who by their wickedness suppress the truth" (Rom. 1:18), refuse to recognize and worship the Creator. By doing so, they stand guilty before God. Paul writes, "They exchanged the truth about God for a lie and revered and worshiped and served the creature rather than the Creator" (v. 25). As a result of this rebellion against the Creator, "God gave them up to a debased mind and to things that should not be done" (v. 28). God permits the people to rebel against him and then leaves them up to their own devices and to endure the consequences that follow from their sinful rebellion.

### Testimony from the Tradition

Turning to the larger Christian tradition, we will cite evidence from some prominent thinkers who likewise ground the intelligibility of the world in its being created by God. In a very famous essay, Josef Pieper makes the case that the doctrine of creation plays an integral, though understated, role in Thomas Aquinas's account of truth and human knowing.[11] To begin with, Pieper notes the close connection between ontological truth ("the truth of things in the world") and logical truth ("the truth of knowledge") for Aquinas.[12] In his *Disputed Questions on Truth*, Aquinas argues that truth resides primarily in the mind of the knower: "Truth is the adequation of thing and intellect. But this adequation can exist only in an intellect. Therefore truth exists only in an

11. See Pieper, "Negative Element," 43–71.
12. Pieper, "Negative Element," 50.

intellect."[13] In light of such a claim, Pieper writes, "Only what is thought can be called in the strict sense 'true,' but real things *are* something thought."[14] In other words, things are "true" because they are known by a subject. However, in this account, the knower who constitutes the truth of things is not a human knower, but rather *God the Creator*. Things are "ontologically true" and intrinsically intelligible because they are thought into being by the Creator.

To explain further, Pieper calls attention to another section of the same text by Aquinas. Here, Aquinas situates the truth of things in relation to God's knowing and to human knowing: "A natural thing, then, set up between two intellects, is said to be true by an adequation to both."[15] The two intellects of which Aquinas speaks are God's intellect and the human intellect. Created things are thus situated between these two intellects. Aquinas continues, "For according to the divine intellect [a thing] is said to be true so far as it fulfills that to which it is ordered by the divine intellect."[16] By this, Aquinas means that things are ontologically true and intelligible to others because things reflect an archetypal idea in God's mind. The intelligible nature of things (i.e., their essences) stems from their participating in God's ideas. Pieper adduces the following text from the *Summa Theologica* in this regard: "Every creature has its own proper species [i.e., essential nature], according to which it participates in some degree in the likeness to the divine essence. So far, therefore, as God knows His essence as capable of such imitation by any creature, He knows it as the particular type and idea of that creature."[17] In other words, it is because creatures reflect and participate in the wisdom of the Creator that they possess essential natures and an intrinsic intelligibility, which makes them knowable to us. It is because things are first "creatively thought by the Creator" that they can in turn be thought and known as true by others.[18]

Pieper discerns an important consequence in this situating of the truth of things between God's knowing and human knowing. Namely, things are both intelligible and yet can never be exhaustively grasped by the human mind. On the one hand, Aquinas holds that in the act of knowing, the human being does

13. Aquinas, *Disputed Questions on Truth* q. 1, a. 2, cited in James F. Anderson, ed. and trans., *An Introduction to the Metaphysics of St. Thomas Aquinas* (1953; repr., Washington, DC: Regnery, 1997), 66. By "adequation," Aquinas has in mind something like the *cognitive assimilation* of the intelligibility of the thing known to the knower.

14. Pieper, "Negative Element," 51.

15. Aquinas, *Disputed Questions on Truth* q. 1, a. 2, in Anderson, *Metaphysics of St. Thomas Aquinas*, 68.

16. Aquinas, *Disputed Questions on Truth* q. 1, a. 2, in Anderson, *Metaphysics of St. Thomas Aquinas*, 68.

17. Aquinas, *Summa Theologica* I, q. 15, a. 2, in Pieper, "Negative Element," 66.

18. Pieper, "Negative Element," 61.

grasp and assimilate the intelligibility of the thing known. But on the other hand, the intelligible reality of created things is grounded in their participation in God's mind (which is incomprehensible). Thus, the essential nature of things can never be wholly grasped by a created intellect: "The ultimate reality of things is something to which we can never finally penetrate, because we can never fully grasp these likenesses of the Divine Ideas precisely as likenesses."[19] While Aquinas is an epistemological realist (i.e., he holds that the mind obtains extramental reality in the act of knowing), there is a good deal of epistemological humility in this vision. There is no end to the human intellectual inquiry into things, because of the surplus richness in the intelligible reality of things. As Pieper concludes, "Things are inaccessible to human knowledge precisely because they are all too knowable."[20]

Joseph Ratzinger makes a similar argument in his *Introduction to Christianity*.[21] He begins by stating that anyone who claims to believe in God today is making a deliberate decision. It is a decision about what is good and important in the world, and it is a decision also between competing accounts of reality. In particular, Ratzinger argues that it is a "decision in favor of the primacy of the *logos* as against mere matter."[22] Here Ratzinger sets up Christian theism in contrast to materialism. By "the primacy of the *logos*," Ratzinger means that there is an intrinsic intelligibility, meaning, and value in reality itself. He writes, it "implies opting for the view that the *logos*—that is, the idea, freedom, love—stands not merely at the end but also at the beginning, that [*logos*] is the originating and encompassing power of all being."[23] Whereas a materialist vision would see such notions as truth and love as "a chance by-product of being" with "no structural, authoritative meaning for reality as a whole," Christian theism regards them as ingredient to the very structure of reality itself.[24]

According to Ratzinger, the intrinsic intelligibility of things stems from their being created by God: "The objective mind we find present in all things . . . is the impression and expression of subject mind."[25] God's creative mind impresses intelligibility into creatures in the act of creation. The intelligibility that things receive from the Creator in turn enables them to be thought and known by knowers. For Ratzinger, then, in the act of knowing of reality, a person "re-thinks" what God has already "thought" in the act of creating that reality:

---

19. Pieper, "Negative Element," 67.
20. Pieper, "Negative Element," 70.
21. Here we explicate argumentation from Ratzinger, *Introduction to Christianity*, 151–61.
22. Ratzinger, *Introduction to Christianity*, 151.
23. Ratzinger, *Introduction to Christianity*, 152.
24. Ratzinger, *Introduction to Christianity*, 152.
25. Ratzinger, *Introduction to Christianity*, 152.

"The intellectual structure that being possesses and that we can *re*-think is the expression of a creative *pre*-meditation, to which they owe their existence."[26]

Aquinas, Pieper, and Ratzinger all speak of the intelligibility of created things with reference to notion of "measuring."[27] Aquinas puts the matter succinctly: "The divine intellect measures but is not measured; natural things measure and are measured; but our intellect is measured, and it does not measure natural things but only artificial things."[28] That is to say, God's creative intellect imparts intelligibility to things (it "measures" them) and does not receive intelligibility from them (it is not "measured" by them). The created things receive their intelligibility from God (they are measured by God's intellect), and they also impart their intelligibility to knowing subjects (things measure the intellect of the knower). The human intellect receives the intelligibility of things and is so measured by them.

The upshot of this last point is that in the act of knowing, the human mind takes in (and becomes in some manner conformed to) the intelligibility of extramental things. The mind is in-formed by reality. This latter point is especially significant because it is rejected in some very influential sectors of modern thought. That is, in certain modern (and postmodern) accounts of the mind-and-world relationship, either reality as such is deemed unknowable, or it is the knower, not reality as such, who is determinative in the act of knowing, or both. This is especially the case in the highly influential thought of Immanuel Kant (1724–1809). Given the importance of this point (i.e., the mind takes in the intelligibility of things in the act of knowing) and the deleterious consequences of its denial, we must pursue the matter further.

## Modern Dilemmas

### The "Egocentric Predicament"

Many modern philosophical accounts of human knowing are caught up in what Robert Sokolowski has called the "egocentric predicament."[29] It follows from the claim that what a human being knows directly is an idea in his or her individual mind, not extramental reality as such. That is, we do not know

26. Ratzinger, *Introduction to Christianity*, 152.
27. So Aquinas, *Disputed Questions on Truth* q. 1, a. 2; Pieper, "Negative Element," 54; Ratzinger, *Introduction to Christianity*, 152–53. The explication that follows reflects Pieper, "Negative Element," 54.
28. Aquinas, *Disputed Questions on Truth* q. 1, a. 2, cited in Anderson, *Metaphysics of St. Thomas Aquinas*, 67–68.
29. Sokolowski, *Introduction to Phenomenology*, 9.

the extramental world but rather our mental representations of the world: our ideas. Sokolowski describes the problem in this way:

> In the Cartesian, Hobbesian, and Lockean traditions, which dominate our culture, we are told that when we are conscious, we are primarily aware of ourselves and our ideas. Consciousness is taken to be like a bubble or an enclosed cabinet. . . . Impressions and concepts occur in this enclosed space . . . and our awareness is directed towards them, not directly towards the things "outside." We can try to get outside by making inferences: . . . but we are not in any direct contact with them. . . . All we can really be sure of at the start is our own conscious existence and the states of that consciousness.[30]

The "egocentric predicament" entails that the individual knower is trapped within his or her mental subjectivity. All that one can really know are the ideas in one's mind. Since an individual's ideas are what he or she directly knows, any knowledge of extramental reality can only come by way of inference from his or her subjective ideas. In theories beset by the egocentric predicament, the mind is separated from the world (as well as the body) and set over against them—for the mind and its contents are all that the knower directly knows. And as Louis Dupré observes, "No rational argument can securely relink the mind to reality after we have defined it [i.e., the mind] as an isolated entity."[31] Once the bridge between the mind and the world has been destroyed, it cannot be rebuilt.

Such modern theories of knowledge isolate the human knower from the world and from other knowers. This severing of mind and world has further repercussions, writes Sokolowski: "If we are bereft of intentionality, if we do not have a world in common, then we do not enter into a life of reason, evidence, and truth. Each of us turns to his own private world, and in the practical order we do our own thing: the truth does not make any demands on us."[32] When worked out to its conclusions, the egocentric predicament rules out the possibility that human beings genuinely experience the world together, can engage in meaningful discussion and debate about it, and can come to know it accurately. Given that the human knower is cut off from the world and directly knows only his or her subjective ideas, it is difficult to see the egocentric predicament as ultimately resulting in anything but relativism: there is no commonly accessible truth, just individual subjective "takes" with no means to adjudicate rationally between them.[33]

---

30. Sokolowski, *Introduction to Phenomenology*, 9.
31. Louis Dupré, *Passage to Modernity: An Essay in the Hermeneutics of Nature and Culture* (New Haven: Yale University Press, 1993), 86.
32. Sokolowski, *Introduction to Phenomenology*, 10.
33. Sokolowski, *Introduction to Phenomenology*, 10.

These modern philosophical views stand in marked contrast with the general view held in classical and medieval philosophy. Josef Pieper provides an illuminating sketch of the classical account of the mind-and-world relationship.[34] According to the general view of classical philosophy, the world as such has an intrinsic intelligibility of its own. The human mind is receptive to the world's intelligibility and takes it in. For the premoderns, Pieper writes, "there was an element of purely receptive 'looking,' not only in sense perception but also in intellectual knowing or, as Heraclitus said, '*Listening-in to the being of things.*'"[35] With respect to human reasoning, Pieper notes that the medievals further "distinguished the intellect as *ratio* [i.e., reasoning] and the intellect as *intellectus* [i.e., understanding]."[36] Pieper further defines these terms: "*Ratio* is the power of discursive thought, of searching and re-searching, abstracting, refining, and concluding . . . whereas *intellectus* refers to the ability of 'simply looking' . . . to which the truth presents itself as a landscape presents itself to the eye."[37] According to these premoderns, Pieper concludes, human knowing has both active and contemplative dimensions: "The path of discursive reasoning is accompanied and penetrated by the *intellectus*' untiring vision, which is not active but passive, or better, *receptive*—a receptive operating power of the intellect."[38] In this view, it is extramental reality that is fundamentally determinative in the act of knowing. Reality impresses on the mind its intelligibility, which the mind not only receives but also actively investigates to understand more deeply.

This point—that the mind takes in the intelligibility of being in the act of knowing—is famously rejected by Immanuel Kant. For Kant, it is the individual knower, not reality as such, who is fundamentally determinative in the act of knowing.[39] In many ways, Kant has had an enormous impact on modern thought, and his influence extends to theology and thinking about Scripture. The influence of Kant is especially problematic for our appreciation of Scripture as putting people in living contact with divine reality, and therefore, Kant's thinking needs to be addressed. Though we are going to be

34. Josef Pieper, *Leisure: The Basis of Culture*, trans. Gerald Malsbary (South Bend, IN: St. Augustine's Press, 1998).

35. Pieper, *Leisure*, 11. The citation of Heraclitus in Pieper (*Leisure*, 11n5) is from Hermann Diels and Walther Kranz, eds., *Die Fragmente der Vorsokratiker*, 3 vols. (Berlin: Weidmannsche Verlagsbuchhandlung, 1952), frag. 112.

36. Pieper, *Leisure*, 11.

37. Pieper, *Leisure*, 11.

38. Pieper, *Leisure*, 11–12.

39. Language adapted from Francis Martin, "Reflections on Professor Bockmuehl's 'Bible versus Theology,'" *Nova et Vetera*, English edition 9 (2011): 49. Here, Martin speaks of "the Kantian principle that the subject is determinative in the act of knowledge."

critical of Kant's theories and take a different conceptual road, one cannot doubt his genius and the power of his contributions.

### The Kantian Account

Fundamental for Kant is the claim that human beings do not know things-in-themselves (i.e., the noumenal) but only appearances (i.e., the phenomenal). With this distinction, Kant makes a characteristically modern move by separating the reality of things from the ways in which things appear.[40] According to Kant, all that human beings can know is the way in which things appear to them; we cannot know things-in-themselves: "It is only the form of sensuous intuition . . . by which we can know objects only as they *appear* to us (to our senses), not as they are in themselves."[41] For Kant, the individual human knower takes in unorganized sense perceptions, which arise from things-in-themselves. Other than the fact that these unorganized sensations arise from things, human beings can know nothing about things-in-themselves. Kant states, "I say that things as objects of our senses existing outside us are given, but we know nothing of what they may be in themselves, knowing only their appearances, i.e., the representations which they cause in us by affecting our senses."[42] Since the knower can only know appearances (and appearances tell us nothing about things), one cannot make blanket claims about things-in-themselves on the basis of one's individual perception of them: "A grave error may arise due to illusion, in which I proclaim to be universally valid what is merely a subjective condition of the intuition of things and certain only for all objects of sense."[43]

According to Kant, the individual knower takes in these unorganized sense perceptions. These perceptions are then organized by the mind's faculty of judgment according to the universal structures of human cognition that are present in every human mind (i.e., what Kant calls the "categories").[44] The end product of this cognitive process of the mind's organization of brute sensations is "experience."[45]

The fundamentally important point here is that for Kant, the mind *imposes* intelligibility and organization onto unordered sense perceptions arising from

40. See Robert Sokolowski, *Eucharistic Presence: A Study in the Theology of Disclosure* (Washington, DC: Catholic University of America Press, 1993), 179–86.

41. Immanuel Kant, *Prolegomena to Any Future Metaphysics* #283, trans. James W. Ellington (Indianapolis: Hackett, 1977), 27.

42. Kant, *Prolegomena* #289 (Ellington, 33).

43. Kant, *Prolegomena* #292 (Ellington, 35).

44. For Kant's categories of cognition, see Kant, *Prolegomena* #303 (Ellington, 46–47).

45. Kant writes, "Experience consists in the synthetic connection of appearances (perceptions) in consciousness, so far as this connection is necessary." *Prolegomena* #305 (Ellington, 48).

external things. This is Kant's "Copernican revolution" in philosophy: it is not that an intelligible world gives itself to be understood by a knowing subject, but rather that the knowing subject imposes intelligibility and order onto sense perceptions.[46] According to Kant, the individual human being does not know reality as such or things-in-themselves, but only his or her own subjective experiences. In this account of human cognition, "the human mind is incapable of transcending its own consciousness to know things-in-themselves."[47] Furthermore, the individual's mind is fundamentally determinative in the synthetic creation of experiences, and these experiences constitute the object of consciousness. Intelligibility is not something discovered by the knower as much as it is imposed by the knower.

The basic Kantian claim that the individual cannot know things-in-themselves but only his or her subjective experiences, which are determined by cognitive categories, has for an intellectual descendant much contemporary historical and cultural relativism. Whereas for Kant the categories of cognition are present in every human mind, certain post-Kantian lines of thought relocate these reality-structuring categories from the individual's mind to his or her particular historical and cultural settings. In these post-Kantian accounts, Clarke writes, "we still impose intelligibility on the world from within our own a priori's [but in this case] . . . they are a priori's of culture and of language imprinted in us by the society in which we are brought up."[48] Since the experience that the individual knows receives its intelligibility from the imposition of particular historical, cultural, and linguistic categories (which are themselves relative to particular times and places), "there can be no culture- or history-transcending knowledge . . . [and no] metaphysical knowledge of real being with any claim to universally valid, objective truth."[49] Or as Matthew Lamb

46. Kant writes in his preface to the second edition of his *Critique of Pure Reason*, "Up to now it has been assumed that all our cognition must conform to the objects; but all attempts to find out something about them *a priori* through concepts that would extend our cognition have, on this presupposition, come to nothing. Hence let us once try whether we do not get farther with the problems of metaphysics by assuming that the objects must conform to our cognition. . . . This would be just like the first thoughts of Copernicus, who, when he did not make good progress in the explanation of the celestial motions if he assumed that the entire celestial host revolves around the observer, tried to see if he might not have greater success if he made the observer revolve and left the stars at rest." Kant, "Preface to the Second Edition," in *Critique of Pure Reason*, trans. Paul Guyer and Allen W. Wood (Cambridge: Cambridge University Press, 1998), b.xvi (p. 100).

47. W. Norris Clarke, SJ, "Action as the Self-Revelation of Being: A Central Theme in the Thought of St. Thomas," in *Explorations in Metaphysics*, 58.

48. W. Norris Clarke, SJ, *The One and the Many: A Contemporary Thomistic Metaphysics* (Notre Dame, IN: University of Notre Dame Press, 2001), 12.

49. Clarke, *The One and the Many*, 13.

puts the matter, "If intelligence were intrinsically conditioned by space and time, then we would need different sciences and scholarship for different places and times. There would be one chemistry for France and another for England."[50]

Since—on this view—the human being can only know his or her own subjective experience (which results from sense perceptions organized according to the categories of cognition), anything that cannot be known by sense perception cannot be said to be known at all. Only what is empirical and sensible can count toward knowledge. This restriction on "what counts" as knowledge has important ramifications for metaphysical and theological thinking. For one, Kant's theory of knowledge restricts the extent of what can be known in metaphysical thinking. As we have seen, Kant holds that mind imposes intelligibility onto the world, and consequently, conventional metaphysical principles and properties cannot be said to inhere things as such. Moreover, all that "counts" toward knowledge comes from sense perception, and many metaphysical truths are not directly available in sense perception. Thus, we cannot be said to have knowledge of metaphysical truths: "Metaphysics has to do not only with concepts of nature, which always find their application in experience, but also with pure rational concepts, which can never be given in any possible experience whatsoever. Consequently, the objective reality of these concepts . . . and also the truth or falsity of metaphysical assertions cannot be discovered or confirmed by any experience."[51]

Since divine realities are beyond the sensible, they are beyond experience and thus beyond knowledge. Accordingly, Kant's restrictive account of reason eliminates the possibility that human beings can have any knowledge that God appears or acts in the world. Within Kant's epistemology, as Joseph Ratzinger states, "something or someone Wholly Other, a new beginning from another plane, has no room to occur."[52] With regard to the Bible, the Kantian view holds that all biblical accounts of divine action in the world, such as the incarnation or miracles, cannot have "really" happened as described—or at least, human beings cannot possibly be said to "know" them. Therefore, such accounts of divine revelation or interventions must be explained in terms of sensible, natural realities that gave rise to such beliefs.[53]

---

50. Matthew L. Lamb, "Eternity and Time," in Lamb, *Eternity, Time, and the Life of Wisdom* (Naples, FL: Sapientia Press, 2007), 48.

51. Kant, *Prolegomena* #326 (Ellington, 69).

52. Joseph Cardinal Ratzinger, "Biblical Interpretation in Conflict: On the Foundations and the Itinerary of Exegesis Today," in *Opening Up the Scriptures: Joseph Ratzinger and the Foundations of Biblical Interpretation*, ed. José Granados, Carlos Granados, and Luis Sánchez-Navarro, essay trans. Adrian Walker (Grand Rapids: Eerdmans, 2008), 18.

53. Ratzinger thus concludes, "The events recounted in the Bible cannot really have happened as the Bible recounts them, and [exegesis that presupposes this Kantian premise] elaborates

The Kantian restriction on knowledge rules out the possibility of divine revelation in the world. It also means that human beings cannot make any realistic truth-claims about God, even by analogy. The space for God in the Kantian system is in the realm of subjectivity, and moral reasoning in particular: "Morality, thus, leads ineluctably to religion, through which it extends itself to the idea of a powerful moral Lawgiver."[54] For Kant, the idea of God is necessary to explain why someone ought to choose duty to the moral law over personal incentive and to guarantee right and wrong.[55] In much Kantian-informed theological thinking (e.g., theological liberalism), knowledge of God comes by way of the individual's subjectivity and not by any intelligible or manifest form in extramental reality.[56]

Another implication of the Kantian account for our project concerns its view of the human subject vis-à-vis the intelligible voice of being. A Kantian-informed theory of knowledge denies that the human being can know reality as such or have any real knowledge of God by way of the world. On this view, the individual knower cannot receive any kind of intelligible message or reality from without.[57] Since the mind imposes intelligibility onto the world and does not receive it from the world, the individual knower, not the external reality, is fundamentally determinative in the act of knowing.

The Kantian vision keeps the knowing subject (the reader of Scripture) from being receptive to the intelligibility and voice of extramental realities.

Since, for Kant, all that one can be said to know is his or her individual "experience," his account of human knowing ends up isolating the human knower from the world and from other knowers. The individual cannot get beyond his or her own subjectivity. For Kant, the individual knower cannot know anything about things-in-themselves aside from the fact that they give rise to disorganized sense data. As in those modern theories beset by the egocentric predicament, so also here, the mind is separated from the extramental world and set over against it—for the mind and its contents are all that the knower directly knows.

For a variety of reasons, therefore, we contend that a Kantian-informed account of human knowing and the world cannot be squared with the belief that Scripture can put people in living and life-giving contact with the divine

---

methods for uncovering how these events must really have happened." "Biblical Interpretation in Conflict," 19.

54. Immanuel Kant, *Religion within the Limits of Reason Alone*, trans. Theodore M. Green and Hoyt H. Hudson (New York: Harper Torchbooks, 1960), 5.

55. See Kant, *Religion within the Limits*, 4–5, 90–91.

56. See Francis Martin, *The Feminist Question: Feminist Theology in the Light of Christian Tradition* (Grand Rapids: Eerdmans, 1994), 168–75.

57. So Clarke, "Interpersonal Dialogue," 31–44.

realities that it mediates. Such an account rules out the possibility of divine revelation in the world, denies that human beings can have any positive knowledge of God, and keeps the human being from being receptive to the voice of intelligible, extramental realities.

We can also recognize that despite their influence, many of the implications of the Kantian account, as well as the egocentric predicament, are quite counterintuitive.[58] We do in fact communicate successfully with other people. We can successfully dialogue with others about matters that are external to both parties and yet commonly experienced by them. The whole endeavor of the natural sciences presupposes that there is an intrinsic intelligibility to the world that human beings can discover by use of their reasoning.[59] Moreover, as Clarke points out, if the basic Kantian account of things is true—that the mind imposes intelligibility on the world—then it becomes difficult to account for how and why our mental constructs accurately match up with the world and allow us to act on it.[60] Furthermore, post-Kantian forms of historical and cultural relativism are notoriously self-contradictory. For they claim as being universally and absolutely true that all truth-claims are relative to historical and cultural context: it is universally true that nothing is universally true. Now, it is one thing to say that our thinking and speaking are accidentally conditioned by the historical, cultural, and linguistic settings in which we find ourselves. But it is another thing to say that human beings cannot possibly get beyond their historical and cultural circumstances and cognitively access ontological truth as it is on its own terms.[61] Indeed, as Clarke points out, that "we can transcend own culture enough . . . is shown by the fact that we can translate more or less accurately from one language to another, between all the major languages in the world."[62] Such ordinary human experiences should point us away from these modern accounts of knowing and toward the public character of truth, human knowing, and reasoning.[63]

Creation, understood theologically and philosophically, is essential for grasping how Scripture puts people in living and life-giving contact with the divine realities it mediates. Our reading of Aquinas's metaphysics of creation is much indebted to W. Norris Clarke, who shows participation and relationality to be integral dimensions of being. Clarke also applies his analyses of

58. Sokolowski, *Introduction to Phenomenology*, 10–11; Clarke, *The One and the Many*, 13.

59. So Feser, *Scholastic Metaphysics*, 9–24.

60. Clarke, *The One and the Many*, 12–13.

61. See Matthew L. Lamb, "Temporality and History: Reflections from St. Augustine and Bernard Lonergan," *Nova et Vetera*, English edition 4 (2006): 838–50.

62. Clarke, *The One and the Many*, 13.

63. Sokolowski, *Introduction to Phenomenology*, 11–16, 42–51.

Aquinas's metaphysics to matters of human cognition and the problems raised by Immanuel Kant in particular. Given our indebtedness to his interpretation of Aquinas's metaphysics, we will continue to follow Clarke in his extension of metaphysical principles to human cognition in his case for what he calls "relational realism."[64]

## W. Norris Clarke on "Relational Realism"

### Beginning with Interpersonal Dialogue

To illustrate the basic structures of relational realism (and also to show flaws in the Kantian account), Clarke reflects on the common experience of interpersonal dialogue.[65] Reflections on this common human experience, Clarke argues, allow us to confirm at least five key truths about the self and the world. First, the fact that one engages in a dialogue with another confirms the real existence of one's own self. The experience of dialogue makes one aware that one is "actively thinking, communicating, and receiving (being acted upon)." Second, interpersonal dialogue also confirms the real existence of the other party with whom one converses. One becomes aware of being "in touch with, present to, *another real being*, on whom [one acts] and who acts in return on [one] by exchanging information." Sharing information, questioning, and answering are all modes of action. It is through this reciprocal action of the parties that the real existence of each party in the dialogue is known and confirmed. Third, the experience of interpersonal dialogue confirms not only the reality of the self and the other but also that oneself and the other are of like kind. Clarke comments, "The real other is truly *like* me, because it *acts* like me, by talking, communicating in a way that I can understand, through words, gestures, writing, etc." These similarities in action indicate some more basic similarities in each party's mode of being.[66]

Fourth, interpersonal dialogue shows that one does in fact "*receive a pre-structured, pre-formed message from without*, an intelligible message which [one understands] and can act on to confirm [e.g., by asking questions]."[67] In interpersonal dialogue, one receives information from the other, which the other has already articulated and communicated intelligibly. Interpersonal dialogue depends on this giving and receiving of information, which has its own intelligible

---

64. The phrase "relational realism" is that of Clarke, "Action as the Self-Revelation of Being," 59.

65. Clarke, "Interpersonal Dialogue," 31–44. In this section, we summarize Clarke's argumentation in this essay.

66. All citations in this paragraph are from Clarke, "Interpersonal Dialogue," 34.

67. Clarke, "Interpersonal Dialogue," 34 (emphasis original).

structure and form. Moreover, the knowing subject receives this already intelligibly formed information from without. When we take in such preformed,
intelligible information, we can make further associations between the received
message and our unique field of experiences, cultural and historical situation,
and so on; but these personal associations build on the basic reception of preformed information.[68] Clarke thus concludes, "Our cognitive equipment is able,
and naturally disposed, [to take] in already *formed* messages, formed by another
real knowing subject . . . distinct from me, through the pathways of my senses
. . . and reciprocally I can send similar messages of my own to the other."[69]

Fifth, interpersonal dialogue enables the dialogue partners to recognize
themselves as "a 'We' [and together we] can then turn to explore, share, and
discuss the messages coming in to both from a non-human world beyond."[70]
Through interpersonal dialogue, the parties identify with each other as the
same kind of being, who are able to communicate intelligibly about the commonly shared world. Interpersonal dialogue thus opens up into the publicness
of the world and of human reasoning and dialogue about our common world.

Clarke argues that the experience of interpersonal dialogue provides significant pushback against some basic tenets in a Kantian theory of knowledge.[71] Recall that for Kant, the individual can know only his or her subjective
experience, which is the end product of unformed sense perceptions ordered
by the mind according to its cognitive categories. The basic Kantian vision
also ends up isolating the mind from reality and from other knowers. The
experience of interpersonal dialogue, however, highlights the individual's
place in relation to other knowers and in relation to a common world about
which information can be exchanged. Moreover, Kant holds that the mind
does not receive intelligibility from the world, but rather the mind imposes
intelligibility onto unformed sense data. This notion that the mind imposes,
and does not receive, intelligibility cannot be squared with the experience of
receiving preformed, intelligible information from another in interpersonal
dialogue. Therefore, this common human experience gives us reason not to
adopt a Kantian account of human knowing.

### Self-Communication through Action

Clarke brings the insights of relational metaphysics to bear on the topic
of human knowing in his essay "Action as the Self-Revelation of Being: A

68. Clarke, "Interpersonal Dialogue," 34–35.
69. Clarke, "Interpersonal Dialogue," 35 (emphasis original).
70. Clarke, "Interpersonal Dialogue," 35.
71. See Clarke, "Interpersonal Dialogue," 32–33.

Central Theme in the Thought of St. Thomas."[72] Recall that for Aquinas, all real beings are a composite of two ontological coprinciples: essence and the act of existing (*esse*). Since created beings do not have their act of existing by virtue of their own essences, they must receive their limited act of existing at every moment from a noncontingent source, one whose essence is the pure act of existing itself: God. This is the creation metaphysics of participated *esse*: all created beings continually receive their *esse* by way of a participatory share (limited by their essential natures) in God's unlimited *esse*, which is identical with God's essence.

Participatory ontology is also intrinsically relational. Clarke argues that for Aquinas, the act of existing (*esse*) is intrinsically active. The participatory share in *esse* constitutes the depths of any creature's being, and thus at their innermost depths, real beings are not static but dynamic. The active depths of being give rise to further action performed by things. As Clarke writes, "The act of existence of any being . . . is its 'first act,' its abiding inner act, which tends naturally, by the very innate dynamism of the act of existence itself, to overflow into a 'second act,' which is called action or activity."[73] This metaphysical vision understands the world as an interconnected system of things acting on and being acted on by others.

The notion of action as the self-manifestation of being is the linchpin for Clarke's account of relational realism in contradistinction to a Kantian theory of knowledge—and in particular, the Kantian claim that the mind imposes intelligibility onto the world and does not receive it from the world. According to Clarke, "The self-communication of being is also necessarily a *self-revelation* or *self-manifestation* of being."[74] By virtue of their possession of *esse*, created realities are fundamentally active and tend to manifest their own being through activity. For Clarke, such self-communicative action is intelligible: action says something about the actor: "Since the action that flows out from a being is not simply an indeterminate surge of raw energy, but pours out from, and is self-expressive of, the whole unified inner being of the thing, both its act of existence and its essence, its action cannot help but be *essence-structured action*."[75] So understood, the activities and influences of an agent on another are revelatory of that agent's being. An agent's activities

---

72. Clarke, "Action as the Self-Revelation of Being," 45–64. In this section, we summarize Clarke's argumentation in this essay and apply it to our case. We also develop material given in Francis Martin, "Joseph Ratzinger, Benedict XVI, on Biblical Interpretation: Two Leading Principles," *Nova et Vetera*, English edition 5, no. 2 (2007): 303–311.
73. Clarke, "Action as the Self-Revelation of Being," 46.
74. Clarke, "Action as the Self-Revelation of Being," 51 (emphasis original).
75. Clarke, "Action as the Self-Revelation of Being," 54 (emphasis original).

and influences encode information about the agent. A being's self-revealing action is intelligible and informational because it manifests the intelligibility of the being that produces the action.

We can consider the same dynamic from the point of view of the thing acted on or influenced by the other. When a thing is affected or influenced in some manner by the action of another, it comes to light as "a receiving center for the surrounding world."[76] When a being realizes that it is "the recipient of self-revealing action from the surrounding world, . . . it is now enabled to interpret the messages, the *information*, contained within this incoming action, . . . *as* the self-revelation of these beings to it through the mediation of their structured action upon it."[77] Through our being affected by the activities of things, we can learn information about the kind of things that act upon us from the kinds of actions that they perform. On this account, Clarke writes, "all human knowledge of the real is an interpretation of action."[78]

Similar to the preceding example of interpersonal dialogue, Clarke's analysis in this essay pushes back against a Kantian theory of knowledge. Recall that for Kant, the individual knower cannot know anything about things-in-themselves other than that they give rise to unformed sense perceptions. According to Clarke, Kant's theory puts him in an untenable position: Kant "cannot hold *both* that things in themselves truly act upon us, penetrate our consciousness, and at the same time that this action is non-informative, non-communicative of anything in the nature of the agents."[79] In other words, how can Kant say that things act upon us and yet also that those actions say absolutely nothing about the agents that perform them? Furthermore, recall that for Kant, the mind then imposes intelligibility onto unformed sense perceptions, making the knower, not the known, fundamentally determinative in the act of knowing. As with his analysis of interpersonal dialogue, Clarke reiterates that by being acted upon, the knower receives intelligible information from an external source and about realities outside of him- or herself. That human beings receive intelligible information from outside themselves should lead us to recognize that in the act of knowing, the mind is "receptive and not creative of its objects."[80] When we know things, our minds are in-formed by intelligible reality outside ourselves.

We saw in Pieper's essay that created things receive their intelligibility from God and impart their intelligibility to knowing subjects. Clarke adds to this

76. Clarke, "Action as the Self-Revelation of Being," 54.
77. Clarke, "Action as the Self-Revelation of Being," 54 (emphasis original).
78. Clarke, "Action as the Self-Revelation of Being," 46.
79. Clarke, "Action as the Self-Revelation of Being," 59 (emphasis original).
80. Clarke, "Action as the Self-Revelation of Being," 54.

picture that the intelligibility of things is given through their self-manifesting action. Here, intelligible reality (and not the individual knower) is fundamentally determinative in the act of knowing: the knower is "measured" by the thing known.

We can also think of these dynamics in terms of gift giving and gift welcoming. To begin with, the relational and active character of being means that things "have the capacity to manifest themselves and thus play an active role in their being known" by others.[81] Things manifest, or "give," themselves and their intelligibility to other things through activity. Intellectual beings possess the capacity to "receive" the intelligibility of the other, which it manifests (or "gives") through activity. Things make a gift of themselves to others through self-revelatory action, and knowing subjects welcome that gift of intelligibility in the act of knowing. There exists, as Jacques Maritain would claim, a kind of "nuptial relationship between mind and reality."[82]

This nuptial relationship between mind and world entails a cognitive union between them. For instance, while Aquinas never develops a full-fledged epistemology in the way that modern philosophers do, he does maintain that the intelligibility of the thing known comes to exist in a cognitive mode of existence in the mind of the knower.[83] Aquinas follows Aristotle in holding that all human knowledge begins with sense experience of things in the world. Through sensation, human beings take in the intelligibility of things, which (as Clarke argues) is communicated through modes of self-manifesting action.[84] Through the processes of intellection, the mind transposes the communicated intelligibility of the thing known into a cognitive form. The mind forms a concept (also known as "the inner word" or an "intention").[85] In this respect, Aquinas holds to what is called an "identity theory" of knowledge.[86] In a Thomistic theory of knowledge, the same intelligibility (or "form") that exists in a thing comes to exist cognitively in the knower. As Aquinas succinctly

81. Martin, "Bockmuehl's 'Bible versus Theology,'" 4.

82. As cited in Clarke, *The One and the Many*, 39.

83. Frederick Copleston, *A History of Philosophy*, vol. 2, *From Augustine to Duns Scotus* (New York: Image, 1993), 388–97.

84. Martin, "Bockmuehl's 'Bible versus Theology,'" 62.

85. See Harm Goris, "Theology and Theory of the Word in Aquinas: Understanding Augustine by Innovating Aristotle," in *Aquinas the Augustinian*, ed. Michael Dauphinais, Barry David, and Matthew Levering (Washington, DC: Catholic University of America Press, 2007), 75; Sokolowski, *Phenomenology of the Human Person*, 286–303; cf. Martin, "Bockmuehl's 'Bible versus Theology,'" 64–65.

86. See Norman Kretzmann, "Philosophy of Mind," in *The Cambridge Companion to Aquinas*, ed. Norman Kretzmann and Eleonore Stump (Cambridge: Cambridge University Press, 1993), 138–39; Scott MacDonald, "Theory of Knowledge," in Kretzmann and Stump, *Cambridge Companion to Aquinas*, 160–62.

puts it, "A thing is known in as far as its form is in the knower."[87] For Aquinas, concepts (or intentions) are not the object of what we know but that *by which* the mind enjoys union with extramental reality.[88] Through the processes of sensation and intellection, the human knower takes in the intelligibility of a reality and transposes it into a cognitive mode of existence. In the act of knowing, there is a union of knower and known.

The metaphysics of creation involves us in a relational, epistemological realism. Through the intelligible self-manifestation of being through action and its cognitive reception, human beings can enjoy genuine cognitive contact with extramental reality. At the same time, Clarke points out that human knowledge of reality, though genuine, always remains limited and incomplete.[89] Things reveal themselves to us through their action, and no amount of action can exhaustively reveal a thing's being.[90] This is because at the depths of any created reality's being is its relationship to the Creator, its participation in God's *esse*.[91] Moreover, there are the built-in limitations of human knowing.[92] Human knowledge depends on sensation and discursive reason. We can know only what is given us by external realities, and we know them from within a limited perspective.[93] And so, the metaphysics of creation both holds that human beings can genuinely know the intelligible reality of things and that there is an inexhaustible richness to the reality of things, which we can never fully grasp.

87. Aquinas, *Summa Theologica* I, q. 75, a. 5. For this and further references, see MacDonald, "Theory of Knowledge," 160–61, 188n5.

88. Aquinas writes, "The intelligible species [i.e., a thing's intelligibility in cognitive form] is to the intellect what the sensible image is to the sense. But the sensible image is not what is perceived, but rather that by which sense perceives. *Therefore the intelligible species is not what is actually understood, but that by which the intellect understands*" (*Summa Theologica* I, q. 85, a. 2 [emphasis added]). Edward Feser explains with an (admittedly imperfect) example, "If you need glasses in order to see the cat, you might say that the glasses are also something 'by which' you see it; but it is still the cat you see, and not the glasses, which are only a means of helping you to see it." Feser, *Aquinas: A Beginner's Guide* (Oxford: Oneworld, 2009), 146.

89. Clarke, "Action as the Self-Revelation of Being," 56.

90. Clarke, "Action as the Self-Revelation of Being," 56.

91. And thus, with reference to the previously discussed essay by Pieper, Clarke ("Action as the Self-Revelation of Being," 55) writes that to "know even the least finite thing fully . . . we would have to know it precisely as an image of God and how it proceeds from and expresses the original, which is hidden from us [in God]."

92. In this respect, Clarke points to Aquinas's dictum: "Whatever is received is received according to the mode of the receiver." "Action as the Self-Revelation of Being," 56, citing Aquinas, *Summa contra Gentiles* 2.74. The English translation of the larger discussion in which this dictum appears can be found in Thomas Aquinas, *Summa contra Gentiles*, 5 vols., trans. Anton C. Pegis, FRSC, James F. Anderson, Vernon J. Bourke, and Charles J. O'Neil (Notre Dame, IN: University of Notre Dame Press, 1975), 2:227–32, esp. 230.

93. Clarke, "Action as the Self-Revelation of Being" 56–57.

As we have discussed, things act in a manner appropriate to their mode of being, and thus not all acting is necessarily volitional or conscious. Action, therefore, is an analogous notion. One way in which things can be regarded as acting upon other things—and thus revealing themselves through action—is by *appearing*. By appearing, things present themselves and disclose their intelligibility to the other things. In this way, things act upon and influence other things. By conceiving of appearances in this way, we can connect Clarke's metaphysical reflections with the phenomenological contributions of Robert Sokolowski.[94] More specifically, we look to incorporate into our account elements from Sokolowski's philosophical analyses of intentionality, words, and things to show how the intelligibility of things can be captured and mediated by language.

## Sokolowski on Intentionality, Words, and Things

A central category in phenomenology is intentionality. Intentionality designates the directedness of human consciousness, "its being directed toward something, as it is an experience of or about some object."[95] Whereas in theories of knowing beset by the egocentric predicament, human consciousness is wholly self-enclosed (i.e., I directly know only my own self-consciousness and the ideas in my mind), intentionality holds that human consciousness is always directed toward something. So understood, "to intend" something is to be conscious of it and so to be in a kind of cognitive relationship with it. The human subject can intend things that are present (i.e., "filled intentions") but also things that are absent (i.e., "empty intentions").[96]

Given that intentionality designates "the conscious relationship we have to an object," this phenomenological doctrine can interface with the relational ontology previously discussed.[97] Clarke himself appeals to the notion

94. It should be noted that not all interpreters of Edmund Husserl would agree with Sokolowski's interpretation, which we follow here. By his own admission, Sokolowski (*Introduction to Phenomenology*, 223) represents the "'East Coast' interpretation" of Husserl in the United States. For a larger view of issues in Husserlian study, see Barry Smith and David Woodruff Smith, eds., *The Cambridge Companion to Husserl* (Cambridge: Cambridge University Press, 1995).

95. David Woodruff Smith, "Phenomenology," *The Stanford Encyclopedia of Philosophy* (Winter 2016 edition), ed. Edward N. Zalta, https://plato.stanford.edu/archives/win2016/entries/phenomenology.

96. On empty and filled intentions, see Sokolowski, *Introduction to Phenomenology*, 33–40.

97. Sokolowski, *Introduction to Phenomenology*, 8. He notes that this phenomenological use of intentionality differs in kind from the more psychological use of "intention" associated with willful action or planning.

of intentionality to interpret the self-communication of being through action and the reception of a thing's intelligibility by a knower. Clarke identifies a "double movement of intentionality" at work in this relational realism.[98] On the one hand, there is "the incoming *ontological intentionality of action* itself into the knower" (i.e., a directedness from the thing to the knowing subject).[99] By the various modes of essence-structured action, things communicate their intelligibility to other things. In the act of knowing, a subject takes in the communicated intelligibility of a thing, and the subject transposes this intelligibility into a cognitive mode. On the other hand, there is a "second, complementary movement of *cognitive intentionality*" (i.e., a directedness from the knowing subject to the thing).[100] The knowing subject traces this received intelligibility back to the thing from which it originates and interprets it as informative of the thing's being and cognitive achievements. Intentionality thus provides a way to integrate ontology and epistemology, relationality and realism, knower and known. As Clarke concludes, "Such is the dynamism of action, as it originates in the order of consciousness, passes into the ontological order, then transforms itself again into the order of consciousness, thus synthesizing being and consciousness into a single unified cosmic process of self-manifestation."[101]

Related to the notion of intentionality is a robust appreciation for appearances. The status of appearances is a long-standing issue in Western philosophy, going back to the ancient Greeks.[102] For thinkers such as Pythagoras and Plato, visible appearances either concealed or weakly imitated "the really real." For a modern thinker such as Kant, the individual subject knows only appearances (phenomena). These appearances are separate from things-in-themselves (noumena) and tell us nothing about those things. In such accounts, appearances either are regarded as "mere appearances" or are reified into a kind of thing or psychological entity that constitutes the object of our knowing.[103]

By contrast, Sokolowski argues that phenomenology holds that appearances are intrinsic to the reality of a given thing: "The way things appear is part of the being of things; things appear as they are, and they are as they appear."[104] Things

98. Clarke, "Action as the Self-Revelation of Being," 57–58, here 57.

99. Clarke, "Action as the Self-Revelation of Being," 57 (emphasis original).

100. Clarke, "Action as the Self-Revelation of Being," 57 (emphasis original). Clarke explains this complementary, cognitive intentionality in this way: the subject "recognizes it [i.e., the received, conceptualized intelligibility] explicitly *as a sign* or message from another and reaches out dynamically in the cognitive order, through the mediation of the sign, to *refer it by an intending relation* back to the thing itself from which it came" (57, emphasis original).

101. Clarke, "Action as the Self-Revelation of Being," 58.

102. See Dupré, *Passage to Modernity*, 15–29; Sokolowski, *Eucharistic Presence*, 179–86.

103. Sokolowski, *Introduction to Phenomenology*, 15; cf. 50–51.

104. Sokolowski, *Introduction to Phenomenology*, 14.

manifest themselves to a conscious subject through appearances, and in doing so, they reveal something of their identity. In this way, a certain connection can be made between Sokolowski's phenomenological analysis of appearances and Clarke's Thomistic metaphysics. On Clarke's reading of Aquinas, things naturally communicate their own being through essence-structured action—they act on or influence other things in ways appropriate to their own natures, and in doing so, they manifest their own intelligible natures. One way in which things can be said to "act" upon other things is by appearing to them. While not a kind of action in a volitional sense, appearances can nevertheless be reckoned as a way in which things have influence on other things. So understood, appearances are a means by which the intelligibility of things is made manifest to others.

One and the same thing can be presented to a subject in a variety of ways (e.g., through direct perception from this angle or that, through language, through pictures). Through all these modes of manifestation, it remains the same thing—a phenomenological notion known as "identity in manifolds."[105] As Sokolowski puts it, "The identical fact can be expressed in a manifold of ways, and the fact is other to any and all of its expressions."[106] The more ways in which a thing is given and intended by subjects from different vantage points, the more "heightened" is the thing's being and our appreciation of it.[107] Of course, people can be misled by appearances, and appearances certainly can be manipulated to create false impressions. But when we are misled or deceived by appearances, we make a mistake in judgment: we take the world in a particular way when in fact it actually exists in another way (and is revealed to be so upon further inspection). The mistake in judgment presupposes a similarity between what is taken or proposed to be the case and the ways in which things actually appear.[108]

Things manifest their identities by appearances that are correlated with the intelligible structures of their being. Sokolowski explains that a chief endeavor of phenomenological reflection is to distinguish and clarify the different ways in which a subject can intend something (e.g., by perceiving, remembering, picturing, signifying) and the ways in which these different intentionalities can interact with one another.[109] The kind of intending proper to language (written or spoken) is signitive intending.

When a person reads or hears words, he or she is conscious both of the words and also that to which the words point. But given their referential status,

105. Sokolowski, *Introduction to Phenomenology*, 27–33.
106. Sokolowski, *Introduction to Phenomenology*, 28.
107. Sokolowski, *Introduction to Phenomenology*, 32.
108. Sokolowski, *Introduction to Phenomenology*, 14–15.
109. Sokolowski, *Introduction to Phenomenology*, 12–16.

the words have a subordinate status to the things that they signify. Words and verbal articulations direct a person's consciousness away from him- or herself and toward the things that the words present. So understood, words are a means by which a person comes into a conscious, cognitive relationship with the things that the words present.

The human capacity to use language and the kinds of intentionalities involved with language are intimately related to human reasoning.[110] According to Sokolowski, we human beings move from simple perception and into reasoning when we register distinctions and associations between things and between parts and wholes of individual things and/or when we form judgments about them.[111] Thus, a person registers item A as having such and such a quality or as being distinct from item B (e.g., "this mug is blue" or "a human being differs in kind from a chair"). To articulate such registrations and judgments is to insert linguistic syntax into experience.[112]

Linguistic syntax allows us to articulate a particular state of affairs as being the case; in phenomenological jargon, it is to constitute "a categorial object."[113] Such judgments and articulations of being can in turn be presented to others through words. We can present things or the world as being in a certain way (which, of course, may prove to be accurate or inaccurate in one respect or another, depending on verification).[114] Sokolowski writes, "By speaking to you, I can 'give' you the same categorial object that I see and articulate now. You can articulate that selfsame object even in its absence."[115] Through language, we can articulate things as being in a certain way and present them as such to others. On this account, meanings, judgments, and propositions are not so much subsistent entities in a speaker's mind (as they are in many modern philosophical accounts of knowing) as they are "a dimension of presentation [of things]. . . . It is how the world is being projected as being, through what someone is saying."[116] Put differently, "Words and sentences do not represent reality, they reveal it."[117]

110. Here, we follow Sokolowski, *Introduction to Phenomenology*, 88–111.

111. Sokolowski states that this is what is technically called "*categorial* intentionality . . . the kind of intending that articulates states of affairs and propositions, the kind that functions when we predicate, relate, collect, and introduce logical operations into what we experience." *Introduction to Phenomenology*, 88 (emphasis original).

112. Sokolowski writes, "Syntax in language simply expresses the relations of part and whole that are brought out in categorial consciousness." *Introduction to Phenomenology*, 91.

113. Sokolowski, *Introduction to Phenomenology*, 90.

114. Sokolowski, *Introduction to Phenomenology*, 101–2.

115. Sokolowski, *Introduction to Phenomenology*, 103.

116. Sokolowski, *Introduction to Phenomenology*, 100.

117. Francis Martin, introduction to *Acts*, Ancient Christian Commentary on Scripture: New Testament 5 (Downers Grove, IL: InterVarsity, 2006), xxv. We acknowledge our indebtedness to Robert Sokolowski for this language.

As a means of presentation, words are a way by which people can intend things and larger states of affairs. Words and linguistic articulations mediate to a knower the intelligibility of things. Through language, people achieve cognitive contact with the intelligible identity of things. As Sokolowski writes, words "capture and carry the intelligibilities of things, and weave them syntactically into statements, arguments, narratives, and conversations."[118]

Sokolowski has intimated that this phenomenological analysis of language, while differing in some respects, has some commonalities with Aquinas's identity theory of knowledge. For Aquinas, in the act of knowing, the same intelligible form that exists in the thing known comes to exist in another mode of being (i.e., cognitively) in the mind of the knower—it is the same intelligible form in two modes of existence. Since the same form exists in both the known and the knower (albeit in different modes), the knower comes into cognitive union with things through the cognitive presence of the same form.[119]

By words and syntax, a person can capture, articulate, and mediate the intelligibility of things to others. Sokolowski argues, "There is an identity between the thing known and the *word* by and in which it is known. . . . The thing we know does not just enjoy a cognitive existence in our minds, but . . . as a thing *named* it enjoys something like a cognitive existence *in its name*."[120] Like concepts in Aquinas's theory of knowledge, words and verbal articulations capture and mediate the intelligibility of being: verbalizations constitute the thing's intelligibility in a different modality of existence.[121] When a person takes in the verbalized intelligibility of things through sensation and intellection, that same intelligibility comes to exist cognitively in the knower. Through the mediation of language, the intelligibility of things becomes present to a knowing subject. There exists, on this account, a union of mind, words, and world.

## Looking Back and Looking Forward

The belief that Scripture can put people into living and life-giving contact with God invites us to reflect on how people come into cognitive contact with external realities through language. In this chapter, therefore, we have climbed one more step on the expository ladder in part 2 by applying some elements

118. See Robert Sokolowski, "God's Word and Human Speech," *Nova et Vetera*, English edition 11 (2013): 199.
119. See Sokolowski, *Phenomenology of the Human Person*, 286–303.
120. Sokolowski, "God's Word and Human Speech," 196 (emphasis original).
121. See also Sokolowski, *Phenomenology of the Human Person*, 301–2.

of the Distinction and participatory ontology to human cognition and the relationship between the mind, words, and the world.

Creation provides the larger context for these reflections on human cognition. Human beings have a natural desire to know the truth of things in themselves. Corresponding to this natural human drive to know is the notion that things have an intrinsic intelligibility that makes them knowable. Witnesses in both Scripture and Christian tradition root the intrinsic intelligibility of things in their being created by God and so reflecting his Word (*logos*) or Wisdom. This claim that things have an intelligibility of their own that the mind receives has been contested in some modern philosophical circles. This is especially the case in the influential vision of Immanuel Kant, for whom the individual knower, not reality itself, is fundamentally determinative in the act of knowing. The Kantian influence, we contend, is a significant obstacle to a proper appreciation of the belief that Scripture can put people in living contact with God. The Kantian restriction on cognition not only precludes any possibility of human beings having intellectual knowledge of God but also makes the human knower the one who imposes intelligibility on things. The human mind becomes isolated, and since it does not receive intelligibility from the world, it is, if you will, deaf to the voice of external, intelligible realities. If the human knower cannot be receptive to the voice of intelligible being among created realities, it surely cannot be receptive to the Word of God mediated through Scripture.

We have argued that Clarke's interpretation of Thomistic metaphysics and Sokolowski's phenomenology provide a way to maintain the union of mind and world in contradistinction to certain modern theories of cognition. Evidence from the experience of interpersonal dialogue and the self-communication of being through action, including the ways in which things are given through appearances, shows how human knowers can come into genuine contact with the intelligible reality of other people and things. Things communicate their intelligibility through action and appearance.

The intelligibility of things can also be captured and mediated through words and the articulations of linguistic syntax. The human subject is capable of receiving the intelligibility of things, which is given through action and appearance. Through sensation and intellection, humans take in the intelligibility of things, which comes to have a kind of cognitive existence in the knower. In this way, there is genuine communion of mind and world, of subject and object, in the act of knowing.

This understanding of human cognition, set within the context of creation, provides the conceptual space for thinking about how human beings can come into cognitive contact with external realities, including the realities given in

Scripture. We are now, accordingly, in a position to reflect theologically on the mediation of divine reality through the biblical texts. For as we will argue, God makes himself and his will known through the various realities of the divine economy, which the biblical text mediates. By coming into cognitive contact with these biblical realities, human beings come into cognitive contact with the God whose mysterious presence these realities bear.

# 9

# The Mediation of Divine Reality
# through the Biblical Text

The survey of biblical witnesses in part 1 brought to light various associations that the Word of God has with causal power and modes of presence. Taken together, these biblical witnesses provide substance and warrant for identifying Scripture, a form of inspired human discourse, as putting people in living and life-giving contact with the Word of God. Thus far in part 2, we have been considering some philosophical and theological principles that help us to grasp the intelligibility of this biblical teaching. Prioritizing the doctrine of creation, we have reflected on how the distinctive understanding of God in the biblical tradition shapes our thinking about ontology, transcendence, and the union of minds, words, and the world.

We are now in position to take the next step: we will bring the biblical material and the philosophical and theological reflections together and offer a theological account of how Scripture can put its audience in living and life-giving contact with the divine realities that it mediates. Given the multifaceted character of our topic, we are going to divide our reflections on Scripture into two chapters. In the present chapter, we will focus on how Scripture mediates divine reality to people, and in the next, we will consider how the divine reality, mediated by Scripture, becomes present and active in them.

The exposition in this chapter will unfold in four principal sections. First, we will frame our account with some important elements from the Second Vatican Council's *Dogmatic Constitution on Divine Revelation (Dei Verbum)*. Drawing on established elements in the Christian tradition, *Dei Verbum* teaches that God reveals himself and his will in the words and realities of the divine economy for the salvation of humanity. Scripture mediates divine reality by verbally presenting and interpreting the various realities in the economy that bear the divine mystery. Second, building on the account of cognition and signitive intentionality given in chapter 8, we will explore how the biblical texts mediate the reality (or *res*) of which they speak. The texts present the intelligibility of the realities or states of affairs of which they speak, and in so doing they allow the audience of Scripture to come into a conscious, cognitive relationship with these realities—that is, to intend them. Third, we will reflect on the realities of the divine economy that the biblical text mediates. The various realities of the divine economy can be said to bear divine mystery, for in them God is mysteriously and actively present. God also illumines select individuals to perceive his active presence in these realities and interpret them appropriately. Fourth, the incarnation of the Word of God in Jesus Christ modifies the understanding of God and all things in relation to God, including the divine economy. The incarnation and paschal mystery cause all other realities in the divine economy to appear as having dimensions wherein they participate (in some manner) in the mystery of salvation in Christ. On these bases, we therefore contend that *by coming into cognitive union with the realities mediated by the biblical text, the audience of Scripture can come into contact with the divine mystery that those realities bear.*

## Getting Our Bearings with *Dei Verbum*

We begin our account of how Scripture mediates an encounter with divine reality and power with some key passages in the Second Vatican Council's *Dogmatic Constitution on Divine Revelation (Dei Verbum).*[1] *Dei Verbum* §2 contains a theologically rich, yet dense, statement that sheds light on Scripture's capacity to mediate divine reality and power. Given the importance of this passage for our exposition, we provide both the official English translation and the Latin original:

> This plan of revelation is realized by deeds and words having an inner unity: the deeds wrought by God in the history of salvation manifest and confirm the teaching and realities signified by the words, while the words proclaim the deeds and clarify the mystery contained in them.

1. All English citations of *Dei Verbum* are taken from http://www.vatican.va/archive/hist_councils/ii_vatican_council/documents/vat-ii_const_19651118_dei-verbum_en.html. Latin citations are taken from http://www.vatican.va/archive/hist_councils/ii_vatican_council/documents/vat-ii_const_19651118_dei-verbum_lt.html.

*Haec revelationis oeconomia fit gestis verbisque intrinsece inter se connexis, ita ut opera, in historia salutis a Deo patrata, doctrinam et res verbis significatas manifestent ac corroborent, verba autem opera proclament et mysterium in eis contentum elucident.*

*Dei Verbum* speaks of God revealing himself in an "economy of revelation" (*revelationis oeconomia*).[2] This statement appears in the first chapter of *Dei Verbum*, which treats divine revelation as such. As commentators have pointed out, divine revelation is described here in historical and sacramental terms.[3] The chapter opens by speaking of revelation as God's action "to reveal Himself and to make known to us the hidden purpose [*sacramentum*] of His will" (*DV* §2). The text then states that God's revelation is directed toward a salvific end. God reveals himself and his will so that "through Christ, the Word made flesh, man might in the Holy Spirit have access to the Father and come to share in the divine nature" (*DV* §2). God's revelation of himself and his will in the divine economy is ordered toward the salvation of human beings. This salvation consists in God's bringing human beings to participate in his own trinitarian life through Jesus Christ. In short, divine revelation is for human salvation.

The above quoted text from *Dei Verbum* aligns two phrases for the arena in which God reveals: the "economy of revelation" and the "history of salvation." Across its compositions, the Christian Bible furnishes us with a succession of God's actions in the history of Israel, the life of Jesus, and the church—it narrates the divine economy. At various moments within this succession and often in concert with his saving acts, God enters into a covenant relationship with select individuals and groups. He does so, in part, to draw people into communion with himself and advance his designs for the world. God's revelatory and salvific designs are accomplished fully in the life, death, and resurrection of Jesus of Nazareth, the incarnate Word of God. Jesus transposes (and does not void) God's covenant with Israel into the new, eschatological covenant wherein all peoples are gathered into relationship with the Father through Christ and his ecclesial body, the church.[4]

---

2. Translation ours. Later references and citations of this Latin phrase will reflect this translation of ours.

3. René Latourelle, SJ, *Theology of Revelation: Including A Commentary on the Constitution "Dei Verbum" of Vatican II* (Staten Island, NY: Alba House, 1966), 460–62; Joseph Ratzinger, *Dogmatic Constitution on Divine Revelation*, chap. 1, in *Commentary on the Documents of Vatican II*, ed. Herbert Vorgrimler, trans. William Glen-Doepel et al. (New York: Herder & Herder, 1969), 3:171.

4. Following the lead of Pope John Paul II, in his remarks at the synagogue in Mainz in November 1980, one can agree that it is vital "to elaborate a theological position that takes

In this way, *Dei Verbum* identifies the divine economy as the macrocontext for understanding God's saving and revelatory actions in the history of salvation—and by extension, the interpretation of Scripture.[5] Individual biblical books and passages need to be interpreted in light of the whole sweep of the divine economy, which has as its telos the salvation of all humanity in Jesus Christ. In so teaching, the council accords with the fundamental principle in early Christian theology that Scripture must be interpreted in light of its essential, unifying scheme—its *skopos* or *hypothesis*—which is ultimately christological. As Frances Young writes, "The notion of the Bible having a particular *hypothesis*, which Irenaeus identified with the Canon of Truth or Rule of Faith, and characterized implicitly as . . . the Christological reference, emerged along with the doctrine of the unity of the Bible."[6]

Moreover, by speaking of the economy of revelation, *Dei Verbum* points not only to the canon of Scripture but also, in a tacit way, to the church as the context for interpreting Scripture. As Lewis Ayres reminds us, the notion of a canon implies a community for whom it is canonical.[7] In the case of the Christian biblical canon, the community is the church. Thus, *Dei Verbum* intimates in §2 what it more explicitly states elsewhere: proper interpretation of Scripture requires attention to the church's faith and tradition (cf. §§8, 12, 23).

*Dei Verbum* further specifies that the economy of revelation "is realized by deeds and words having an inner unity [*fit gestis verbisque intrinsece inter se connexis*]" (§2). This statement pairs "deeds" (*gestis*) with words. While it does not come across in English tradition, the Latin text of our focal passage uses three different terms for that which is associated with words (*verbis*): the text uses *gesta* ("deeds"), *opera* (also translated as "deeds" but which we will render as "works"), and *res* ("realities"). For the sake of consistency in exposition, we will continue to employ the third of these terms (*res*) and speak of "realities" in the broad manner akin to the Latin term *res*.

---

account of the genuine newness of the New Testament while respecting the permanent value of the Old Covenant that has never been revoked." John Paul II, quoted in Francis Martin, "Election, Covenant, and Law," *Nova et Vetera*, English edition 4 (2006): 858.

5. Accordingly, *Dei Verbum* §12 later teaches that the proper interpretation of the Bible requires attention to the unity of the biblical canon: "No less serious attention must be given to the content and unity of the whole of Scripture if the meaning of the sacred texts is to be correctly worked out."

6. Frances M. Young, *Biblical Exegesis and the Formation of Christian Culture* (New York: Cambridge University Press, 1997; repr., Peabody, MA: Hendrickson, 2002), 20.

7. Lewis Ayres, "On the Practice and Teaching of Christian Doctrine," *Gregorianum* 80 (1999): 50. Cf. George A. Lindbeck, *The Nature of Doctrine: Religion and Theology in a Post-liberal Age* (Philadelphia: Westminster, 1984), 119–20.

As we will use the term, the *res* of the biblical text is that which a text presents to its audience—it is "what the text is about."[8] Depending on the text, the *res* might be historical or concrete persons, things, or events (e.g., Jesus, the Jerusalem temple, Moses's leading an exodus group out of Egypt). But in other texts, the *res* (i.e., the contents or realities) may not have the same kind of historical character. Examples of this sort would include various laws and legal prescriptions, spiritual insights given through poetic discourse (e.g., the psalms) or figurative story discourse (e.g., Jonah), as well as the meaning of the beginning and end of all things (e.g., creation and the eschaton).[9] To use the technical, phenomenological category discussed in the previous chapter, the *res* can be reckoned as the "categorial object" constituted and conveyed by the linguistic articulations of the biblical text.

*Dei Verbum* specifies that these realities in the divine economy are both revelatory and salvific. Considered as "deeds," they are done "by God in the history of salvation," and they also "manifest" what the words signify (§2). Significantly, these realities in the divine economy have "the mystery contained in them [*mysterium in eis contentum*]" (§2). As we will discuss, "mystery" is a biblically warranted category for divine revelation, especially the eschatological revelation of God's hidden plan of salvation in Christ. Moreover, "mystery" came to be used in early Christian exegesis to designate the inner dimensions of biblical realities wherein they participate in the work of Christ, dimensions that are revealed only in his light. The term "mystery" not only expresses the hidden, yet revelatory, presence of God in these realties but also intimates that all realities in the history of salvation participate in some manner in the life and work of Christ (cf. *DV* §§15, 17).

The revelation of God in the divine economy, however, is not wholly manifestational—there is also a propositional component to it.[10] Hence, *Dei Verbum* §2 also speaks of revelatory words in the divine economy. The text specifies several different aspects of these words in the divine economy. At a basic level, the words signify the realities of the economy (*res verbis significatas*) and proclaim the works of God (*opera proclament*). The council also affirms that in the divine economy, God provides teaching (*doctrinam*) through words, though this passage does not specify how God communicates his Word through

8. So Francis Martin, "Revelation and Its Transmission," in *Vatican II: Renewal within Tradition*, ed. Matthew L. Lamb and Matthew Levering (New York: Oxford University Press, 2008), 68.

9. Following Thomas Joseph White, OP, *Exodus*, Brazos Theological Commentary on the Bible (Grand Rapids: Brazos, 2016), 8–9.

10. On the necessity of divine revelation as having a propositional dimension to complement the manifestational dimension, see Mats Wahlberg, *Revelation as Testimony: A Philosophical-Theological Study* (Grand Rapids: Eerdmans, 2014), esp. 28–33, 52–59.

human speech.[11] Moreover, the biblical language also serves to "clarify the mystery contained in" the realities of the divine economy (§2). This correlation of the words with the mystery borne by the realities gives us perspective on the "intrinsic connection" between the deeds and words in the divine economy.

This "intrinsic connection" exists between the deeds and words, the signified and sign, in salvation history.[12] Both the deeds and words in salvation history are revelatory, and each sheds interpretive light on the other. The words of the biblical text are revelatory in that through them, God delivers divine teaching and interprets the meaning of the realities in salvation history that the words present: "The words proclaim the deeds and clarify the mystery contained in them." These mystery-bearing realities of salvation history also "manifest and confirm" what the biblical words signify.

*Dei Verbum* §2 thus provides us with helpful teaching about how Scripture mediates divine realities to people, and in what follows, we will follow its basic coordinates. We now turn to fill out this picture by reflecting on the mediation of God through the words and realities in the divine economy that Scripture presents.

## Biblical Language as Mediating Realities

We will continue to employ the traditional distinction between words (*verba*) and things (*res*). Not only does this basic distinction have purchase in phenomenology, but also it has a long-standing history in the Christian tradition for talking about Scripture and its contents. In *On Christian Doctrine*, Augustine famously discusses "signs" (*signa*) and "things" (*res*) in terms of each other: "A sign, after all, is a thing, which besides the impression it conveys to the senses, also has the effect of making something else come to mind."[13] The preeminent example of what Augustine calls a conventional sign is a word. He writes, "Words, after all, are far and away the principal means used by human beings to signify the thoughts they have in their minds."[14] Augustine also holds that things signified by words can in turn be signs of other things, such as Old Testament things serving as signs of Christ.[15] Thomas Aquinas

11. Cf. *Dei Verbum* §§11–13.

12. The remainder of this paragraph first appeared in William M. Wright IV, "Inspired Scripture as a Sacramental Vehicle of Divine Presence in the Gospel of John and *Dei Verbum*," *Nova et Vetera*, English edition 13 (2015): 177.

13. Augustine, *On Christian Doctrine* 2.1.1, in Augustine, *Teaching Christianity*, trans. Edmund Hill, OP, Works of Saint Augustine I/11 (Hyde Park, NY: New City, 1996), 129.

14. Augustine, *On Christian Doctrine* 2.3.4. (Hill, 130).

15. Augustine, *On Christian Doctrine* 1.2.2; 3.9.13.

continues this tradition by using this language to articulate the two basic senses of Scripture: the literal and the spiritual. In the *Summa Theologica*, Aquinas defines the literal sense as "that first signification whereby words signify things," and the spiritual sense as the "signification whereby things signified by words have themselves also a signification."[16]

Robert Sokolowski's phenomenological analysis of words, things, and intentionality can help us grasp how the Bible's language mediates the realities of which it speaks.[17] Sokolowski observes that when we read any written text, including Scripture, we must be very attentive to the referential nature of language and the kinds of intending that occur in reading. When a person reads written words, recognizes them as written language (and not random markings or blotches of ink), he or she is conscious not only of the written markings on a page but also of whatever those words present to the consciousness: "When the words stand out, we no longer intend just what is before us. A new kind of intending comes into play, one that makes these perceived marks into words and at the same time makes us intend not just the marks that are present, but the [thing], which is absent."[18] In such "signitive intending," the person intends not only the words but also (by going through the words) that to which the words refer.[19] Words are a means by which things, even absent things, are presented to an individual as a dative of manifestation. So understood, words are a kind of appearance, a means of disclosure. As Sokolowski puts it, "Words, whether spoken or written, present things. We never have 'just' words: words are vehicles to articulate and disclose things."[20]

Recognition that language is a means of presenting *things* is crucial because it makes the reality or the state of affairs presented by the words to be the proper object of consciousness—not simply the words, texts, or the authors' ideas per se. These are all means *by which* a reality is presented to a subject. To regard any text, including the Bible, as an end, rather than

16. Thomas Aquinas, *Summa Theologica* I, q. 1, a. 10. English citations of the *Summa Theologica* are taken from Thomas Aquinas, *Summa Theologica*, trans. Fathers of the English Dominican Province, 3 vols. (New York: Benziger, 1947–48).

17. A version of the next two paragraphs first appeared in William M. Wright IV, "The Doctrine of God and the Liturgical *Res* in John's Gospel: Reading John 8:12–20 with the Theology of Disclosure," *Nova et Vetera*, English edition 12 (2014): 952–53. The present text is a revision and expansion of that original.

18. Robert Sokolowski, *Introduction to Phenomenology* (Cambridge: Cambridge University Press, 2000), 78.

19. Sokolowski, *Introduction to Phenomenology*, 79.

20. Robert Sokolowski, *Eucharistic Presence: A Study in the Theology of Disclosure* (Washington, DC: Catholic University of America Press, 1994), 141–42.

a means by which things are presented, would be to commit the fallacy of "misplaced concreteness."[21] Treating the written text as an end resembles, according to Sokolowski, "rationalism, historicism, and psychologism. . . . In each case a form of manifestation—a text, a thought, a situated appearance, a perception—is taken to replace the thing manifested."[22] To detach appearances from things, to reify appearances into a kind of thing or reduce them to purely subjective matters, and to regard such subjective realia as the objects of human knowing are all characteristic features of the egocentric predicament of modern epistemology.[23]

When a person encounters the words of Scripture and recognizes them as language, he or she also comes into cognitive contact with what those words articulate. It is an act of signitive intentionality: a person intends not only the words but also the things that the words present. As a mode of disclosure, the biblical language can "capture and carry the intelligibilities of [the] things," realities, and states of affairs of which the language speaks.[24] When the audience of Scripture takes in the words of Scripture through sensation and intellection, the audience takes in the intelligibilities of the biblical *res*, which the words capture and mediate. The biblical words thus mediate the intelligibility of the biblical reality (or *res*), enabling people to come into a cognitive relationship with that reality. To use the classic Augustinian and Thomistic terminology, it is the *res* presented by the *verba* or *signa* of the biblical text that one properly intends when reading Scripture. The words (*verba*) of Scripture give us the reality (*res*), for they make the intelligibility of the *res* present in Scripture's audience.

This phenomenology of biblical language, including the recognition that words enable a person to intend things, provides a way to reconnect with premodern Christian accounts of the literal sense of Scripture. As we have seen, Thomas Aquinas defines the literal sense of Scripture in comparable terms: "That first signification whereby words signify things [*voces significant res*] belongs to the first sense, the historical or literal."[25] This notion that the biblical text, in its many genres and modes of discourse, presents the realities in the history of God's revelatory and saving action accords with the definition

21. Sokolowski, *Introduction to Phenomenology*, 25.
22. Sokolowski, *Eucharistic Presence*, 143.
23. See Sokolowski, *Eucharistic Presence*, 182–84; Sokolowski, *Introduction to Phenomenology*, 9–11; Peter Casarella, "Questioning the Primacy of Method: On Sokolowski's *Eucharistic Presence*," *Communio* 22 (1995): 669–75.
24. Robert Sokolowski, "God's Word and Human Speech," *Nova et Vetera*, English edition 11 (2013): 199.
25. Thomas Aquinas, *Summa Theologica* I, q. 1, a. 10. Latin text from www.corpusthomisticum.org.

of the literal sense summarized by Augustine of Dacia: "*Littera gesta docet: The letter teaches us what was done.*"[26]

This manner of parsing things also provides a helpful way for thinking about the "communicative intention" of the biblical authors.[27] The place of the author's intention in biblical interpretation has fallen on hard times in some circles, especially under the influence of postmodern literary theory. With respect to the Bible, the complexity of the topic has not lessened with the recognition that the biblical writings are themselves products of many authors, who wrote in different times, drawing on diverse traditions, and in response to different situations. In such cases, we might ask, with Olivier-Thomas Venard, "Who is the author of a Gospel, for example? The final redactor? The composer of the first accounts? Does the presumed author of the hypothetical Q source hold the key to the literal sense of the passages in question?"[28]

But if we conceive of intentionality more in terms of ontological than psychological terms (as Aquinas and Sokolowski do), we might get a bit more leverage on the matter—though this route does not resolve all problems and complexities. For instance, in the same article of the *Summa Theologica* cited above (I, q. 1, a. 10), Aquinas offers another definition of the literal sense in terms of the author's intention: "Since the literal sense is that which the author intends, and since the author of Holy Writ is God, Who by one act comprehends all things by His intellect, it is not unfitting . . . if, even according to the literal sense, one word in Holy Writ should have several senses."[29] This latter definition of the literal sense speaks of what "the author intends,"

26. Henri de Lubac, *Medieval Exegesis*, trans. Mark Sebanc and E. M. Macierowski, 3 vols. (Grand Rapids: Eerdmans, 1998–2009), 2:41 (emphasis original). For an in-depth discussion of de Lubac's thought on the literal sense of Scripture, see William M. Wright IV, "The Literal Sense of Scripture according to Henri de Lubac: Insights from Patristic Exegesis of the Transfiguration," *Modern Theology* 28 (2012): 252–77.

27. See Stephen E. Fowl, "The Role of Authorial Intention in the Theological Interpretation of Scripture," in *Between Two Horizons: Spanning New Testament Studies and Systematic Theology*, ed. Joel B. Green and Max Turner (Grand Rapids: Eerdmans, 2000), 71–87. Fowl distinguishes the authors' communicative intentions from authorial motives, and he acknowledges his own indebtedness to Mark Brett, "Motives and Intentions in Genesis 1," *Journal of Theological Studies* 42 (1991): 1–16, and Quentin Skinner, "Motives, Intentions, and the Interpretation of Texts," *New Literary History* 3 (1971): 393–408.

28. Olivier-Thomas Venard, OP, "Problématique du sens littéral," in *Le sens littéral des Écritures*, ed. Olivier-Thomas Venard, OP (Paris: Les Éditions du Cerf, 2009), 312, translation ours.

29. Aquinas, *Summa Theologica* I, q. 1, a. 10. The Latin text reads as follows: "Quia vero sensus litteralis est, quem auctor intendit, auctor autem sacrae Scripturae Deus est, qui omnia simul suo intellectu comprehendit, non est inconveniens, ut dicit Augustinus XII confessionum, si etiam secundum litteralem sensum in una littera Scripturae plures sint sensus." Cited from www.corpusthomisticum.org.

but Aquinas immediately identifies the author of Scripture as God. Even if this claim is applied to the human beings, we should not assume that what Aquinas means by "intention" (*intentio*) is the same as what the category "author's intention" means in modern biblical scholarship. For Aquinas, the *intentio* (in human beings) is the cognitively existing intelligibility, or form, of a thing. Given its metaphysical grounding in formal causality, Aquinas's notion of "intention" cannot simply be equated with what the category "author's intention" means in much modern biblical scholarship, which gives no attention to formal causality. For the former, intention is anchored in ontology and metaphysical epistemology, and for the latter, intention is a matter of psychology (or of an epistemology beset by the egocentric predicament) without the metaphysical associations.

Nevertheless, modern historical and literary analysis has provided invaluable help in determining the communicative intention, or the illocutionary acts, expressed by the human authors of the biblical books.[30] These modes of analysis help in "establishing cultural sympathy" with the ancients, and thus they "can result in a reasonably successful attempt to understand the correct tenor of the author's work, what he 'intended to say.'"[31] Or to use Mats Wahlberg's way of putting it, modern biblical criticism can help determine both the expression (i.e., what an author invites his audience to envision) and the assertion (i.e., what an author claims is true and in what respect) made in a particular genre or mode of discourse.[32] Even if, with Aquinas, we grant that the literal sense of Scripture may admit multiple meanings, historical and literary analysis can help readers of Scripture who are at a temporal and cultural remove from the books' contexts of composition

---

30. The category "illocutionary acts" comes from speech-act theory. Nicholas Wolterstorff explains the matter: "Fundamental to [speech-action] theory is the distinction between *locutionary acts* and *illocutionary acts*. Locutionary acts are acts of uttering or inscribing words. *Il*-locutionary acts are acts performed *by way of* locutionary acts, acts such as asking, asserting, commanding, promising, and so forth." Wolterstorff, *Divine Discourse: Philosophical Reflections on the Claim That God Speaks* (Cambridge: Cambridge University Press, 1995), 13. Compare Fowl, "Role of Authorial Intention"; Nicholas Wolterstorff, "The Promise of Speech-Act Theory for Biblical Interpretation," in *After Pentecost: Language and Biblical Interpretation*, ed. Craig Bartholomew, Colin Greene, and Karl Möller (Grand Rapids: Zondervan, 2001), 73–90.

31. Francis Martin, "Some Aspects of Biblical Studies since Vatican II: The Contribution and Challenge of *Dei Verbum*," in *Sacred Scripture: The Disclosure of the Word* (Naples, FL: Sapientia Press, 2006), 230.

32. Following Wahlberg, *Revelation as Testimony*, 38–39. Wahlberg gives the following example: "The books of Jonah and Job in the Bible are pieces of fiction, and many of the propositions that the declarative sentences in the books express are not asserted—that is, not claimed (by the human authors, or by God) to be true" (39). By "true," here, Wahlberg seems to have in mind facticity.

to acquire a better grasp of the truth-claim being made in a given text or mode of discourse.[33]

We can also think of the authors' intention in more phenomenological or ontological terms. For an author's "statement is about *something* and that too is what the author intends; his mind intends some reality, some aspect of being and interpreting his text includes participating in the knowledge that the author is communicating."[34] Put differently, when reading the biblical text, a person enters into a conscious, cognitive relationship both with the words and, through the words, with the intended reality. Thus, "in order to participate more fully in the reality mediated by the words— *intentio* understood metaphysically—it is imperative that we grasp what, in terms of his own context, the author 'wants to say'—*intentio* understood psychologically."[35] In short, to grasp "what the text is about," we should first grasp what the authors are saying in that text and presenting to our consciousness.

The words do not simply signify things—as if "signify" were to mean just signaling or pointing toward things. By using language, we cause things to appear to others in a particular way.[36] As Sokolowski remarks, when we take in an articulated state of affairs (a categorial object), we take in "how the world is being projected as being, through what someone is saying."[37] Through language, things are presented—in a sense—as interpreted by another.[38] Accordingly, when we intend the intelligibility of things, given through words, we intend those things as they are made to show up by another. Applying this principle to the biblical discourse, we can say that in verbally presenting a reality of some sort, the biblical writers are also interpreting that reality theologically. How biblical realities are presented is quite significant, for the various realities mediated by the biblical text are revelatory and salvific: in them is concealed and revealed the living God, who works in the course of the divine economy to bring about the salvation of the world.

---

33. See Mark F. Johnson, "Another Look at the Plurality of the Literal Sense," *Medieval Philosophy & Theology* 2 (1992): 117–41; Stephen E. Fowl, "The Importance of a Multivoiced Literal Sense of Scripture: The Example of Thomas Aquinas," in *Reading Scripture with the Church: Toward a Hermeneutic for Theological Interpretation*, by A. K. M. Adam, Stephen E. Fowl, Kevin J. Vanhoozer, and Francis Watson (Grand Rapids: Baker Academic, 2006), 35–50; Mark D. Jordan, *Ordering Wisdom: The Hierarchy of Philosophical Discourses in Aquinas* (Notre Dame, IN: University of Notre Dame Press, 1986), 26–31.

34. Martin, "Contribution and Challenge," 230 (emphasis original).

35. Martin, "Contribution and Challenge," 231.

36. Robert Sokolowski, *Phenomenology of the Human Person* (Cambridge: Cambridge University Press, 2008), 299; Sokolowski, *Introduction to Phenomenology*, 158–59.

37. Sokolowski, *Introduction to Phenomenology*, 100.

38. Sokolowski, *Introduction to Phenomenology*, 5.

## The Mystery-Bearing Realities of the Divine Economy

### Mystery-Bearing Realities

The biblical tradition recognizes that the radically transcendent God reveals something of himself and his will in the course of the divine economy. It is especially through God's self-revelatory and saving *actions* that human beings are given to know something of who God is personally. As Gilles Emery puts it (with reference to the revelation of God's sacred name in Exod. 3:14), "God reveals 'who he is' by his life-giving action in history."[39] God's revelatory and saving actions in salvation history are a kind of "word," because these actions say something about who God is.[40] In short, humans can know something of who God is (in part) on the basis of what God does in the economy of salvation.[41]

This theological position converges somewhat with W. Norris Clarke's analysis of the self-communication of being through action. Since action is "essence-structured" (i.e., creatures act in a range of ways proper to what they are), action can be taken as revealing the intelligibility of the actor. Although God is not any kind of being, we can discern an analogical point of convergence here on the basis of *esse*. When God chooses to reveal himself to human beings in intelligible ways, we come to know something of who God is on the basis of God's actions. Thus, the "acts of a person (even or especially when this 'person' is God) are revelatory; they manifest the person, the subject who acts, and not merely the source of the act as agent."[42]

To say that God is actively present in the realities of salvation history, revealing himself and exercising his saving power, is to say that these realities of salvation history bear "mystery." Within the biblical writings (as well as many noncanonical writings from the Second Temple period and later first century), "mystery" has a range of connotations that often involve the notion of hiddenness.[43] The term "mystery" generally connotes heavenly truths or

39. Gilles Emery, OP, *The Trinity: An Introduction to Catholic Doctrine on the Triune God*, trans. Matthew Levering (Washington, DC: Catholic University of America Press, 2011), 45 (italics removed).

40. This theological point coincides with the semantic flexibility of the Hebrew noun *dābār*, which can mean both "word" and "thing." See Martin, "Revelation and Its Transmission," 57.

41. As Emery (*Trinity*, 59–60) points out, the trinitarian heresy of monarchianism denies this very point by disconnecting the immanent and economic Trinity.

42. Francis Martin, "Reflections on Professor Bockmuehl's 'Bible versus Theology,'" *Nova et Vetera*, English edition 9 (2011): 62.

43. A helpful introduction and survey of the relevant material remains Raymond E. Brown, SS, "The Pre-Christian Semitic Concept of 'Mystery,'" *Catholic Biblical Quarterly* 20 (1958): 417–43; Brown, "The Semitic Background of the New Testament *Mysterion* (I)," *Biblica* 39

realities, which are hidden with God and become accessible to humans only if God should reveal them (cf. Dan. 2). Uses of this term in the New Testament often have a more focused, christological meaning. For instance, in the Pauline letters, the term "mystery" is often synonymous with "gospel" (e.g., Rom. 16:25; 1 Cor. 1:17–18; 2:1). In Ephesians especially, "mystery" designates God's hidden plan to bring about the salvation of all people through Jesus Christ (cf. Eph. 1:9–10; 3:1–12).

While God is present to all things as the source of their existence and intelligibility, God may choose to be actively present in the realities of salvation history in a different, more intensive and salvific manner. In such a light, we can speak of these realities as bearing divine mystery. Henri de Lubac speaks of the realities in salvation history as having a "religious consecration" on account of God's active presence in them: "God acts in history and reveals himself through history. Or rather, God inserts himself in history and so bestows on it a 'religious consecration.' . . . As a consequence historical realities possess a profound sense and are to be understood in a spiritual manner: *historika pneumatikōs*; conversely, spiritual realities appear in a constant state of flux and are to be understood historically: *pneumatika historikōs*."[44]

Since God is actively present in the realities of the divine economy, these realities bear an abundance of revelatory and spiritual significance. As de Lubac puts it, in Scripture, "the very facts have an inner significance; although in time, they are yet pregnant with an eternal value."[45] The mystery-bearing biblical realities have a spiritual fullness that cannot be exhausted in a single textual rendering. Hence, various biblical realities are the subject of reflection and interpretation in a variety of biblical texts and genres. Gerhard von Rad approaches this point in his *Old Testament Theology* when he speaks of the "openness" of the events in Israel's history. He writes, "All presentation of history in the Old Testament is in one form or another inherently open to a future."[46] He bases this claim on the recognition that a given reality or action of God in the history of Israel can be interpreted in different ways,

---

(1958): 426–48; Brown, "The Semitic Background of the New Testament *Mysterion* (II)," *Biblica* 40 (1959): 70–87.

44. Henri de Lubac, *Catholicism: Christ and the Common Destiny of Man*, trans. Lancelot C. Sheppard and Sister Elizabeth Englund, OCD (San Francisco: Ignatius, 1988), 165. The Greek in de Lubac's text has been transliterated above.

45. De Lubac, *Catholicism*, 168. He quotes Gregory of Nyssa, *Against Eunomius* 12 (PG 45:940).

46. Gerhard von Rad, *Old Testament Theology*, vol. 2, *The Theology of Israel's Prophetic Traditions*, trans. D. M. G. Stalker (Edinburgh: Oliver & Boyd, 1965), 361. Here we develop argumentation found in Francis Martin, "Historical Criticism and New Testament Teaching on the Imitation of Christ," in *Sacred Scripture*, 44–55.

in different texts, and at different historical moments—a phenomenon cor-related with the practices of innerbiblical exegesis.[47] These saving acts of God in the history of Israel are naturally "open to a future" because they lend themselves to being reinterpreted in future historical contexts. Von Rad continues, "Their intrinsic openness to a future actually needed such fresh interpretation on the part of later ages; and for the latter it was essential to their life to take up tradition in this way and give it a new meaning."[48] The full spiritual significance of the mystery-bearing realities may exceed the particular linguistic formulations that mediate them. But those linguistic for-mulations remain essential, and they do mediate something of those realities and their intrinsic intelligibility.[49] For it is through the biblical discourse that the audience of Scripture attains cognitive contact with the mystery-bearing realities mediated by the text.

### Perceiving and Interpreting the Mystery

Since God reveals "mysteries"—realities and truths that are above the natural comprehension and reach of human beings—voices in the biblical tradition recognize a correlate action of God in people to grace them with the ability to receive and discern what God is revealing.[50] For instance, in Isaiah 6, a seraph touches a fiery coal from the heavenly/temple altar to the prophet Isaiah's mouth (vv. 6–7). The text specifies that this act was to purge Isaiah of his sinfulness (v. 7), and having been so cleansed, Isaiah then receives his prophetic mission and message from God (vv. 8–13). God not only provides the message but also enables the prophet with the means to receive and speak it. Similarly, in the dream vision episode of Daniel 2, Daniel and his compan-ions are declared "wise" and as possessing "understanding" in the respect that heavenly mysteries are revealed to them (v. 21).

This basic dynamic—that God both reveals and enables people to receive this revelation—appears, for instance, in Aquinas's treatment of the gift of prophecy. Aquinas speaks of God providing the prophet with a "supernatural

47. The landmark study on this practice is Michael Fishbane, *Biblical Interpretation in Ancient Israel* (Oxford: Clarendon, 1985).

48. Von Rad, *Old Testament Theology*, 2:361.

49. We are indebted here to Guy Mansini, OSB, in his unpublished paper "Dogma Yesterday and Today," for his reinforcement of these points and for kindly sharing his unpublished text with us.

50. As Francis Martin writes, "God imparts knowledge in a twofold manner: first by sup-plying something with the light, or the capacity, to understand what is presented, and second by presenting what is to be known." "*Sacra Doctrina* and the Authority of Its *Sacra Scriptura* according to St. Thomas Aquinas," in *Sacred Scripture*, 3.

light"—that is, the graced capacity to perceive what God is revealing.[51] This divine illumination enables the prophet, for instance, to receive revealed knowledge from God, to interpret Scripture and the words of Jesus, and to make correct judgments about natural realities in light of God's truth.[52] God not only reveals the mysteries to be believed but also provides individuals with the internal capacity to perceive and interpret them.[53] God gifts select people with the faith illumination to perceive aspects of what he is revealing and doing in various realities in the history of salvation.

Among the many contributions of literary and rhetorical scholarship on the Bible has been a heightened appreciation for the interrelationship between form and content in the biblical books. The poetics of the biblical discourse—its literary and rhetorical dynamics—is an essential component in how the texts mediate the biblical realities.[54] As Michael Fishbane writes, "Form is inseparable from content, such that every textual formulation of an event constructs a unique literary reality; to imagine a different formulation of it would be to construct a different reality."[55] Similarly, Adele Berlin writes, "We must look not only for *what* the text says, but also *how* it says it."[56] The linguistic medium is ingredient to the message of the biblical texts. Put differently, there is an appropriate congruence between sign and signified.

The Second Vatican Council's *Dogmatic Constitution on Divine Revelation* (*Dei Verbum*) makes a comparable point when it speaks of the "intrinsic connection" (*intrinsece inter se connexis* [translation ours]) between the deeds and words in the history of salvation (§2). There is a kind of revelatory reciprocity between the words and realities in the divine economy.[57] René Latourelle argues that this revelatory reciprocity is explicitly sacramental: "The sacramental character of revelation appears in the interpenetration and

---

51. Aquinas, *Summa Theologica* II-II, q. 173, a. 2. For further discussion, see Martin, "*Sacra Doctrina*," 4–8, which we draw on here.

52. Aquinas, *Summa Theologica* II-II, q. 173, a. 2.

53. This twofold dynamic was often articulated in the tradition with reference to Psalm 36:9: "In your light we see light." See Francis Martin, *The Feminist Question: Feminist Theology in the Light of Christian Tradition* (Grand Rapids: Eerdmans, 1994), 6–7.

54. See Francis Martin and Sean McEvenue, "Truth Told in the Bible: Biblical Poetics and the Question of Truth," in *The International Bible Commentary*, ed. William R. Farmer (Collegeville, MN: Liturgical Press, 1998), 116–27; Martin, *Narrative Parallels to the New Testament*, Resources for Biblical Study 22 (Atlanta: Scholars Press, 1988), 1–24.

55. Michael Fishbane, *Biblical Text and Texture: A Literary Reading of Selected Texts* (Rockport, MA: Oneworld, 1998), xi.

56. Adele Berlin, *Poetics and Interpretation of Biblical Narrative* (Winona Lake, IN: Eisenbrauns, 1994), 20.

57. Contents in the next two paragraphs first appeared in Wright, "Scripture as a Sacramental Vehicle," 177–78. They have been reworked and expanded here.

mutual support that exists between word and work. God performs the act of salvation and at the same time develops its meaning; He intervenes in history and tells us of the import of His intervention; He acts and comments on His action."[58]

As a fruit of divine inspiration, the Bible's linguistic articulations, its *verba*, possess a privileged congruence with the divine actions and mystery-bearing realities in salvation history. Various texts and genres in Scripture interpret the realities of the divine economy in such a way that the divine mystery that they bear is brought to light in some measure (*DV* §2). Thus, Henri de Lubac, commenting on this passage in *Dei Verbum*, writes, "It is the same Word of God who, on the one hand, 'realizes the plans of God in history' and, on the other, 'translates in human words, on the lips of God's messengers, to make the meaning of this revelation through the realities understood.'"[59] The biblical *verba* constitute linguistic articulations especially apt for the disclosure of these sacred realities, having, as they do, an inspired, "intrinsic" relation with them. The biblical discourse thus "has a unique capacity to transpose, express, and mediate the action, the *res*, or the *mysterion*."[60]

The words of the biblical compositions articulate and interpret the realities such that ways in which God is actively present in those realities are to an extent brought to light. This was observed, for instance, in our study of 2 Kings 17, where the Deuteronomists discern in the Assyrian conquest of the northern kingdom the hand of God to punish for unrepentant sin. In doing so, they provide a "prophetic interpretation of reality."[61] The words are "intrinsically connected" to the realities in that they bring to light in a privileged and unique manner something of the mystery within the realities. The mystery, properly speaking, lies within the realities, not in the words per se, and in this respect, the words are subordinate to the realities of which they speak.

But given that they are "intrinsically" connected to the realities, the verbal articulations are indispensable. For it is in and through the verbalizations that the audience of Scripture has access to the realities of divine economy and the divine mystery concealed and revealed in them. By speaking of an intrinsic connection between revelatory words and realities in the divine economy, *Dei Verbum* offers an integration of what has been termed manifestational and

58. Latourelle, *Theology of Revelation*, 462.

59. Henri de Lubac, *La Révélation divine*, in Cardinal Henri de Lubac, *Œuvres completes*, ed. Éric de Moulins-Beaufort and Georges Chantraine (Paris: Les Éditions du Cerf, 2006), 4:68–69, translation ours.

60. Martin, "Revelation and Its Transmission," 57.

61. Walter Kasper, *The God of Jesus Christ*, trans. Matthew J. O'Connell (New York: Crossroad, 1984), 66–67.

propositional revelation.[62] God not only manifests himself in actions and realities, but also communicates information about himself, his will, and designs through propositions given in verbal discourse. Indeed, as Wahlberg has persuasively argued, if divine revelation is to have any epistemic purchase, it must have a propositional dimension wherein information is communicated in verbalizations. That is to say, revelation must involve the communication of knowledge and have "a determinate *cognitive content*" that provides a measure for adjudicating various interpretations.[63] Moreover, Wahlberg argues that human beings simply cannot have a personal relationship with God unless divine revelation involves a propositional component: "God wants personal communion with humans. Personal relationships (unlike impersonal relationships) require knowledge. It is impossible for me to relate in a personal way to somebody or something without knowing (or justifiably believing) something about that person or thing. . . . I cannot stand in a personal relationship—such as the relationship of loving, hating, fearing, or praising—to somebody or something without knowing something about that object or person."[64] Taken as a whole, the Christian Bible provides a narrative succession of God's revelatory and saving actions in these mystery-bearing realities, which have a spiritual fullness and are the subject of interpretation in various biblical texts and genres. This economy of salvation, given in the Christian Bible, culminates in the life, death, and resurrection of Jesus Christ. Thus, God's revelatory and saving actions in the course of the divine economy cannot be understood adequately apart from Jesus Christ.

## The Incarnation and Economic Participation

### Shifts Introduced by the Incarnation

The incarnation of the Word of God in Jesus Christ has far-reaching effects on how God, the world, the divine economy, and all things within it (including Scripture) are understood. First, the incarnation introduces some basic modifications into the Distinction and the understanding of God that it entails. As discussed in chapter 5, the incarnation presupposes the Old Testament

---

62. See Wahlberg, *Revelation as Testimony*, 28–33. As Wahlberg (*Revelation as Testimony*, 26) defines the term, propositions "are what declarative sentences express." He goes on (33–42) to correct many misconceptions about propositional revelation (e.g., a proposition is identical with a sentence; it can only be given in literal speech; it must convey timeless or eternal truths; every propositional claim is a revealed truth).

63. Wahlberg, *Revelation as Testimony*, 36 (emphasis original).

64. Wahlberg, *Revelation as Testimony*, 25.

notion of the Distinction between Creator and creation, but the incarnation also reveals the Distinction to be even more mysterious and profound. To reiterate, in the incarnation, as Sokolowski writes, "God is revealed to be so transcendent that he can enter into his creation without suffering limitation in his divinity."[65] The incarnation thus brings about an "intensification" in the biblical understanding of God and his transcendence.[66]

Second, the Christian belief that God becomes human in Jesus Christ, without any diminishment of his divinity, modifies the understanding of who the God of Israel is. Richard Bauckham and Larry Hurtado, in particular, have helpfully examined the intelligibility of Christian belief in Jesus's divinity within the context of Second Temple Jewish monotheism such that Jesus was included (to use Bauckham's language) in the "identity of God."[67] As we have seen in chapter 1, the New Testament writings employ various biblical images, categories, and texts to depict Jesus as intrinsic to who God is. The upshot is that the understanding of God in the New Testament is not wholly identical with that given in the Old Testament. Sokolowski writes, "There is a difference even though there is not an otherness"—as would be the case for Marcion.[68]

Third, if the incarnation so modifies the understanding of God, it also modifies the understanding of all things in relation to God.[69] This includes, for instance, creation. Many New Testament writings identify Jesus, as the Word and Wisdom of God, as the one through whom God (the Father) creates (e.g., John 1:3–4; 1 Cor. 8:6; Col. 1:16; Heb. 1:2). Since all creation exists in relation to the Creator, to identify Jesus as the agent of creation entails that all created things exist in continual relation to him as the Son (or Word) of God. Thus, the prologue of the Fourth Gospel says of the divine Word, "All things came into being through him, and without him not one thing came into being" (John 1:3). Similarly, Hebrews speaks of the Son as the one who "sustains all things by his powerful word" (Heb. 1:3).

Fourth, the incarnation also impacts how one understands the divine economy. In Christian understanding, the overarching course of God's revelatory and salvific action in the divine economy culminates in Jesus Christ. In this light, Jesus comes to be seen as the center point of God's designs for the

65. Sokolowski, *Eucharistic Presence*, 54.
66. Sokolowski, *Eucharistic Presence*, 54.
67. See Richard Bauckham, *Jesus and the God of Israel: God Crucified, and Other Studies on the New Testament's Christology of Divine Identity* (Grand Rapids: Eerdmans, 2008); Larry W. Hurtado, *How on Earth Did Jesus Become a God? Historical Questions about Earliest Devotion to Jesus* (Grand Rapids: Eerdmans, 2005), esp. 31–55; Hurtado, *The Lord Jesus Christ: Devotion to Jesus in Earliest Christianity* (Grand Rapids: Eerdmans, 2003).
68. Sokolowski, *Eucharistic Presence*, 54.
69. See Wright, "Doctrine of God and the Liturgical *Res*," 966–67.

world and the whole of human history. As the agent of God's definitive act of salvation, Jesus is the one in whom God makes good on his saving promises given in Scripture (e.g., Luke 4:21; John 19:28; Acts 13:32–33; 1 Cor. 15:3–8). As the incarnate Word, Jesus is the supreme revelation of who God is—he is the Son, the only one who knows the Father and so can reveal the Father to others (Matt. 11:27; John 1:18). As the head of the church, he is the one in whom all humanity is reconciled with and gathered to the Father (e.g., Col. 1:15–20). The New Testament claim that the risen and ascended Jesus reigns over all creation and will serve as the eschatological judge further entails that all creation is also subject to his sovereign rule.[70] In short, the incarnation leads us to understand the divine economy as leading up to, culminating in, and circling around the person of Jesus Christ.

Fifth, the events of Jesus's life, death, and resurrection also impact what we understand to be included in the mystery borne by the biblical realities. As mentioned previously, the term "mystery" in the New Testament writings often designates the hidden plan of God to bring about the salvation of the world in Christ. Thus, the opening benediction in Ephesians declares that God "has made known to us the mystery of his will," which is "to gather up all things in [Christ]" (Eph. 1:9–10). The "mystery" that God has revealed to Paul is God's hidden plan to bring about the salvation of all people through Jesus Christ and to gather them to participate in his risen life as members of his body, the church (Eph. 3:5–6; cf. 5:32).[71] This mystery of salvation in Christ had been hidden with God from eternity, but "it has now been revealed to his holy apostles and prophets by the Spirit" (3:5; cf. Col. 1:26–27). Paul similarly writes in Romans that this mystery of salvation in Christ "was kept secret for long ages but is now disclosed, and through the prophetic writings is made known to all the Gentiles" (Rom. 16:25–26). This text from Romans exemplifies the connection, which Paul discerns here and elsewhere, that the revelation of the mystery of salvation in Christ has been prepared for in the Scriptures (cf. Rom. 1:1–2). Here, "mystery" and the divine economy of salvation in Christ coincide.

---

70. Cf. Matt. 25:31–46; 28:18; John 5:19–30; Acts 10:42; 17:31; 2 Cor. 5:10; 2 Tim. 4:1; Rev. 1:17–18.

71. For an overview of issues pertaining to the category "mystery" in Paul, see Markus Barth, *Ephesians 1–3*, Anchor Bible 34 (New York: Doubleday, 1974), 18–21, 123–27; Brown, "Semitic Background of the New Testament *Mysterion* (I)," 434–48; Brown, "Semitic Background of the New Testament *Mysterion* (II)," 70–87; James D. G. Dunn, *Romans 9–16*, Word Biblical Commentary 38B (Dallas: Word, 1988), 677–79; Joseph A. Fitzmyer, SJ, *Paul and His Theology: A Brief Sketch*, 2nd ed. (Upper Saddle River, NJ: Prentice Hall, 1987), 38–41; Benjamin L. Gladd, *Revealing the* Mysterion: *The Use of Mystery in Daniel and Second Temple Judaism with Its Bearing on First Corinthians*, BZNW 160 (Berlin: de Gruyter, 2008).

Furthermore, the incarnation and the paschal mystery introduce a new context or horizon for viewing the realities given in the Old Testament. In various ways, New Testament writings frequently present the resurrection of Jesus as furnishing his disciples with a new way of understanding the Scriptures.[72] This is most vividly depicted in the resurrection narratives in Luke 24, wherein the risen Jesus "opened their minds to understand the scriptures" (Luke 24:45). This belief finds other articulations in the New Testament, from Paul's rehearsal of the early Christian kerygma that Christ died and rose "in accordance with the scriptures" (1 Cor. 15:3–5), to the use of Scripture to interpret Jesus's death and resurrection in the speeches in Acts (e.g., Acts 2:14–36; 13:26–41), to the postresurrectional understanding of Jesus and the Scriptures given to the apostles by the Paraclete in John (e.g., John 14:26; 16:7–15).

Taken together, these considerations lead to an important theological point: if all the biblical realities participate in the divine economy and if the divine economy has as its core the mystery of salvation in Christ, then all biblical realities, insofar as they participate in the divine economy, also participate in the mystery of salvation in Christ. The "mystery" borne by the biblical realities includes their manner of participating in the life and work of Jesus Christ.

### Economic Participation

One way to think about the mystery-bearing realities of the divine economy in relation to Christ is in terms of "economic participation."[73] In chapter 6, we discussed the notion of participation as an aspect of the Thomistic metaphysics of creation. W. Norris Clarke identified three principal elements in a participatory relationship.[74] First, there is a source, which has (or is) a given perfection or attribute in its fullness. Second, there is a participating subject, which partakes in a limited way of the perfection or attribute in question. Third, there is a relation of derivation or dependence: the participating subject receives or derives its limited possession of the perfection from the source, which derives the perfection from none.

Recall that Aquinas discerns this participatory relationship in the most fundamental structures of being. Aquinas speaks of God as the pure, unlimited act

---

72. Helpful discussion can be found in Donald Juel, *Messianic Exegesis: Christological Interpretation of the Old Testament in Early Christianity* (Philadelphia: Fortress, 1988).

73. See Martin, "Imitation of Christ," 43–55, 69–71; Martin, "Contribution and Challenge," 239–42; Martin, "The Spiritual Sense (*Sensus Spiritualis*) of Sacred Scripture: Its Essential Insight," in *Sacred Scripture*, 271–75; Martin, "Election, Covenant, and Law," 863–65.

74. W. Norris Clarke, SJ, "The Meaning of Participation in St. Thomas," in *Explorations in Metaphysics: Being—God—Person* (Notre Dame, IN: University of Notre Dame Press, 1994), 93.

of existing (*ipsum esse subsistens*) from whom all creatures receive their own limited act of existing (*esse*) at every moment of their being. God is the source, who is *esse* (i.e., the perfection) itself. Contingent creatures are the participating subjects, who, since they do not have *esse* by virtue of their own natures, derive it from God at all times. Within this basic picture of participatory ontology, God is the radically transcendent yet immanently present Creator, and all creatures are grounded, in the depths of their being, in God's own life. Creation is fundamentally an "open system" because it cannot exist at any time apart from the transcendent Creator, who is immanently and noninvasively present to it. This participatory relationship of creatures to their Creator involves an "inner" or "vertical" dimension of things. This participatory relationship can be called "inner" because its core lies in the hidden depths of a thing's being: its act of existing. This participatory relationship can also be called "vertical" because it tracks ontologically "downwards." As participants in God's *esse*, all creatures are grounded, in the depths of their being, in God.

These elements of participatory ontology provide a way for thinking about the divine economy and the ways in which its various realities participate in the mystery of salvation in Christ—that is, a kind of "economic participation." We begin by identifying "the perfections" that the source and the participating subjects possess in different ways. Recall that *Dei Verbum* teaches that God reveals himself and his will in the words and realities of the divine economy and that divine revelation is aimed at salvation. The "mystery" borne by these realities of the divine economy is the active presence of God, who reveals himself and exercises his saving power in and through them. Following *Dei Verbum*, we can identify revelation and salvation as the focal perfections in the divine economy.

The divine economy, narrated in the Christian biblical canon, reaches its climax in the life, death, and resurrection of Jesus Christ. As the incarnate Word of God, Jesus is the fullness of divine revelation, for the human words and deeds of Jesus are the human words and deeds of God himself. Jesus's death and resurrection is also God's definitive act of salvation for all people wherein God makes good on his saving promises. Reconciling sinners to God, Christ enables all people to be gathered into the life of God by giving them a share in his own risen life. Articulated within a participatory structure, the life, death, and resurrection of the incarnate Word are the center and source point in the divine economy. Jesus Christ is the fullness of revelation and salvation, the very purpose to which the divine economy tends.[75]

75. For a very illuminating analysis of the teaching of *Dei Verbum* on this matter in light of its development, see Jared Wicks, SJ, "The Fullness of Revelation in Christ in *Dei Verbum*," *Josephinum Journal of Theology* 23 (2016): 176–204.

Identifying Jesus as center and source point in the divine economy causes all mystery-bearing realities in the divine economy—including those before and after the mortal life of the incarnate Word—to appear as participating, in some manner, in his life and work.[76] Within the participatory structure, these mystery-bearing realities of the economy (e.g., Old Testament realities) are the participating subjects.

The mystery borne by the biblical realities involves the active presence of God, who reveals himself and exercises his saving power in them. These two aspects—God's revelation and saving action—are constituted fully in the incarnate Word. God does in a definitive and complete manner in Jesus what he does in real, but limited, ways in other biblical realities: "Long ago God spoke to our ancestors in many and various ways by the prophets, but in these last days he has spoken to us by a Son" (Heb. 1:1–2). In this way, other mystery-bearing biblical realities come to light as "anticipated participations" in the mystery of Christ.[77] Understanding the biblical realities as anticipated participations does not (and should not) detract from the abiding theological and spiritual value of these biblical realities in their own right. Rather, to think of the biblical realities in this participatory way is just to affirm that within the divine economy, the mystery borne by these realities includes dimensions wherein they participate in the mystery of Christ by way of anticipation.

This understanding of the biblical realities as participating in the mystery of Christ in an anticipatory manner reflects elements in the traditional doctrine of the spiritual sense of Scripture. As Paul used the term "mystery" to designate God's hidden plan of salvation in Christ now revealed by the Holy Spirit, so did the term "mystery" come to be used in early Christian exegesis of the Old Testament to designate its hidden christological dimensions, which are brought to light by the paschal mystery and work of the Holy Spirit. Henri de Lubac notes that in premodern Latin exegesis, the term *mysterium* was often paired with *sacramentum*.[78] The latter term, *sacramentum*, designated what was exterior and commonly accessible, and the former term, *mysterium*, designated what was interior and hidden.[79] De Lubac writes that for exegetes such as Ambrose and Augustine, "the

76. Thus Martin writes, "For the New Testament, the Lord Jesus Christ, particularly in his death and resurrection, constitutes the center of history, giving a new and fulfilled meaning to the ancient tradition and providing a context and direction for the lives of all who come to believe in him." Martin, "Imitation of Christ," 50.

77. Martin, "Election, Covenant, and Law," 865–71, 886–90; Martin, introduction to *Sacred Scripture*, xii–xiv.

78. De Lubac, *Medieval Exegesis*, 2:19–27.

79. De Lubac, *Medieval Exegesis*, 2:21, quotation from 2:22.

mystery . . . is the interior component, the reality hidden under the letter and signified by the sign. . . . The sacrament contains the mystery, it relates to the mystery."[80] Within this theological vision, the *sacramentum* and the *mysterium* are different aspects of the same biblical reality: one is patent, while the other is latent.

According to de Lubac, it is very important to recognize that the "mystery" (or spiritual sense) is more a dimension of the biblical reality itself than it is a property of the biblical texts. De Lubac writes in his first major theological work, *Catholicism*, "The spiritual meaning, then, is to be found on all sides, not only or more especially in a book but first and foremost *in reality itself*."[81] In this regard, he cites Augustine's remarks from his *Enarrations on the Psalms*: "In the very fact itself and not only in what is said about the fact we ought to seek the mystery."[82] De Lubac makes the same point even more emphatically in *Medieval Exegesis*. Speaking of the biblical *historia*—that which the words present—de Lubac writes, "All these historical things . . . convey a mystery to us. Once again, beyond the immediate content of the history or the primary sense of the letter, let us look for *the spiritual meaning that is in it*."[83] The spiritual sense (or mystery of Christ) is an inner dimension of the reality mediated by the text: "To discover this allegory [i.e., mystery or spiritual meaning], one will not find it properly speaking in the text, but in the realities of which the text speaks; not in history as recitation, but in history as event." De Lubac later adds, "The text acts only as spokesman to lead to the historical realities; the latter are themselves the figures, they themselves contain the mysteries that the exercise of allegory [i.e., spiritual exegesis] is supposed to extract from them."[84]

As explicated by de Lubac, the spiritual sense "is based, not on a theory of text, but on a theology of history."[85] More specifically, as Susan Wood observes, the spiritual sense is really a sacramental theology of history.[86] It discerns the invisible, divine mystery given in and through sensible historical realities. Theologically, the same parsing of the interior and exterior dimensions of a reality finds an analogue in the hypostatic union of the incarnate Word. As the humanity of Jesus concealed and revealed his deity, so too does

---

80. Quotations from de Lubac, *Medieval Exegesis*, 2:21 and 2:22, respectively.

81. De Lubac, *Catholicism*, 169 (emphasis original).

82. De Lubac, *Catholicism*, 169, quoting Augustine, *Enarrations on the Psalms* 68.2.6 (trans. de Lubac, *Catholicism*, 169n14).

83. De Lubac, *Medieval Exegesis*, 2:84 (emphasis original).

84. De Lubac, *Medieval Exegesis*, 2:86.

85. Martin, "Election, Covenant, and Law," 867.

86. Susan K. Wood, *Spiritual Exegesis and the Church in the Theology of Henri de Lubac* (Grand Rapids: Eerdmans, 1998), 37–39.

the *sacramentum* of the biblical reality conceal and reveal the *mysterium* within it.[87] As we have seen, the mystery borne by a biblical reality requires God's gift of the prophetic light in order to be perceived and interpreted. Similarly, the specifically christological dimensions of this mystery require a kind of understanding conferred by the Holy Spirit in order to be perceived. It is the *spiritual* sense because its discernment requires the light of the Holy *Spirit*, poured forth by the risen Christ. Within this account, the senses of Scripture are neither "levels" or "layers" of textual meaning, nor dimensions of the human authors' thinking, nor different meanings intended by the divine and human authors (as in the theory of the *sensus plenior*). Rather, they are better understood as "four dimensions of the event [or reality] that is being mediated by the words."[88]

A helpful way to think about the spiritual sense is in terms of the previously discussed phenomenological doctrine of identity in manifolds. This phenomenological doctrine holds that a thing's identity can be given through a variety of appearances (i.e., manifolds) to a conscious subject. Sokolowski explains with the example of a cube.[89] A person who looks at a cube from a particular angle sees only certain sides of the cube at that particular moment. But as the person moves to another vantage point—or turns the cube to another side or position—other sides of the cube come into view. These newly visible sides are aspects of the cube's identity, but they come into sight only when viewed within a certain context.

Sokolowski applies these theological and phenomenological insights to the christological dimensions of the Old Testament.[90] The life, death, and resurrection of Jesus Christ modify the biblical understanding of God and all things in relation to God. The incarnation and the paschal mystery thus cause new aspects of the biblical realities to come to light, and they also create a new context from within which the biblical realities are seen. The christological dimensions (i.e., the mystery, or the spiritual sense) should be understood as aspects of the biblical realities, mediated by the texts, which come into view only when seen from within a christological context: "It is not the case that there was one meaning in the mind of the human authors and another meaning intended by God, but that the one *thing* intended by the human author had dimensions that had not yet come into view, dimensions

87. De Lubac, *Medieval Exegesis*, 2:22; cf. Wood, *Spiritual Exegesis*, 39. De Lubac is much indebted here to Origen's exegesis of the transfiguration in his *Commentary on Matthew* 12.36–38. See Wright, "Literal Sense of Scripture," 254–59.
88. Martin, introduction to *Sacred Scripture*, xiii.
89. See Sokolowski, *Introduction to Phenomenology*, 17–21, 27–33.
90. Sokolowski, *Eucharistic Presence*, 138–58.

that could not appear until more had happened."[91] As different sides of a cube come into view when the cube is seen from a particular angle, so do new "sides" or dimensions of the biblical realities come into view when those realities are viewed in light of the paschal mystery. The newly visible "sides" do not erase the other sides—any more than looking at a cube from a different vantage point does. It just means that new aspects of the identity of the biblical realities have become visible and do not come into view outside the paschal mystery. Christian readers of the Scripture do well to consider all aspects of the realities mediated by the biblical text: the abiding teaching, wisdom, and spirituality given in these realities' literal dimensions in the Old Testament as well as those dimensions wherein they participate in the mystery of Christ.

## Looking Back and Looking Forward

Let us bring the main elements of this exposition together. The biblical text puts its audience in a cognitive relationship with the various realities of which the text speaks. The words of the text capture and mediate the intelligibility of the various realities of the divine economy. Through sensation and intellection, the audience of Scripture takes in these verbally mediated intelligibilities such that the intelligibilities come to enjoy a kind of cognitive existence in the audience. The various realities of the divine economy that are mediated by the biblical text bear the divine mystery, for in these realities, God is actively, mysteriously present. In them, God is revealing himself and his will and working his saving power. The biblical texts not only present these realities to their audience but also do so in such a way that some of the realities' mysterious depths are elucidated. The incarnation of the Word of God in Jesus Christ modifies the biblical understanding of God and all things in relation to God, including the divine economy and the biblical realities within it. The life, death, and resurrection of the incarnate Word constitute the fullness of divine revelation and the accomplishment of God's definitive saving act. When seen from within the context of the paschal mystery, all other biblical realities come to light as caught up in the salvific economy of the Word and are shown to have dimensions wherein they participate in his saving work. By coming into cognitive union with the realities mediated by the biblical text, the audience of Scripture comes into contact with the divine mystery that those realities bear. In this way, Scripture can put people into contact with the divine realities that it mediates.

---

91. Sokolowski, *Eucharistic Presence*, 149.

However, there is more to the matter than this. The mystery-bearing realities mediated by the biblical text are, in a respect, historically past and therefore absent to audiences in later generations. The words of Scripture capture and mediate the intelligibilities of the biblical realities, enabling us to intend them as absent. And yet witnesses from both Scripture and tradition affirm that people can encounter in their present moment the mysterious reality of God through the biblical text. Ignace de la Potterie summarizes this line of thinking: "The inspired text does not merely tell the history of salvation, it is also an actual and living word, directly addressed to the Church of today, that she may live by it; it is a word which, in the Church and through her preaching, addresses all christians."[92] Scripture is not just a record of past events from which people of later generations can learn; it is also a vehicle for present encounter with the Word of God in its power. In the final chapter, therefore, we will take up the topic of how Scripture's mediation of the divine realities becomes a living and life-giving encounter in the audience's present moment.

---

92. Ignace de la Potterie, SJ, "The Efficacy of the Word of God," *Lumen Vitae* 10 (1955): 48.

# 10

# Encountering the Living God in Scripture

## *The Holy Spirit and Spirituality*

We have reflected on how the words of Scripture mediate to their audience the mystery-bearing realities of which they speak. By taking in the intelligibilities of the realities of the divine economy, mediated by the biblical text, the audience of Scripture comes into contact with the divine mystery that those realities bear. Even though the biblical accounts and the realities of which they speak are temporally past to us, voices in both Scripture and the subsequent tradition affirm that Scripture's audience can still encounter these biblical realities in their present moment. Henri de Lubac writes, "The human authors of the holy Books have died, the events that they have reported have passed away. . . . But the Word of God was expressed through both. It is he who speaks to us still; it is he who reveals himself . . . present on every page."[1] Accordingly, the biblical tradition invites us to explore how this encounter with the divine realities mediated by the biblical text becomes living and life giving in the audiences' present moment. We will do so in the present chapter as we take the final step on the expository ladder of part 2.

Drawing on witnesses from both Scripture and the tradition, we will argue that the encounter with the divine realities mediated by the sacred

---

1. Henri de Lubac, *Medieval Exegesis*, trans. Mark Sebanc and E. M. Macierowski, 3 vols. (Grand Rapids: Eerdmans, 1998–2009), 2:81.

text becomes living and life giving through the action of the Holy Spirit in those who read (or hear) Scripture with appropriate spiritual and moral dispositions.

Our exposition in this chapter has four major parts: the first two parts primarily concern the Holy Spirit, and the last two primarily concern the readers' spirituality. First, we will reflect on the work of the Holy Spirit to make the divine mystery borne by the biblical realities present in and to Scripture's audience. Second, we will consider evidence from both Scripture and tradition that speaks of the Spirit's activity to impart the gift of understanding these divine realities. Third, we will consider Luke's account of the parable of the sower, which provides important teaching on those dispositions that facilitate people's fruitful reception of the Word of God. Fourth, we will reflect on the lives of four saints whose lives were powerfully affected by their encounters with God through Scripture. Their lives help us identify certain spiritual and moral virtues that dispose people to the powerful reality of God's Word given in Scripture.

### The Holy Spirit and the Present Encounter with God in Scripture

A number of biblical witnesses surveyed in part 1 attest that the Word of God, proclaimed in inspired (or Spirit-anointed) human discourse, can make present or bring about that which it articulates. For instance, Jeremiah states that he "ate" (*'ākal*) the Word of God, and the Word became "like a burning fire" in him (Jer. 15:16; 20:9). In 5:14, the Lord announces to Jeremiah, "I am now making my words in your mouth a fire . . . and the fire shall devour [*'ākal*]" the false prophets and people of Judah. The Word of God, given in the inspired discourse of the prophet, will bring about the destruction that it announces. Similarly, the apostle Paul speaks of his own proclamation of the gospel as being attended by "power and . . . the Holy Spirit" (1 Thess. 1:5; cf. 1 Cor. 2:4). This clothing of Paul's proclamation of the Word of God with Spirit and power enables that Word of God to become actively present within believers: "When you received the word of God that you heard from us, you accepted it not as a human word but as what it really is, *God's word, which is also at work in you believers*" (1 Thess. 2:13, emphasis added). Paul's apostolic proclamation is a means by which the Word of God comes to indwell and work believers in their present moment. First Peter similarly speaks of the Word of God, proclaimed by Christian evangelists in the Holy Spirit, as communicating the reality and power of the risen Jesus (1 Pet. 1:12). Peter states that God the Father "has given us a *new birth* into a living hope *through* the *resurrection of Jesus Christ* from the dead" and similarly speaks of Christians being "*born anew . . . through* the living and enduring *word of God*" (vv. 3, 23, emphasis added).

The capacity of the Word of God to make present what it articulates also applies to inspired written discourse. The author of Hebrews interprets Psalm 95 as the discourse of the Holy Spirit (Heb. 3:7), which speaks directly to his own audience. The words of Psalm 95 address not only the wilderness genera-tion of Israelites but also the contemporary Christian audience of Hebrews, to whom they are united in the divine economy. The word of the "living God" (Heb. 3:12), spoken by the Holy Spirit, is itself "living and active" (4:12), and it speaks to Hebrews' audience through the words of Scripture in their present moment. The Gospel according to John likewise understands itself as a vehicle by which later generations of people can encounter the reality of the risen Jesus and believe in him as the Lord. The resurrection narrative of John 20 presents a personal encounter as necessary for coming to believe in him as the Lord. Such an encounter is available to later generations of believers "who have not seen and yet have come to believe" (John 20:29). The way by which this faith-causing encounter comes about is through the Spirit-touched testimony of Jesus's disciples, which the Fourth Gospel itself contains (17:20; 21:24).

It is not simply that Paul, Peter, and John are communicating informa-tion about Jesus. Rather, these authors present their inspired discourse as a vehicle by which the risen Jesus himself becomes actively present in those who faithfully take in their discourse. Theologically, one of the reasons why this belief is intelligible is the eternity of the divine realities, meditated by inspired human discourse.

Although the biblical realities are (in many cases) created and thus histori-cally past, the divine mystery that they bear is eternal. The same God who was actively present in the realities mediated by the biblical text is eternal and thus continuously and actively present to the world.[2] The same Jesus Christ, crucified and risen from the dead, now sits at the Father's right hand, and the church, as his mystical body, participates in his risen life now. The same Holy Spirit who inspired the Scriptures and guided it to canonization continues to indwell the church and work in the lives of believers.[3] The same mysteries and heavenly realities that were revealed in the course of salvation

2. On God's eternity as a fullness of presence that embraces created, temporal existence, see Matthew L. Lamb, "Temporality and History: Reflections from St. Augustine and Bernard Lonergan," *Nova et Vetera*, English edition 4 (2006): 815–50.

3. We are indebted to Denis Farkasfalvy for this emphasis on the Spirit's role in inspiration as spanning the complex process of the books' composition up to and including their canonization.

history are genuinely enjoyed in the normative doctrines and practices of the faith community.[4]

Similarly, the humanity and human experience of Jesus Christ now enjoys a divine mode of being and presence.[5] The resurrection of Jesus involves the glorified transformation of his whole humanity, and in that glorified humanity, he now reigns over all creation. Upon entering into the Father's glory, the risen Jesus does not leave his human nature and experience behind but makes them part of his glorified existence. This is evident from the fact that the body of the resurrected Jesus bears the wounds of the cross (cf. Luke 24:39–40; John 20:20, 27). The Lamb, whom John sees standing alive in heaven and receiving worship, still bears the marks of his slaughter (cf. Rev. 5:6, 9–14). The glorified humanity of Jesus constitutes an ever-present source of grace and living-giving power, which people can encounter and experience themselves.[6] The eternal, glorified existence of the risen Jesus is what enables various New Testament authors, such as Paul, John, and Peter, to speak of Christ as being actively present within believers. Indeed, "the life of the Church and of each believer is an active participation in the life [of the risen Jesus] still available to us by the action of the Holy Spirit."[7]

A further theological reason why the human discourse of these apostles and prophets can mediate divine realities to their audiences is the action of the Holy Spirit upon them and their discourse. As we have seen, the biblical tradition recognizes the action of God to provide select individuals (prophets and apostles) with the graced insight to discern what God is revealing in the realities of the divine economy. These individuals are gifted by God with the prophetic insight to perceive something of the divine mystery being revealed and to interpret it correctly.

Further insight into the Spirit's action here can be obtained by drawing an analogy with the character of human cognition and communication sketched in chapter 8. As we discussed, in the act of knowing, there is a communion between knower and the thing known. Through diverse modes of activity, things manifest and communicate their own intelligibility to other things, and the intelligibility of things can also be captured and mediated through

4. See Francis Martin, "Election, Covenant, and Law," *Nova et Vetera*, English edition 4 (2006): 865–71.

5. Francis Martin, "Revelation and Understanding Scripture: Reflections on the Teaching of Joseph Ratzinger, Pope Benedict XVI," *Nova et Vetera*, English edition 13 (2015): 261–62.

6. See Columba Marmion, *Christ in His Mysteries*, trans. Mother M. St. Thomas (London: Sands, 1939), 3–30; Francis Martin, "Historical Criticism and New Testament Teaching on the Imitation of Christ," in *Sacred Scripture: The Disclosure of the Word* (Naples, FL: Sapientia Press, 2006), 69–71.

7. Martin, "Imitation of Christ," 70.

language and linguistic syntax. Through sensation and intellection, knowing subjects take in the mediated intelligibility of things and transpose it, giving it a cognitive mode of existence.

We might think of the Holy Spirit as intensifying and elevating these natural dynamics by grace. God is actively and mysteriously present in the realities of the divine economy, and in these realities God reveals himself and exercises his power. The Holy Spirit not only graces select individuals with the prophetic light to perceive something of the divine mystery borne in these realities but also makes the discourse of those individuals apt to mediate the divine mystery to others. That is, the Holy Spirit anoints (or inspires) human discourse, making it able to capture and mediate something of the divine mysteries, which are given in the realities of salvation history and have a divine mode of existence. When the audience of Scripture comes into cognitive contact with the mystery-bearing realities of Scripture, the Holy Spirit works in the inspired human discourse of the Scripture to make the same divine mystery, borne by the biblical realities, present in and to believers.

We might also think of the Spirit's work of inspiration as encompassing both the subjective inspiration of the human authors and the objective inspiration of biblical books.[8] So understood, the inspired Scripture not only mediates realities and communicates truths from the inspired authors of the past but also mediates an encounter with God in the present, who speaks and acts through the inspired texts. Such an understanding squares with a traditional understanding of inspiration described by Henri de Lubac: "It is not only the sacred writers who were inspired one fine day. The sacred books themselves are and remain inspired. . . . The Spirit immured himself in it, as it were. He lives in it. His breath has always animated it. . . . It is full of the Spirit."[9] Or as Denis Farkasfalvy likewise has written, "The chief effect of [such an understanding of inspiration consists] . . . in the presence of a spiritual fullness in the biblical text, a capability to reveal not only truths but ultimately the One who said 'I am the Truth.'"[10]

At the same time, witnesses from both Scripture and tradition also identify the action of the Holy Spirit within the readers of Scripture, giving them a penetrating understanding of the realities mediated by the text. We now turn to a consideration of the Spirit's gift of understanding.

---

8. The remainder of this paragraph first appeared in William M. Wright IV, "Inspired Scripture as a Sacramental Vehicle of Divine Presence in the Gospel of John and *Dei Verbum*," *Nova et Vetera*, English edition 13 (2015): 174–75.

9. De Lubac, *Medieval Exegesis*, 1:81–82.

10. Denis Farkasfalvy, O.Cist., "How to Renew the Theology of Biblical Inspiration?," *Nova et Vetera*, English edition 4 (2006): 249.

## The Holy Spirit's Gift of Understanding

When we speak of the Holy Spirit's gift of understanding the Scriptures here, we mean "the work of the Holy Spirit, bringing the mind and spirit of the reader into contact with the divine realities" mediated by the sacred text.[11] To understand the sacred Scripture means first of all to understand the realities mediated by the Scriptures. It is to receive a penetrating insight into these divine realities, to have a genuine faith-experience of them, and to have one's mind and heart touched by them. To explore the Spirit's work in giving people this kind of understanding, we will consider two sources: first, the Gospel according to John's teaching about the teaching activity of the Holy Spirit, the Paraclete; second, Henri de Lubac's exposition of "spiritual understanding," especially in light of Origen.

### The Paraclete in the Gospel according to John

The Fourth Gospel provides important theological teaching concerning the Holy Spirit's action both to give Jesus's disciples a penetrating insight into the realities of the divine economy and to make the reality of Jesus powerfully active in them. Of particular importance are places in the Gospel narrative where the disciples "remember" something about Jesus that occurred during his ministry and the relation of this remembering to the action of the Holy Spirit.[12]

In three places in the Gospel narrative the narrator interrupts his storytelling to comment on the disciples' remembering something about Jesus. Two of the three cases appear in the episode of Jesus's temple action in John 2:13–22. The first instance occurs immediately after Jesus's prophetic action in the temple. He drives out the animals being sold in the temple precincts, empties out the money boxes used for the currency exchange, and overturns tables. He then prophetically declares, "Take these things out of here! Stop making my Father's house a marketplace" (2:16). After reporting Jesus's words, the narrator comments that his disciples associated Jesus's action with the words of Psalm 69:9: "His disciples remembered that it was written, 'Zeal for your house will consume me'" (2:17).[13] The disciples' remembering involves a reciprocal interpretation between Jesus and Scripture. The disciples come

---

11. Francis Martin, introduction to *Sacred Scripture*, xiii.

12. In this section, we bring together and rework argumentation given in William M. Wright IV, "The Theology of Disclosure and Biblical Exegesis," *The Thomist* 70 (2006): 404–9.

13. When John cites Ps. 69:9 in 2:17, he changes the verb tense to give the psalm a more prophetic tone. The LXX of Ps. 69:9 reads, "Zeal for your house *consumed* me" (LXX Ps. 68:1, translation ours), with the verb *katesthiein* in the aorist tense (*katephagen*). The quotation of

to understand something about Jesus's action in the temple in light of Psalm 69: the text speaks of ardent zeal for the temple as devouring the psalmist much as the temple incident (and what it signifies) will contribute to Jesus's own death. Conversely, Jesus's actions shed new light on Psalm 69, allowing it to appear as a prophetic anticipation of Jesus's actions.

The second instance of the disciples' remembering occurs in the very next narrative episode. After his prophetic actions, a group of "Jews," most likely some of the temple authorities, demand that Jesus provide a "sign" to legitimate his provocative actions in the temple (John 2:18). Jesus responds to them with another prophetic challenge: "Destroy this temple, and in three days I will raise it up" (v. 19). The Jewish authorities misunderstand Jesus, thinking that he is threatening the temple proper and promising to literally rebuild the structure. The narrator then clarifies for the Gospel's audience the true meaning of Jesus's statement: "But he was speaking of the temple of his body" (v. 21). Jesus's words thus come to light as a prophecy of his own death and resurrection, the sign that would legitimate his actions in the temple. This insight into Jesus's words, however, came only after Jesus rose from the dead. John continues, "After he was raised from the dead, his disciples remembered that he had said this; and they believed the scripture and the word that Jesus had spoken" (v. 22). The disciples' remembering takes place after Jesus's resurrection, and it facilitates their believing in Jesus's words and the Scripture. It is not a matter of simple recollection, but rather a kind of deeper insight into the meaning of Jesus's words and Scripture in relation to Jesus.

The third instance of the disciples' remembering occurs with Jesus's entry into Jerusalem for his final Passover (John 12:12–19). Upon hearing that Jesus is approaching the city, a group of pilgrims go out to meet Jesus and welcome him as a messianic King.[14] The crowd hails Jesus with the words of Psalm 118:25–26, calling him "the King of Israel" and shouting "Hosanna," a petition for God to save his people (John 12:13). In response to the crowds' accolades, Jesus makes an implied messianic claim of a different sort. He gets on a donkey and rides it to the city, thus enacting the messianic oracle of Zechariah 9:9. John then specifies that Jesus's actions were anticipated in the prophets and proceeds to quote two prophetic texts—Zephaniah 3:16 and Zechariah 9:9—as illumining Jesus's prophetic actions (John 12:14–15).

After quoting these two texts, the narrator states, "His disciples did not understand these things at first; but when Jesus was glorified, then they

this psalm in John 2:17 ("Zeal for your house will consume me"), however, features the same verb, *katesthiein*, but in the future tense (*kataphagetai*).

14. Francis Martin and William M. Wright IV, *The Gospel of John*, Catholic Commentary on Sacred Scripture (Grand Rapids: Baker Academic, 2015), 219–21.

remembered that these things had been written of him and had been done to him" (John 12:16). This statement has several important aspects in common with the other two "remembering" passages. First, as was seemingly the case with Jesus's saying in 2:21, the disciples did not grasp the significance of the events surrounding Jesus's arrival in Jerusalem at the time when they occurred. Second, it is only after Jesus's resurrection ("when Jesus was glorified") that they are said to "remember" (cf. v. 22). Third, that which the disciples remember are events in Jesus's ministry as well as passages in the Old Testament that they recognize as anticipating these events (vv. 17, 22). This "remembering" is not simple recollection, but rather is a deeper insight into the significance of Jesus's words and actions and other things in relation to Jesus, especially the Scripture.

These three "remembering" passages have much theological significance because, when situated within the larger Gospel narrative, they all point to the activity of the Holy Spirit, the Paraclete. In the second Paraclete promise, Jesus tells his disciples, "The Holy Spirit, whom the Father will send in my name, will teach you everything, and *remind* you of all that I have said to you" (John 14:26, emphasis added). Since the Holy Spirit is promised to "remind" the disciples of Jesus's words, it is implied that when the disciples "remember" things about Jesus, they are "reminded" by the Holy Spirit. Moreover, the timing of this "remembering" as located after Jesus's resurrection also points to the Holy Spirit, for the Gospel repeatedly places the coming and action of the Paraclete after Jesus's resurrection. For instance, the narrator explains that Jesus's words about "rivers of living water" (7:38) referred to the Holy Spirit, but believers had not yet received the Spirit "because Jesus was not yet glorified" (v. 39). The Holy Spirit comes to Jesus's believers only after the resurrection. Later, in the Farewell Discourse, Jesus tells his disciples that the Holy Spirit can come to them only after Jesus has returned to the Father: "If I do not go away, the Advocate will not come to you; but if I go, I will send him to you" (16:7). The fulfillment of these anticipations appears in the resurrection narrative in John 20. When the risen Jesus appears to his disciples on Easter Sunday evening, he breathes the Holy Spirit on his disciples, empowering them for their mission to the world (vv. 21–22).

The "reminding" activity of the Paraclete is ingredient to his action to teach Jesus's disciples and give them a deeper understanding of Jesus. To reiterate some matters discussed in chapter 4: the Holy Spirit is the "Spirit of truth" (John 14:17; 15:26; 16:13). The Spirit, who "will guide [them] into all the truth" (16:13), brings the disciples into a deeper understanding of Jesus, who is himself "the truth" (14:6; 17:17). The Spirit does nothing independently of Jesus (and thus the Father): "He will not speak on his own. . . . He will take what is mine and declare it to you. All that the Father has is mine" (16:13–15). The Spirit does not bring a new revelation but rather reveals to the disciples the depths and significance of Jesus.

The Spirit also impresses the truth and reality of Jesus onto the disciples' hearts and minds. This is the principle at work in the statements about the Spirit's work to "prove the world wrong about sin and righteousness and judgment" (John 16:8).[15] In the first Paraclete promise, Jesus specifies that the all of the Spirit's activity, which he sets forth in the Farewell Discourse, takes place within the disciples (14:17). The Spirit works on the disciples' interiority, their hearts, minds, and spirits. Through this inner activity, the Spirit so impresses the truth and reality of Jesus on the disciples' spirits that they are convinced that "the world," which rejects Jesus, is wrong. Put positively, the Spirit provides the conviction and assurance that Jesus and his word are true. In doing so, the Spirit makes the truth of Jesus a living, powerful reality within the disciples.

Seen against this background, the "reminding" activity of the Paraclete is part of his teaching activity within the disciples. The Spirit confers on the disciples a deeper understanding of Jesus, his words and deeds, things in relation to him, and especially how select Old Testament passages relate to Jesus. The Spirit leads them to grasp an inner significance that was not available to the disciples or others at a time prior to Jesus's death and resurrection. Indeed, these deeper meanings become perceptible only through the Spirit's inner activity within the disciples.

To use the categories given in the previous chapter: the Spirit leads the disciples to a deeper grasp of the mystery of Christ and other realities in the divine economy as participating in him. The Holy Spirit imparts this "spiritual understanding" to the disciples, by which they are given to perceive the depths of truths about Jesus and things in relation to Jesus. It is this "spiritual understanding" that enables the disciples to discern the mystery of Christ in the biblical realities (i.e., to discern the "spiritual sense") and experience the truth and convicting power of the reality of Jesus for themselves.

### *Henri de Lubac on Spiritual Understanding and Assimilating the Mystery*

Like almost all terms and categories associated with the doctrine of the fourfold sense, "spiritual understanding" is fraught with challenges and confusion.

---

15. See Martin and Wright, *Gospel of John*, 265–67; Francis Martin, *The Life-Changer: How You Can Experience Freedom, Power and Refreshment in the Holy Spirit* (Ann Arbor, MI: Servant, 1990), 141–46.

We have argued that the senses of Scripture are not, properly speaking, different authorial or textual meanings. Rather, they are different dimensions of the mystery-bearing realities mediated by the biblical text. Just as the disciples in John's Gospel needed the Spirit's activity to discern inner dimensions of Jesus and the Scriptures in relation to him, so also do readers of the Christian Scriptures need the Spirit's assistance to discern and experience the mystery of Christ and the hidden ways in which biblical realities participate in him. Accordingly, we can define "spiritual understanding" as "a Spirit-conferred faith experience of the reality mediated by the Sacred Text, and a perception of how that reality shares in the mystery of the Whole Christ [i.e., the mystical union of Christ and the church]."[16] Spiritual understanding is *spiritual* primarily because it comes from the Holy Spirit's work within Jesus's disciples.[17]

According to de Lubac, Origen's account of both the spiritual sense (i.e., the mystery of Christ and the participation of all biblical realities in this mystery) and its corresponding perception in spiritual understanding involves the dual action of the Holy Spirit. On the one hand, the Holy Spirit works in the production of the biblical books and their assemblage into the canon, giving this diverse collection of books a deeper unity. Moreover, for Origen, the Holy Spirit continues to abide in the books of Scripture.[18] Inspiration thus extends to both the biblical authors (in the past) and the biblical texts (in their present). On the other hand, the same Holy Spirit works in faithful readers to lead them to a deeper understanding of the Scriptures: "The Spirit who inspired it at the time of its writing is also the one who now makes it understood."[19] Origen's remarks in his *Homilies on Ezekiel* are illustrative: "Just as the one who was ordered to speak these things has need of the Holy Spirit, so he who wishes to expound their hidden significance has need of the same Spirit."[20] Similarly, in his *Homilies on Numbers*, Origen speaks of "considering in the Spirit what has been written through the Spirit."[21] This is what Origen, and the later voices in the tradition (including the Second Vatican Council in *Dei Verbum* §12), know as interpreting Scripture "in the [same] spirit in which it was written."[22]

---

16. Francis Martin, "Some Aspects of Biblical Studies since Vatican II: The Contribution and Challenge of *Dei Verbum*," in *Sacred Scripture*, 250.

17. Henri de Lubac, *History and Spirit: The Understanding of Scripture according to Origen*, trans. Anne Englund Nash and Juvenal Merriell (San Francisco: Ignatius, 2007), 443–47.

18. De Lubac, *History and Spirit*, 337–39.

19. De Lubac, *History and Spirit*, 361.

20. Origen, *Homilies on Ezekiel* 2.2, in de Lubac, *History and Spirit*, 361n144.

21. Origen, *Homilies on Numbers* 16.9, in de Lubac, *History and Spirit*, 339n15.

22. See Ignace de la Potterie, SJ, "Interpretation of Holy Scripture in the Spirit in Which It Was Written (*Dei Verbum* 12c)," in *Vatican II: Assessment and Perspectives—Twenty-Five Years*

According to de Lubac, there is a "reciprocal causality" between this spiritual understanding and conversion to Christ, both of which involve the work of the Holy Spirit.[23] To begin with, the Holy Spirit makes the reality of the risen Jesus present in believers—a point that we have seen similarly attested in the New Testament writings of Paul, John, and Peter. De Lubac observes that Origen often speaks of Jesus, the Word of God, coming to people through the Scripture, and the presence of Jesus in believers enables them to understand. For instance, Origen remarks in his *Homilies on Isaiah*, "Let us pray that his advent will take place even now, for if Jesus does not come, we cannot see these things."[24] De Lubac also adduces the following statement of Origen from the same homily: "If you wish even now to hear, let us pray the Lord together that at last now when the Word comes we may be able to attend to the prophetic sayings."[25] The presence and work of Jesus in believers enable them to arrive at a deeper understanding of his mystery and the Scriptures in relation to him.

The Spirit's work of impressing the mystery of Christ onto the hearts of believers (and thus imparting spiritual understanding) goes hand in glove with the believer's measure of faith and conversion to Christ. Spiritual understanding of the christological mystery is given to believers by the Spirit, and it increases to the extent that believers cooperate with the Spirit's action in them through holiness of life. Hence, this mode of understanding Scripture has a prominent spiritual and ascetical dimension to it. As de Lubac writes, "Understanding is not here a matter of cleverness of mind, even a mind illumined by God, but of purity of heart, or uprightness, and of simplicity."[26] Accordingly, such a mode of understanding requires on the part of Scripture's reader such dispositions as humility, perseverance, submitting one's mind to God and his Word, and recognizing the limits of one's own understanding of the sacred text.[27]

Such "spiritual understanding" is not a method, but it does have certain boundaries and principles of operation.[28] De Lubac argues that, despite

---

*After (1962–1987)*, ed. René Latourelle (Mahwah, NJ: Paulist Press, 1988), 220–66. Though the need to interpret Scripture "in the [same] spirit in which it was written" (*DV* §12) been vastly underappreciated (if not outright ignored) in postconciliar Roman Catholic biblical interpretation, it remains as much an integral part of Catholic biblical exegesis as do the historical and literary modes of analysis. See William M. Wright IV, "*Dei Verbum*," in *The Reception of Vatican II*, ed. Matthew L. Lamb and Matthew Levering (Oxford: Oxford University Press, 2017), 89–91.

23. De Lubac, *History and Spirit*, 447; cf. 362–63.
24. Origen, *Homilies on Isaiah* 5.2, in de Lubac, *History and Spirit*, 363n153.
25. Origen, *Homilies on Isaiah* 5.2, in de Lubac, *History and Spirit*, 363n153.
26. De Lubac, *History and Spirit*, 365–66.
27. De Lubac, *History and Spirit*, 366–74.
28. De Lubac, *History and Spirit*, 448–50.

Origen's own exegetical excesses, this mode of spiritual understanding is possible only within the context of the church and its faith.[29] The Holy Spirit dwells in the church as a community and delivers to the church the deeper meaning of Scripture. Accordingly, the church's "rule of faith," "rule of piety," or "analogy of faith" sets the boundaries for interpretive freedom and also serves as a norm for adjudicating interpretations.[30] Such an approach to Scripture has a definite place for learning and intellectual study, but because it deals in matters that textual and empirical analysis cannot access (i.e., the mystery of God), it is ultimately dependent on God's work in people. As de Lubac describes Origen's view, "We will therefore employ 'all the resources of our mind' in the explanation of the texts . . . [and] after having examined the letter to the best of our ability, we will implore 'the grace of the Spirit to penetrate the mystery of it.'"[31]

This mode of understanding involves the personal assimilation of the mystery borne by the realities mediated by the biblical text. It is an internalizing and personalizing of that mystery-bearing *res*, which facilitates and brings about the transformation of one's life in faith, hope, and love. Since the mystery borne by the biblical *res* is inexhaustible, there is no end to such spiritual understanding of this mystery. De Lubac summarizes these essential features very clearly: "The understanding of Scripture is at the same time the vital assimilation of its mystery. It is a 'visit from Jesus.' It does not consist in ideas, but it communicates the very reality of the One whose riches are unfathomable. It can grow indefinitely, because it expands to the measure of the mind's capacity to receive it."[32] Accordingly, in this world, our understanding of the biblical text and realities will always be partial and imperfect, for our faith and spiritual life will always be imperfect. It is only in heaven that our contemplation of these mysteries will reach their fullness: "The full contemplation of the Scriptures is only for the next life, where it will be our occupation."[33]

The ways in which the mystery of Christ unfolds in the lives of believers (and, conversely, the ways in which they participate in the mystery of Christ) also find expression in de Lubac's account of the moral and anagogical senses of Scripture. In his writings on premodern exegesis, de Lubac finds much significance in the ordering of the biblical senses. He notes that there existed two primary sequences of the biblical senses (both of which came from Origen): a threefold sequence (literal-moral-spiritual) and a fourfold

29. De Lubac, *History and Spirit*, 362–65.
30. De Lubac, *History and Spirit*, 348–60, 363, 372–75.
31. De Lubac, *History and Spirit*, 364, citing Origen, *Homilies on Leviticus* 9.1.
32. De Lubac, *History and Spirit*, 382.
33. De Lubac, *History and Spirit*, 382.

sequence (literal-allegorical-moral-anagogical).[34] One of the critical issues in the sequences is what provides the basis for Christian moral understanding: is it unrelated to the mystery of Christ (as the threefold sequence has it), or does it depend on the mystery of Christ (as the fourfold sense has it)?[35] While he acknowledges the pedagogical value of the threefold sense, de Lubac finds the fourfold sense to be more theologically adequate because of the way it understands the moral sense as flowing from the allegorical (or spiritual) sense.[36] By placing the moral sense as following the allegorical, the fourfold sense grounds Christian life and mysticism on the mystery of Christ. Put differently, the moral sense—or mode of contemplation—is the personal assimilation of the mystery of Christ, given in Scripture.

Given that the moral sense (or tropology) flows from the mystery of Christ, the moral sense is not simply a matter of deriving moral teachings or worthy examples of conduct from Scripture.[37] These are perfectly legitimate exegetical endeavors, but they pertain more properly to the literal sense: the words and the realities that they mediate. Instead, de Lubac argues, the moral sense (or mode of contemplation) concerns the personal appropriation of the mystery of Christ, given through the biblical realities: "This Mystery [of Christ], which was prefigured in the Old Testament, is realized again, is being actualized, is being completed within the Christian soul. *It is truly being fulfilled within us*."[38] The moral sense "is the doctrine of the interiorization of the biblical datum: its history and its mystery."[39]

The moral sense is the mystery of Christ as it takes root in the reader and grows within. De Lubac puts much emphasis on the personal and immediate aspects of this manner of contemplating the biblical realities: "It is by the tropological sense . . . that Scripture is fully *for us* the Word of God, this Word which is addressed to each person, *hic et nunc* ["here and now"] as well as to the whole Church, and telling each 'that which is of interest to his life.'"[40] It is a present, personal encounter with the mystery of Christ, which the reader experiences by contemplating the realities mediated by the text with appropriate dispositions.

34. De Lubac (*Medieval Exegesis*, 1:82–89) acknowledges there existed other sequences and numberings of the biblical senses. For both sequences as having their roots in Origen, see de Lubac, *Medieval Exegesis*, 1:142–50.

35. De Lubac, *Medieval Exegesis*, 1:114–15.

36. De Lubac, *Medieval Exegesis*, 1:146–47.

37. De Lubac, *Medieval Exegesis*, 2:130–31.

38. De Lubac, *Medieval Exegesis*, 2:134 (emphasis original).

39. De Lubac, *Medieval Exegesis*, 2:139.

40. De Lubac, *Medieval Exegesis*, 2:140 (emphasis original), quoting Gregory the Great, *Epistle* 5.46.

A hallmark example of this mode of understanding is Bernard of Clair-vaux.[41] Bernard's exegetical meditations on Scripture display a faith experience of the mystery-bearing realities mediated by the text. For instance, Bernard speaks of an "intermediate coming" of God's Word, situated between Christ's incarnation and parousia.[42] This intermediate coming occurs when the Word of God comes to indwell a person's soul in the present moment to provide spiritual comfort and sustenance. Bernard associates this present encounter with the Word of God with Jesus's promise in John 14:23: "Anyone who loves me will keep my words, and my Father will love him, and we shall come to him."[43] To keep God's words, Bernard explains, is to allow them to penetrate one's mind and heart and shape one's conduct and daily life. De Lubac calls this the personal "assimilation of [Scripture's] mystery."[44]

Bernard's exegesis thus shows how "the mystery interiorizes itself within the heart, where it becomes experience—though always passing over in itself 'the limits of experience' as well as those of reason."[45] The mystery is the "sweetness" and "the honey" that the reader of Scripture savors in the kind of contemplation that is the moral sense. It is this encounter with the mystery of Christ that gives rise to Christian mysticism.[46]

The mystery of Christ, while genuinely experienced in the present by believers, is not yet grasped or revealed in all its fullness. The full enjoyment of the mystery of Christ comes only in the heavenly vision of God in the eschatological, new Jerusalem (cf. Rev. 22:1–5). Similarly, the transformation of Christians, started by Christ in the present time, will reach its completion in heavenly life. The present mode of participating in the mystery of Christ, real but limited, is situated with respect to the heavenly, eschatological mode of sharing in his mystery. In this way, the moral sense segues into the anagogical sense.

De Lubac identifies two, interrelated aspects of anagogy: it is both a looking forward to the parousia and a looking "upward" to heavenly destiny.[47]

41. See de Lubac, *Medieval Exegesis*, 2:162–77.

42. Bernard of Clairvaux, *Advent Sermon 5.2*, in Bernard of Clairvaux, *Sermons for Advent and the Christmas Season*, trans. Irene Edmonds, Wendy Mary Beckett, and Conrad Greenia, OSCO, ed. John Leinenweber, Cistercian Fathers Series 51 (Kalamazoo, MI: Cistercian Publications, 2007), 34. This teaching of Bernard is also cited in Joseph Ratzinger (Pope Benedict XVI), *Jesus of Nazareth: Holy Week from the Entrance into Jerusalem to the Resurrection*, trans. Philip J. Whitmore (San Francisco: Ignatius, 2011), 290–91.

43. Bernard of Clairvaux, *Advent Sermon 5.2* (Leinenweber, 34, emphasis removed from biblical quotation).

44. See de Lubac, *History and Spirit*, 382.

45. De Lubac, *Medieval Exegesis*, 2:174.

46. See Henri de Lubac, "Mysticism and Mystery," in *Theological Fragments*, trans. Rebecca Howell Balinski (San Francisco: Ignatius, 1989), 57–69.

47. De Lubac, *Medieval Exegesis*, 2:179–80.

In both respects, it is concerned with eternal destiny, the telos of the divine economy. Accordingly, anagogy is correlated with the theological virtue of hope: "After allegory which built up faith and tropology which built up charity, there is anagogy which builds up hope."[48] The anagogical mode of contemplating the mystery-bearing realities is a kind of yearning, a looking forward to the full enjoyment of the mystery in heaven. In the historic time of the church, believers "possess the [heavenly] realities . . . not according to their proper mode of existence, but rather in another mode, in signs and symbols, until we are with Christ in heaven."[49] The same heavenly realities that are enjoyed in a real but veiled manner in the present time of the church will be enjoyed immediately in heavenly destiny in their fullness: "That which we realize now in Christ through deliberated will is the very same thing which, freed of every obstacle and all obscurity, will become the essence of eternal life."[50]

Witnesses from both Scripture and the Christian tradition thus speak of the action of the Holy Spirit to lead people into a deeper understanding of the mystery of Christ and to apply its transforming power in their lives. As John's Gospel speaks of the Paraclete, the Holy Spirit gives insight and illumination into the mystery of Christ and the biblical realities that participate in it. The Holy Spirit impresses the reality of Jesus (and by extension the divine mystery borne by the biblical realities) onto believers' hearts, making it a "living and active" force in them. Such experiential understanding does not come primarily by way of human effort and learning. Rather, it is the work of the Holy Spirit in people who contemplate the biblical realities in holiness and assimilate the mystery into their lives. This process of contemplation, conversion, and transformation progresses throughout the present life and reaches its fullness in heavenly glory.

The Holy Spirit imparts the gift of understanding the divine realities mediated by the Scriptures and applies their life-giving power to people's lives. At the same time, readers must also have certain spiritual and moral dispositions. These dispositions make the readers increasingly docile and receptive to the Word of God, impressed by the Holy Spirit on them. For further insight into the human reception and assimilation of the Word of God, we turn to the Lukan version of the parable of the sower. As we will see, this account provides essential teaching on the dynamics whereby the Word of God bears fruit in those who hear it.

48. De Lubac, *Medieval Exegesis*, 2:181.
49. Francis Martin, "Election, Covenant, and Law," 867.
50. De Lubac, *Medieval Exegesis*, 2:202.

## The Parable of the Sower and Receiving the Word

The parable of the sower appears in all three Synoptic Gospels (Matt. 13:1–9; Mark 4:1–9; Luke 8:4–8). Jesus invites his audience to imagine a man going out to plant seeds by scattering them. As he sows the seeds, they fall on various kinds of terrain, and depending on the kind of terrain, different things happen to the seed. Each evangelist locates this parable at a different place in his Gospel narrative and recounts it with different nuances of language. Through such compositional techniques, the inspired evangelists bring to light different aspects of Jesus's teaching in this parable.

Luke's account of the parable plays an important role in the larger narrative, which spans both the Gospel according to Luke and its sequel, the Acts of the Apostles. We examined many aspects of the teaching in Luke-Acts on the proclamation of the Word and power of the Holy Spirit in chapters 1 and 3. The parable of the sower squares with those teachings and gives us additional perspective on the Word of God and its working in response to how people receive it.

The core elements of the parable of the sower that are shared among the synoptic accounts are familiar. However, we wish to call closer attention to Luke's account of the parable with its own set of distinctive features. For the sake of reference, the elements of the parable as well as their interpretation in Luke's account are as follows:

| Verses | Terrain | What Happens | Interpretation |
|--------|---------|--------------|----------------|
| 8:5, 12 | "on the path" | trampled and eaten by birds | When they hear, Satan comes and takes away sown Word, so they might not believe and be saved. |
| 8:6, 13 | "on the rock" | "grew up" and "withered for lack of moisture" | They receive the Word with joy but lack roots. They believe for a while but fall away in times of trial. |
| 8:7, 14 | "among thorns" | grew with thorns, which "choked it" | They hear but are choked by cares, riches, pleasures. Their fruit doesn't mature. |
| 8:8, 15 | "into good soil" | grew up and "produced a hundredfold" | "They hear the word, hold it fast . . . , and bear fruit with . . . endurance." |

A close comparison of Luke's account with those of Matthew and Mark brings to light certain details unique to Luke and reveals certain theological emphases. To begin with, all three Synoptics identify the seed in the parable with the Word (Matt. 13:19; Mark 4:14). But Luke does so very directly, and thus he foregrounds this identification. Only in Luke does Jesus explicitly mention the seed at the beginning of the parable as the object of the sower's action: "A sower went out to sow *his seed*" (8:5, emphasis added; cf. Matt. 13:3; Mark 4:3).[51] This direct naming of the seed at the start of the parable is matched by direct attention to the seed at the start of the parable's interpretation. Only in Luke does Jesus begin the interpretation of the parable by stating directly, "The seed is the word of God" (8:11). In this way, Luke's account focuses the audience's attention more sharply onto the seed as the Word of God and what happens with it.

The parable's constant attention to "hearing" complements this emphasis on the seed as the Word of God. All four forms of terrain (the path, the rock, the thorns, and the good soil) have seed fall to them, and in the interpretation, all four are said to "hear" the Word. The different forms of terrain in the parable correspond to different forms of response to the Word that has been sown in (or heard by) people. The point of distinction is *not whether* the terrain/people hear the Word (they all do) but *how* people respond to that Word in different circumstances.

For instance, sometimes (the path) when people hear the Word, it does not take root in them. One might say that in such circumstances, people may *hear* the Word but do not *listen to* it or take it in with faith—and Jesus speaks of the role of Satan in keeping people from such receptive faith and the eternal, eschatological salvation to which it leads. At other times (the rock), people may hear the Word and "receive it with joy" (Luke 8:13). However, despite this initial, joyous reception, theirs is a shallow, superficial faith, and in "a time of testing" (perhaps a singular moment of strong temptation, difficulty, or tragedy), it fails them, and they "fall away" (v. 13). Another kind of response to the Word is drawn out over time. The seed "among the thorns" speaks to a response when people "hear" the Word and "go on their way." As people go about their lives, "they are choked by the cares and riches and pleasures of life" (v. 14). The Word does take some root in them, and they start to produce some fruit. But "their fruit does not mature" (v. 14). Various worries and allurements can strongly influence people, and this keeps them from bearing mature fruit, born from the Word in them.

Luke describes the fourth mode of response, the seed sown in the good soil, in this way: "These are the ones who, when they hear the word, hold it fast in an honest and good heart, and bear fruit with patient endurance" (Luke 8:15).[52] The two actions associated with the good soil—"hold it fast

---

51. By contrast, Mark 4:3 and Matt. 13:3 both read, "A sower went out to sow."

52. For an illuminating study of the pedagogical and moral context of the phrase "honest and good heart," see John B. Weaver, "The Noble and Good Heart: [*Kalokagathia*] in Luke's Parable of the Sower," in *Scripture and Traditions: Essays on Early Judaism and Christianity*

in an honest and good heart" and "bear fruit with patient endurance"—are unique to Luke's account. The first action suggests an embracing of and holding on to the Word, allowing it to enter deeply into one's interiority ("the heart") and become the object of one's rumination and ongoing reflection. The penetration of the Word of God into the soil of a receptive heart in turn causes an immense production of fruit: "a hundredfold" (v. 8). Also unique to Luke's account is the qualifying phrase "with patient endurance" (v. 15). Patient endurance is a means by which the seed in the good soil produces fruit. The hundredfold fruit is born from the Word in a heart with receptive faith and over an extended time, through difficulties and trial.

The next two units that follow Luke's account of the parable of the sower shed further light on its teachings. First, immediately after the parable, Luke recounts some sayings of Jesus that use the imagery of "lighting a lamp"—and not hiding it—in order to address the way in which people manifest what is within them, because "nothing is hidden that will not be disclosed" (Luke 8:16–17). Jesus then adds a further instruction, "pay attention to how you listen" (v. 18). The mention of "listening" recalls the numerous uses of this same verb in the interpretation of the parable to designate the various modes of receiving the Word of God. Another verbal link to the parable appears in Jesus's subsequent elaboration: "To those who have, more will be given; and from those who do not have, even what they seem to have will be taken away" (v. 18). The verb in 8:18 for "taken away" (Greek: *airein*) also appears in the parable to designate the action of Satan, who "takes away" the Word sown in people (v. 12).

Through these verbal connections, as well as the placement of these sayings immediately after the parable, Luke invites his audience to see the parable with its explanation (8:4–15) and the sayings unit that follows (vv. 16–18) in relation. The that-which-is-hidden or lighted lamp in the sayings unit corresponds to the Word of God, which in sown into people's hearts. The indwelling Word (or lack thereof) will become manifest for others to see. Implicitly, this manifestation comes about through the fruit that it does (or does not) produce in a person. Hence, Jesus encourages people to be receptive to the Word ("pay attention to how you listen"), for, depending on how they listen to and receive the Word, that Word will or will not bear great fruit in them ("more will be given"), and others "may see the light" (vv. 16, 18). But to those who fail to receive the Word, "even what they seem to have will be taken away" (v. 18).

Second, after these sayings, Luke places the episode of Jesus's mother and brothers attempting to reach him in spite of a large crowd (Luke 8:19–21).

---

*in Honor of Carl R. Holladay*, ed. Patrick Gray and Gail R. O'Day, Supplements to Novum Testamentum 129 (Leiden: Brill, 2008), 151–71.

Upon hearing of their presence, Jesus responds, "My mother and my brothers are those who hear the word of God and do it" (v. 21). As in the sayings unit, Luke's word choice connects this episode back to the parable of the sower. While Matthew and Mark have Jesus speaking of "whoever does the will of God" (Mark 3:35) or "whoever does the will of my Father in heaven" (Matt. 12:50), Luke's account mentions "the word of God." Moreover, Luke has two actions—"hear" and "do"—performed with respect to the Word of God. Jesus's true kin are like the good soil in the parable: they "hear the word" (8:15, 21) and then "do" it. The connections between the scene with Jesus's kin and the parable of the sower suggest that the "fruit" produced by the seed in the good soil entails putting God's Word into practice. It involves allowing the Word to sink deeply into the heart and so transform one's life and conduct, making one kin to Jesus.[53] Genuine listening to the Word involves receptivity and faithful obedience to it.

The parable of the sower provides us with two essential spiritual teachings regarding the Word of God and its work in people. First, the parable of the sower presents the Word of God as an acting subject. It can be received into people through their hearing. Once inside people's hearts, the Word can produce effects in them. The Word transforms people from within and issues forth in transformed conduct over time. It enables them to bear fruit "a hundredfold" (Luke 8:8) and "with patient endurance" (v. 15). Through the fruits of transformed lives, the presence and power of the indwelling Word will be made manifest to others (vv. 16–17).

Second, the Word exercises its power to the extent that people receive the Word and yield to it. As we have discussed, the parable and its interpretation present the different kinds of terrain as different modes of response to the Word of God. The Gospel also speaks to the measure of growth that each terrain/mode of response produces: no growth (the path); a little growth (the rock and the thorns); much growth (the good soil). The measure of produce is directly proportional to the receptivity of people to the Word. In other words, the Word bears fruit in people to the extent that people allow the Word to put down roots in their hearts and grow in them. To those who receive the Word of God, "hold it fast in an honest and good heart" (Luke 8:15), and "obey it" (11:28), even "more will be given" (8:18), for through their yielding to the Word, the Word will continue to work its transformative power in them. The Word of God will be powerful in a person's living,

---

53. The same point appears later in the Gospel when a woman praises Jesus's family ties: "Blessed is the womb that bore you and the breasts that nursed you" (11:27). As he does in Luke 8:19–21, Jesus elevates spiritual kinship over natural kinship: "Blessed rather are those who hear the word of God and obey it" (11:28).

a preacher's preaching, and a teacher's teaching to the extent that the Word has first become a powerful reality in that person's own life. The Word exercises its power in people to the extent that people receive that Word and consent to its working in them.[54]

Seen from this perspective, the ones who truly understand the Scriptures are the saints—men and women whose lives have been profoundly touched and transformed by Christ in the Holy Spirit. Accordingly, we will conclude our study of how Scripture puts people in a living and life-giving contact with divine reality by reflecting on four saints whose lives were powerfully changed by an encounter with God, mediated through Scripture. Having been so changed by God through Scripture, these holy men and women changed the church and the world. In reflecting on their lives, we can also identify certain virtues and spiritual dispositions that their lives suggest as being integral to encountering divine reality and power through Scripture.

## Saints and the Scriptures

### Saint Antony of Egypt

We begin with Saint Antony of Egypt (d. 356). In his spiritual classic, *The Life of Antony*, Saint Athanasius recounts how several powerful encounters with God through Scripture changed Antony and led him to the monastic life. When he was about twenty years old and not long after the death of his parents, Antony was walking to church, contemplating how the apostles gave up everything to follow Christ during his ministry and how the first Christians handed over their possessions to the apostles for the sake of those in need (Acts 4:32–37). Athanasius writes that Antony "went into the church pondering these things [from Acts], and just then it happened that the Gospel was being read, and he heard the Lord saying to the rich man, *If you would be perfect, go, sell what you possess and give to the poor, and you will have treasure in heaven.* It was as if by God's design he held the saints [from Acts] in his recollection, and as if the passage were read on his account."[55] Hearing these words of Jesus in the gospel, proclaimed in the liturgy, as spoken directly to himself, Antony obeyed and followed the examples of the apostles and early

---

54. There is coherence here with the saying of Bernard of Clairvaux: "to consent is to be saved [*consentire enim salvri est*]." Bernard of Clairvaux, *De Gratia et Libero Arbitrio* [*On Grace and Free Will*], PL 182:1002.

55. Athanasius, "The Life of Antony," 2, in Athanasius, *"The Life of Antony" and the "Letter to Marcellinus,"* trans. Robert C. Gregg, Classics of Western Spirituality (Mahwah, NJ: Paulist Press, 1980), 31 (emphasis original).

disciples in Acts: "Immediately Antony went out from the Lord's house and gave to the townspeople the possessions he had from his forebears."[56]

It was another, similar experience of hearing the Lord speaking to him through the Scripture that led Antony to the monastic life. Athanasius continues, "But when, entering the Lord's house once more, he heard in the Gospel the Lord saying, *Do not be anxious about tomorrow*, he could not remain any longer."[57] Donating the last of his possessions to the poor and making arrangements for the care of his younger sister, Antony left worldly life and embraced monastic asceticism. Antony became not only a famous exemplar for subsequent Christian spirituality but also the father of Christian monasticism, which in turn changed the world through its intellectual, cultural, and spiritual contributions—not to mention the monastic preservation of Greco-Roman literary culture from its destruction in the early Middle Ages.[58]

Among other things, the example of Antony suggests *ongoing participation in the life of the church* as an important disposition for encountering God in Scripture. The account of Antony's encounter with God through Scripture features him reflecting on biblical stories while he was walking to liturgy. As Guy Mansini observes, that Antony was ruminating on these texts implies his prior Christian formation and knowledge of the Scriptures.[59] Antony had learned the Scriptures and had assimilated their contents to the point where he could ruminate on them in his daily life. Moreover, the liturgy played an important role in Antony's encounter with God through Scripture. Antony was walking to liturgy while reflecting on the example of the apostles in Acts. Athanasius presents Antony as regularly participating in the church's liturgy, and it is there that Antony encountered God through the liturgical proclamation of the Scripture. Antony had heard the Scriptures proclaimed in the liturgy, and they had become part of the fabric of his life.

Not only do spiritual life and grace flow from the risen Christ to members of his ecclesial body, but also ongoing participation in the church's faith and practices forms a kind of character. This ecclesial character disposes one to encounter God in Scripture, and such an encounter with God in Scripture more deeply promotes this character. Hence, Antony moves more deeply into

---

56. Athanasius, "Life of Antony," 2 (Gregg, 31).

57. Athanasius, "Life of Antony," 3 (Gregg, 31).

58. An accessible account of the role of monasticism in this regard is Thomas Cahill, *How the Irish Saved Civilization: The Untold Story of Ireland's Heroic Role from the Fall of Rome to the Rise of Medieval Europe* (New York: Anchor, 1995).

59. Guy Mansini, OSB, "Prayer, the Bible, and Hearing God," *Nova et Vetera*, English edition 6 (2008): 291–92.

his Christian life through his giving to the poor, caring for his family, and embracing the monastic life.

### Saint Augustine

Another example from Christian antiquity is Saint Augustine (d. 430)—perhaps the best-known case of an individual whose life was powerfully transformed by God through Scripture. In book 8 of his *Confessions*, Augustine, speaking to the Lord (and indirectly to his audience), says, "I will now tell the story . . . of the way in which you delivered me from the chain of sexual desire, by which I was tightly bound, and from the slavery of worldly affairs."[60] At this time in his life, Augustine was thirty-one years old and living at a house near Milan with a group of his friends. One day they received a visit from a court official, Ponticianus, who had become a baptized Christian. Instrumental in the conversion of Ponticianus and his friends was Athanasius's *The Life of Antony*, which Ponticianus then recounted to Augustine and his friend Alypius. Upon hearing the story of Antony from Ponticianus, Augustine starting tearing himself up internally over his own weaknesses and inability to give up his sins. Augustine tells his readers that by this point in his life, it was no longer intellectual obstacles that kept him from seeking baptism but moral obstacles. His will was too damaged by sin, and he was too attached to his vices; he could not bring himself to give up his sins and misdirected desires (especially worldly ambition) and fully embrace the Christian life.[61]

Full of inner turmoil, Augustine went out to the residence's garden. He writes, "I heard the voice from the nearby house, chanting as if it might be a boy or girl . . . saying and repeating over and over again, 'Pick up and read, pick up and read.'"[62] Augustine then remembered the life of Antony, as told by Ponticianus, who heard the words of Scripture as spoken to himself and was subsequently changed. Augustine then went back into the house and followed Antony's example: "I hurried back to the place where . . . I had put down the book of the apostle when I got up. I seized it, opened it and in silence read the first passage on which my eyes lit: 'Not in riots and drunken parties, not in eroticism and indecencies, not in strife and rivalry, but put on the Lord Jesus Christ and make no provision for the flesh in its lusts' (Rom. 13:13–14)."[63] Reading these words from Paul's Letter to the Romans changed Augustine's

60. Augustine, *Confessions* 8.6.13, in Saint Augustine, *Confessions*, trans. Henry Chadwick (New York: Oxford University Press, 1991), 141.
61. Augustine, *Confessions* 8.8.19–8.10.22 (Chadwick, 146–48).
62. Augustine, *Confessions* 8.12.29 (Chadwick, 152).
63. Augustine, *Confessions* 8.12.29 (Chadwick, 153).

life: "I neither wished nor needed to read further. At once, with the last words of this sentence, it was as if a light of relief from all anxiety flooded into my heart. All the shadows of doubt were dispelled."[64] Having realized his own inability to bring himself to conversion as well as the need to rely on God, Augustine experienced the transforming and liberating power of God's grace by reading Scripture.[65] He speaks of this event as God's work within him to change his life: "The effect of your converting me to yourself was that I did not now seek a wife [i.e., Augustine received the gift of continence] and had no ambition for success in this world."[66]

Augustine, along with his son Adeodatus and friend Alypius, was baptized the following year by Saint Ambrose in Milan.[67] Upon returning to his native Africa, Augustine eventually became bishop of Hippo Regius and subsequently the most important ecclesiastical figure of the day. Not only was Augustine a hugely important (and unequaled) figure in his own day, but there are few areas of subsequent Western civilization that have not been impacted in some measure by his thinking (e.g., philosophy, theology, psychology, semiotics, politics, law).

Among the moral and spiritual dispositions that Augustine's example commends, two that stand out are his *repentance* and *humility*. By this point in the *Confessions*, Augustine realized that he had to change his life if he was to continue in his pursuit of wisdom. Moreover, he had become a catechumen but had not yet taken the step to be baptized. Augustine knew that his remaining obstacles to becoming a baptized Catholic were moral, not intellectual. He also realized that he could not liberate himself from his sins. Having acknowledged his guilt and his powerlessness to fix his own brokenness, Augustine had been brought by God to a state where he was able to hear God's Word and yield to it. Augustine's spirit of repentance and humility, the recognition of his own sins and weaknesses and his consequent need for God, disposed him to hear God's Word and experience his transforming, healing power.

### Saint Francis of Assisi

Living several centuries after Augustine, Saint Francis of Assisi (d. 1226) is another example of a Christian whose life was powerfully affected by an encounter with the Lord through Scripture. This particular example from

---

64. Augustine, *Confessions* 8.12.29 (Chadwick, 153).
65. Augustine's recognition of his need to rely on God and that only God can change him comes to him from "Lady Continence" (*Confessions*, 8.9.27).
66. Augustine, *Confessions* 8.12.30 (Chadwick, 153–54).
67. Augustine, *Confessions* 9.6.14.

Francis's life pertains not to his conversion to a life of holiness—as with Augustine—but rather to the particular direction of the religious community that had started to form around him.

In his *Life of St. Francis*, Saint Bonaventure reports that soon after Francis's reputation for holiness of life had become publicly known, several men were drawn to follow him and his way of life.[68] The first of these was Bernard, who came to Francis and asked how he might do so. For direction in this matter, Francis and Bernard sought direction from Scripture. They went into a nearby church, and after some prayers together, Francis then prayed that God might corroborate Bernard's intention to follow him with words from Scripture.[69] Francis opened up to the Gospels three times in honor of the Trinity, and the three texts to which Francis opened were these: "The book opened the first time to the text: *If you will be perfect, go, sell* all *that you have*, and *give to the poor* (Matt. 19:21). The second time to the text: *Take nothing on your journey* (Luke 9:3). And the third time to: *If anyone wishes to come after me, let him deny himself and take up his cross and follow me* (Matt. 16:24)."[70] Francis took these sayings of Jesus—all of which speak to poverty and self-denial as ingredient to the life of Christian discipleship—as divine confirmation of Bernard's request. On this basis, Francis then declared, "'This is our life and our rule . . . and the life and the rule of all who wish to join our company. Go, then, *if you wish to be perfect* (Matt 19:21) and carry out what you have heard.'"[71] Thus was born the distinctively joyous embrace of evangelical ("Lady") poverty and self-denial from worldly attachments as central components of the Franciscan way of life. Through this embrace of evangelical poverty, the Holy Spirit breathed (and continues to breathe) life into the Franciscan family of religious, which has been alive for over eight hundred years since its founding, as well as into others—both religious and lay—who have been inspired by the little poor man of Assisi.

Standing out in the example of Francis are his *piety, personal application*, and *obedience*. Despite the specific *way* in which Francis reads Scripture (i.e., opening up to three random pages in the Bible), there is certain virtue that attends what Francis does with Scripture. For instance, Francis surrounds his reading of Scripture with *piety*. He and Bernard pray before reading Scripture, and they open up Scripture three times in honor of the Trinity. Second, the

68. Bonaventure, *The Life of St. Francis* 3, in *Bonaventure: "The Soul's Journey into God," "The Tree of Life," "The Life of St. Francis,"* ed. Ewert Cousins, Classics of Western Spirituality (Mahwah, NJ: Paulist Press, 1978), 200.
69. Bonaventure, *Life of St. Francis* 3 (Cousins, 201–2).
70. Bonaventure, *Life of St. Francis* 3 (Cousins, 201).
71. Bonaventure, *Life of St. Francis* 3 (Cousins, 201).

example of Francis speaks to *personal application*. Like Antony and Augustine before him, Francis receives these words of Scripture as giving him the Word of God. Like the writer of Hebrews in his use of Psalm 95 in Hebrews 3–4, Francis and others hear the words of Scripture as God speaking to them personally then and there. Francis then demonstrates *obedience* to the Word of God. Receiving the Scripture as the Word of God, Francis takes it as being true and as providing reliable direction for his life. With this understanding, Francis not only is willing to obey God's Word but actually carries it out—he puts it into practice. The Word that Francis encounters in Scripture is not just something to be studied or contemplated; ultimately, it is to be put into practice. This can happen only if the Word is received with openness and a spirit of obedience.

### Saint Thérèse of Lisieux

One final example of a saintly life profoundly affected by an encounter with God through Scripture is late-nineteenth-century French nun Thérèse of Lisieux (d. 1897). Like the preceding example of Saint Francis of Assisi, Thérèse found through her prayerful reading of Scripture powerful direction for living out her religious vocation.

By all accounts, Thérèse, who died when she was only twenty-four years old, lived a life of devotion to God from a very young age. When she was fifteen years old, she joined the Carmelite monastery at Lisieux, and in 1890, she took her final vows as a nun. In her "Manuscript B," part of her spiritual autobiography written at the request of her superiors, Thérèse speaks of a time after her vows when she experienced significant turmoil regarding her vocation. Guy Gaucher summarizes her state in this way: Thérèse "was no longer satisfied with her vocation to be a *Carmelite, a spouse, a mother*. She felt immense seemingly contradictory desires welling up within her. She aspired to other, essentially masculine vocations: she would like to be *a warrior, a priest, a deacon, an apostle, a doctor of the Church, a martyr*."[72]

Amid this inner confusion, Thérèse was one day reading 1 Corinthians 12, Paul's teachings about the different members of the one body of Christ. She came to recognize intellectually the positive reality of differences between roles in the ecclesial body and that not every member of the church can have every role—but this recognition did not quell the turmoil within her.[73] Her

---

72. Guy Gaucher, *The Story of a Life: St. Thérèse of Lisieux*, trans. Sister Anne Marie Brennan, OCD (San Francisco: Harper & Row, 1987), 169 (emphasis original).

73. Thérèse writes, "The answer was clear, but it did not fulfill my desires and gave me no peace." Thérèse of Lisieux, *Story of a Soul: The Autobiography of St. Thérèse of Lisieux*, trans. John Clarke, OCD (Washington, DC: ICS, 1976), 194.

spiritual situation changed, however, when she came to Paul's discussion in
1 Corinthians 13 of love as "the more excellent way" (1 Cor. 12:31).

Upon reading this text, something powerful happened in Thérèse's soul:

> I finally had rest. Considering the mystical body of the Church, I had not
> recognized myself in any of the members described by St. Paul, or rather I
> desired to see myself in them *all*. *Charity* gave me the key to my *vocation*. I
> understood that if the Church had a body composed of different members . . .
> [and] *I understood it was Love alone* that made the Church's members act, that
> if *Love* ever became extinct, apostles would not preach the Gospel and martyrs
> would not shed their blood. . . . O Jesus, my Love. . . . My *vocation*, at last I
> have found it. . . . MY VOCATION IS LOVE!
>
> Yes, I have found my place in the Church . . . in the heart of the Church,
> my Mother, I shall be *Love*. Thus I shall be everything, and thus my dream
> will be realized.[74]

As God through Scripture directed Francis of Assisi to embrace evangelical
poverty, so too did he direct Thérèse to embrace love as the fulfillment of
every vocation in the Christian life. By reading Paul's words, Thérèse came to
realize that Christlike love is the heart of the Christian life and that all forms
of the Christian life are variations on the more basic reality of love. By living
the life of Christlike love, Thérèse, in a sense, lived all forms of Christian life,
since love underlies them all.

Thérèse's distinctive insight into this fundamental role of love in the Christian
life is expressed in her little way of spiritual childhood. Recognizing her own
weaknesses and imperfections, she abandoned herself totally to the love and
mercy of God the Father, full of confidence that he would make up for all her
weaknesses and raise her up to the heights of holiness. She speaks of herself as
being like a little girl, playing before her heavenly Father's throne, and "strewing
flowers." These flowers are little (and often unnoticed) acts of love that Christians have many opportunities to perform for others every day. Thérèse writes
the following: "I have no other means of proving my love for you other than
that of strewing flowers, that is, not allowing one little sacrifice to escape, not
one look, one word, profiting by all the smallest things and doing them through
love."[75] According to Thérèse, it is in these small, and often unnoticed parts of
daily life that the real action of Christian living and loving regularly takes place.

The example of Thérèse commends *persevering faith and love* as important
dispositions for encountering God through Scripture. Thérèse was already a

---

74. Thérèse of Lisieux, *Story of a Soul*, 194 (emphasis original).
75. Thérèse of Lisieux, *Story of a Soul*, 196.

professed Carmelite nun, but she had hit a "rough patch" in her life. Despite her angst and feelings of spiritual desolation, she persevered and made her retreat after Easter. Thérèse demonstrated perseverance even in the small-scale example of her meditating on Scripture. While reading over Paul's account of the body of Christ in 1 Corinthians 12, she found no relief from her immediate troubles. But Thérèse continued, and she encountered God and experienced his consolation when reading 1 Corinthians 13. Meditating on this chapter, Thérèse's heart was enflamed by love. Not only did her love for God impel her onward in her perseverance, but also her love for God and for others was further enflamed by what she read. Love for God led her to persevere in her spiritual life, her obligations as a religious sister, and her reading of Scripture, and her encounter with God through Scripture led her to love God and love others more.

The lives of these well-known Christian saints from all periods in Christian history—Antony of Egypt, Augustine, Francis of Assisi, Thérèse of Lisieux—were profoundly impacted by powerful encounters with God through the reading of Scripture. Their lives also give evidence of certain virtues and spiritual dispositions, which accompany a living and life-giving encounter with God in Scripture: active participation in the life of the church, repentance, humility, piety, personal application, obedience, and persevering faith and love.

## Conclusion

Sacred Scripture can put people in living and life-giving contact with the divine realities that it mediates. By putting people in cognitive contact with the realities that it mediates, the biblical text puts people into contact with the divine mystery, which those realities bear. Although much of what the Bible speaks of is historically past, the divine mystery that the biblical realities bear is eternal and can be encountered in the present moment. The Holy Spirit acts upon the discourse of the prophets and apostles, making it apt for mediating the divine mystery and making it present to people. Witnesses from both Scripture and the tradition also recognize the action of the Holy Spirit within people to give them the gift of understanding. This is the gift of a penetrating insight into these divine realities and faith experience of their truth and power.

For this encounter with the divine realities mediated by the sacred text to become living and life giving, the Scripture's audience should have certain spiritual and moral dispositions. As suggested by the parable of the sower, proper dispositions make one receptive to the Word of God and enable it to bear fruit in one's life. The Word bears fruit in people to the extent that people receive and consent to the Word's work in them. The lives of the saints provide further insight into those dispositions that open one up to the power of God's Word. These include active participation in the life of the church (Antony); repentance and humility (Augustine); piety, personal application, and obedience (Francis et al.); and persevering faith and love (Thérèse). These saints provide lived evidence to what we have been reflecting on exegetically and theologically: Scripture puts people in a living and life-giving contact with divine reality.

# Conclusion to Part 2

The focus of this project has been the belief that sacred Scripture can put its audience into living and life-giving contact with the divine realities it mediates. We started in part 1 with a survey of relevant material from both Testaments of the Christian Bible. This survey of biblical witnesses brought to light various associations that the Word of God has with causal power and modes of presence. Through his Word, God exercises his power and brings about various effects, such as in creating and governing the world and in the course of salvation history. God also exercises this power when his Word is proclaimed in inspired human discourse, spoken or written. The Word of God also has associations with various forms of presence. God reveals himself to people through his Word, and we can say that God becomes present to people in the mode of being known (to some extent) through his Word. Witnesses from both Testaments also identify the Word of God as a reality in itself. The Old Testament presents God's Word and Wisdom as a personified agent figure. In the New Testament, the Word of God is intrinsic to God's own life and becomes human in Jesus.

Certain cases in the New Testament bring together both aspects of God's Word—power and presence. The writings of Paul, Peter, and John present the apostolic testimony, spoken or written, as mediating the reality and power of the risen Jesus himself. It is not that Paul, Peter, and John are only communicating information about Jesus. Rather, these authors present their inspired discourse as a vehicle by which the risen Jesus becomes actively present in those who faithfully take in their discourse. Taken together, these biblical witnesses thus provide substance and warrant for identifying Scripture, a form of inspired human discourse, as putting people in living and life-giving contact with the Word of God.

In part 2, we considered some philosophical and theological principles that help us to grasp the intelligibility of this biblically warranted teaching. We have likened our exposition to a ladder or staircase, with each step being a set of principles that build on the previous one. Informing all these principles is the doctrine of creation. Starting from the broadest and most basic setting, we discussed how all thinking about God must be set within the horizon of the Distinction (step 1). The Distinction between God and the world provides the necessary setting for all theological thinking and provides direction so that we do not to start down the wrong theological road. The Distinction provides us with an understanding of God, who is radically transcendent and immanently present to all creation and whose relationship with the world is fundamentally noninvasive and nonviolent.

This theological understanding of God interfaces with the metaphysics of creation explicated by Thomas Aquinas (step 2). Aquinas invites us to see all creation as intimately participating at all times in the mysterious and ineffable life of God. All creation is thus participatory and also relational, given the natural tendency of things to communicate their own intelligibility by action. The doctrine of creation invites us to view Scripture within the setting of the world as an "open system" in contradistinction to the world as a "closed system" and the aberrant understanding of God that often accompanies it (step 3).

We then brought the doctrine of creation and the conceptually congruent ontology of creation to bear on the topic of human cognition (step 4). Participatory metaphysics and the self-communication of being by action provide important leverage against the highly influential theories of Immanuel Kant, which seriously impede a proper reception of this doctrine. The relational realism explicated by W. Norris Clarke and Robert Sokolowski's phenomenological analysis of intentionality, words, and things enables us to preserve the relationships of mind, words, and world against the modern tendency to sunder them. As finite creatures that participate in God's own act of existing, things receive from the Creator their intelligible natures, which they in turn communicate to other things through various modes of action, including appearing. This displayed intelligibility can be captured and mediated through language and taken in by people through sensation and intellection. Through sensation and intellection, a knowing subject takes in the intelligibility of things, and the intelligibility of things comes to exist cognitively in the knower. In this way, a cognitive union between knower and known is achieved, and the union of mind, words, and world is maintained.

We then brought these reflections to bear on the Bible (step 5). We took our coordinates from *Dei Verbum* §2, which speaks of the revelation of God in an economy of salvation, constituted by intrinsically connected words and mystery-bearing realities. Drawing on the work of Robert Sokolowski, we recognize the biblical discourse as a mode of presentation or disclosure for the various realities of which they speak. The words put people in cognitive contact with the realities of which they speak by capturing and mediating their intelligibility. In the various realities of the divine economy, God is mysteriously and actively present, revealing himself and his will and exercising his saving power. So understood, the biblical realities bear divine mystery. The incarnation of the Word of God in Jesus Christ establishes a new setting for understanding God and all things in relation to God. The life, death, and resurrection of Jesus constitute the definitive revelation and saving act of God, and all other realities in the divine economy are revealed to have dimensions whereby they participate in his mystery.

Although the created realities of salvation history are historically past, the divine mystery that they bear is eternal. Through the action of the Holy Spirit, the divine mystery, borne by the biblical realities, becomes present to those who contemplate those realities mediated by the sacred text (step 6). Both Scripture and tradition attest to the vital role of the Holy Spirit in providing a penetrating "understanding" of the mystery of Christ and the biblical realities in relation to him. The Holy Spirit can impress the truth and reality of the divine mystery, borne by the biblical realities, on our spirits, and in doing so, provide a faith experience and intimate understanding of that mystery. Such contemplative, "spiritual understanding" grows in proportion to readers' growth in holiness and conformity to Christ. A similar picture emerges from the Lukan version of the parable of the sower. The Word will bear fruit in people to the extent that they yield to God's work in them: "when they hear the word, [they] hold it fast in an honest and good heart, and bear fruit with patient endurance" (Luke 8:15). Accordingly, some of the best examples for encountering the transforming reality and power of God in Scripture are the lives of the saints. They provide lived evidence for the belief that Scripture can put its readers in living and life-giving contact with the divine realities that it mediates.

In his *Commentary on John*, Origen says that biblical writings "present the sojourn of Christ and prepare for his coming and *produce it in the souls of those who are willing to receive the Word of God*."[1] Not only does Scripture talk about Christ or anticipate his incarnation, but also Scripture makes

---

1. Origen, *Commentary on John* 1.26, in Origen, *Commentary on the Gospel according to John: Books 1–10*, trans. Ronald E. Heine, Fathers of the Church 80 (Washington, DC: Catholic University of America Press, 1989), 39 (emphasis added).

the very reality of Christ, the Word of God, present in the souls of those who welcome him. Scripture does not simply describe Christ and his power; it mediates Christ and his power. Origen then alludes to Christ's words in Revelation 3:20: "Listen! I am standing at the door, knocking; if you hear my voice and open the door, I will come in to you." In the Scripture, the Word of God himself "stands at the door and knocks and wishes to enter [our] souls."[2] What remains is for us is to approach the door that is sacred Scripture and, with a faith-filled, receptive, and obedient heart, heed those same words once spoken to Saint Augustine: "Take up and read."

2. Origen, *Commentary on John* 1.26 (Heine, 39).

# Index

Printed in Great Britain
by Amazon